# The Streets of LIVERPOOL

Published by The Bluecoat Press, Liverpool
Printed in China by Latitude Press
Book design by March Design, Liverpool

ISBN 9781904438984


Acknowledgements
The author wishes to thank the late Frank Dugan, Karl Hughes and Liverpool Record Office for permission to use their photographs in this book. Also to the many followers of the Streets of Liverpool blog for their support and many helpful comments.

Follow The Streets of Liverpool blog at
http://streetsofliverpool.co.uk

# The Streets of LIVERPOOL

**Colin Wilkinson**

THE BLUECOAT PRESS

PREFACE ... 5
INTRODUCTION ... 6
WHATEVER HAPPENED TO THE LIKELY LADS? ... 8
HAVELOCK STREET, c1960 ... 10
ALLERTON TOWERS, 1890 ... 12
WATER STREET, 1880 ... 14
THE SAILORS' HOME, 1860 ... 16
SAILORS' HOME, 1973 ... 18
PLEASANT HILL STREET, 1918 ... 20
SCENES FROM LIVERPOOL LIFE, c1895 ... 22
LIME STREET STATION, c1890 ... 24
HOW THE OLYMPIC MOVEMENT STARTED IN LIVERPOOL ... 26
CHORLEY COURT, c1925 ... 28
NEW BRIGHTON 1890s ... 30
MA EGERTON ... 32
EVERTON TOFFEE SHOP, c1880 ... 34
BEN JONSON STREET, c1890 ... 36
THE GOREE, c1890 ... 40
THEATRE ROYAL, c1965 ... 42
ROE STREET, 1964 ... 44
ST JOHN'S MARKET, 1963 ... 46
LIVERPOOL OVERHEAD RAILWAY, 1957 ... 48
BUNNEY'S, c1955 ... 49
ST GEORGE'S PLACE, c1964 ... 50
RANELAGH STREET, 1965 ... 52
DOES LIVERPOOL HAVE MORE GEORGIAN BUILDINGS THAN BATH? ... 54
WHERE ARE THEY NOW? ... 56
THE SWAN, LONDON ROAD, 1969 ... 58
ORANGE PARADE, LONDON ROAD, 1969 ... 58
DOCK RAILWAY, PIER HEAD, 1953 ... 60
SATURDAY MATINEE, THE GAUMONT, 1953 ... 62
THE NORTHERN HOSPITAL, 1963 ... 64
GOING TO THE MATCH, ANFIELD, 1953 ... 66
ELDON STREET, 1964 ... 68
ST ANNE STREET, 1975 ... 70
WAPPING AND THE BALTIC FLEET, 1929 ... 72
PIER HEAD, AS YOU WILL NEVER SEE IT AGAIN ... 74
HOUGHTON STREET, c1963 ... 78
SQUEAKING JIMMY, CHURCH STREET, 1890s ... 80
MARKET STREET, 1890s ... 82
TATE AND LYLE, 1960 ... 84
THE BLITZ, 1940 ... 86
RAG DAY, 1936 ... 88
NETHERFIELD ROAD, 1927 ... 90
CUSTOM HOUSE c1875 ... 94
COMPTON HOUSE, CHURCH STREET, c1880 ... 96
THE OLDEST PHOTOGRAPH OF LIVERPOOL, 1850 ... 98
PREESON'S ROW, c1905 ... 100
CASTLE STREET, 1875 ... 102
LIMEKILN LANE, c1900 ... 104
LIVERPOOL DOCKERS, c1910 ... 106
BERESFORD ROAD, c1890 ... 108
PARK HILL ROAD, c1910 ... 110
KENT SQUARE, c1930 ... 112
CLAYTON STREET, NUMBER 3 COURT, c1930 ... 114
BYROM TERRACE, c1930 ... 116
CANTERBURY STREET, 1946 ... 118
EDGE LANE, 1939 ... 120
SEFTON PARK, 1890s ... 122
LIME STREET, 1931 ... 124
BUSY CLEANING WINDOWS, 1953 ... 126
INDEX, BARTHOLOMEW'S 1928 POCKET GUIDE TO LIVERPOOL ... 130
KEY MAP TO SECTIONS ... 151
MAPS, BARTHOLOMEW'S 1928 POCKET GUIDE TO LIVERPOOL ... 152

## PREFACE

On 19 January 2010, I started a blog about the photography and history of Liverpool. A blog is an online journal that allows features to be posted chronologically. By regularly updating the blog, with the latest 'article' to appear first on screen, I am able to build up layers of interesting photographs linked to a commentary on each image. The blog http://streetsofliverpool.co.uk has the invaluable option of allowing readers to add their own comments, which greatly enriches its value.

After the conclusion of a successful first year, in which the monthly readership has reached over seven thousand, I decided to take a selection of posts and publish them in this book. The subject matter is varied but that is the joy of blogging; the structure can be quite flexible as long as the core theme – that of presenting Liverpool's history through photographs – is observed. What is important is the attempt to add a context to each photograph posted. The narrative is there to create an understanding of the historical significance of the subject matter – who the photographer was, why it was taken and any other information I can pass on which illuminates the post. My opinions, particularly about Liverpool's lost buildings, might not meet with universal agreement but that is the beauty of blogging; it is my journal but it is open to anyone to add their own comments.

To enhance your enjoyment of the book, I have included the 1928 Bartholomew's Street Atlas. It is a fascinating source of information, published at a time when Liverpool's boundaries were starting to expand beyond Queen's Drive. Not all streets are included, especially the back alleys and courts, but most places mentioned can easily be located. Hopefully, the local and family historian will find it equally invaluable in their studies.

http://streetsofliverpool.co.uk

## INTRODUCTION

In the summer of 1826, Joseph Niepce, successfully took the first permanent photograph, a view from an upper, rear window of his family home in Burgundy, in the village of Saint-Loup-de-Varennes. Photography was born, although it took another thirteen years of refinement before it began to enter the public domain. By May 1841, the first commercial portrait studio was operating in London's Regent Street. Thereafter, the way people saw the world would never be the same again. Coinciding with the first years of the Victorian era, it was the great legacy of the nineteenth century to historical research. The history of the world could be frozen in time, great and small events captured in seconds.

The population of Liverpool, in 1841, had reached 286,000, an astonishing growth from the first Census in 1801, which recorded a population of 77,000. Even in 1831, the population was only 142,000. The port was a boomtown, bolstered by an influx of migrants, particularly from Ireland fleeing the devastating famines, and these dramatic developments coincided with the discovery of photography, with one of the first licences for daguerreotypes being granted for Liverpool in 1841. From a photographic perspective, the next decade was one of slow progress because of restrictions imposed by licensing and copyright. It remained largely an activity for commercial portrait photographers, with a small number of wealthy amateurs who could afford a more experimental approach to the new medium. By the mid-1850s, this band of amateurs had expanded thanks to the removal of copyright and, in true Victorian style, photographic societies sprang up, of which Liverpool Amateur Photographic Association, established in 1853, was one of the earliest (Francis Frith, soon to become famous for his photographs of Egypt and the Middle East, was among the founder members).

So, from the early 1850s onwards, Liverpool had an active photographic culture, but where is the physical evidence? One strand of my blog has been to draw attention to these 'missing years'. Without question, photographs were taken of the city throughout the 1850s and 60s, but precious few have come to light. Somewhere, in a public or private archive, I hope there are images that will fill in these decades and add a new dimension to the way we see Liverpool's dramatic development.

As the century developed, more and more images have survived as records of their time. The real explosion started in the 1890s with the advent of the handheld camera and, soon after, roll film. Photography shifted from being a wealthy person's hobby to a mass medium, with widespread ownership of cameras. The twentieth century witnessed further technical changes, with lighter cameras, faster film, colour and, now, digital imagery. The essence of photography still remains - its unique ability to freeze a moment in time. The hundreds of thousands of images taken of Liverpool that have survived are our windows to the past. Many of these photographs are in public archives, such as Liverpool Record Office. Others are in private collections, including my own. Which is where my blog comes in.

Over 30 years ago, back in 1978, I started Open Eye Gallery, the first photographic gallery in the region. My intention was to showcase the best in local, national and international documentary photography. I opened with the work of Colin Thomas, a Halewood-based photographer, whose striking images of the lives of local children set the tone for the many years to follow. I left Open Eye early in 1982, but my time there had started me on a journey to try and understand the relationship between photography and Liverpool.

Over the years, I have built up an archive of Liverpool photographs, some of which I have used to illustrate the many books I have published with my company, The Bluecoat Press. As part of my work, I have also trawled through other archives and collections for relevant illustrations. What I have realised is there is a wealth of material out there which will greatly advance our appreciation of Liverpool's history but it is not always readily accessible. The blog is there to encourage new thinking about this great photographic heritage and how we can make best use of it. What I have started with my collection in bringing it into the public arena will encourage others to follow. Photographs locked away in drawers serve no purpose if they cannot be seen. The marvellous benefit of the Internet is that photographs can be made freely available without losing physical ownership. The Streets of Liverpool blog has started a process of unlocking these hidden treasures. There is much more to come.

*Colin Wilkinson*

## WHATEVER HAPPENED TO THE LIKELY LADS?

Twenty years ago, back in 1990, a tall, white-bearded American burst into my office holding a box of photographs. His name was Frank Dugan, born in New Jersey in 1925. Frank joined the US Air Force in 1949 and was sent as a control tower operator to Burtonwood in 1950. He met Mary Green, from Anfield, at Speke Airport and they married in 1953 after he had been demobbed. Fancying himself as a photographer, he took wedding photographs for a living, finishing off his rolls of film with the occasional shot of Liverpool life.

As an American in a foreign city, Frank was fascinated by Liverpool, particularly the endless terraced streets and the poverty he witnessed. He returned to the States in 1955 to start up as an antiques dealer and his short career as a photographer was effectively over.

Back in 1990, Frank was hoping to have a book published but there weren't enough images – so I used many of them in a calendar. The images all had that magic quality of freezing time that only photography can achieve. Frank died in 2003 but these photographs will stand the test of time.

Perhaps you know what happened to the three lads in the photograph. They look desperately poor – but how did they turn out? The photograph was taken in 1953, so they will now be in their 60s.

HAVELOCK STREET, c1960.

This photograph of Havelock Street was taken by Karl Hughes and used as an illustration in Liverpool author, Frank Shaw's book *My Liverpool* published in 1971.

What is immediately apparent is the traffic-free street, giving the children the freedom to play outside. With no open space nearby and other amenities very limited, the street became a focal point for the community in a way that no longer exists. There has been quite a heated discussion as to whether the street is Havelock Street, largely due to the absence of a handrail in the photograph. Apparently the handrail was added later and the street is correctly named.

ALLERTON TOWERS, 1890.

In the nineteenth century, Liverpool was second city to London, yet the wealth of its merchant classes is often ignored in local histories. I am as guilty as many, finding the desperate poverty of most of the city's population a more rewarding area of study. The huge disparity between the richest and poorest is today being played out against a background of bankers' bonuses and is perceived largely as London versus the rest of the country. Back in 1890, Liverpool, as second city of the sprawling British Empire, vied with London for commercial supremacy and had a significant number of its own 'fat cats' and the outer fringes of the city were dominated by the estates of merchants and landed gentry.

The Earle family was one such example. Having sold their extensive Spekelands estate, which is where Earle Road is today (St Dunstan's Church was built by the family on the site of their family home), the Earle's decamped to Allerton Towers, adjacent to Allerton golf course.

The Earles are probably best remembered for the statue of General Earle outside St George's Hall. General Earle died in Sudan at the Battle of Dulka Island, when storming the Height of Kerkebam in 1885. His brother, Sir Thomas Earle, lived at Allerton Towers until his death in 1900 and the family moved out to Sandiway, in Cheshire, soon after.

Allerton Towers, which was demolished in the 1930s, was a rather dull Victorian villa, ironically designed by the same Harvey Lonsdale Elmes who produced the masterpiece of St George's Hall. The attractive lodge, orangerie and stable block have survived. The land is owned by Liverpool Council and is one of the city's finest small parks.

WATER STREET, 1880.

Back in the 1980s, I bought a broken up album of Liverpool photographs. Taken in the early 1880s, they covered a rather eclectic range of buildings including the Masonic Hall on Hope Street, the Orphanage on Myrtle Street as well as the Custom House, Town Hall and Sailors' Home. There is evidence of a photographer's blind stamp on the edge of one photograph but it is indecipherable. The quality of the set does suggest a professional photographer, perhaps compiling an album of Liverpool views for his own interest.

The photograph of Water Street is typical, centering on the Cunard Company headquarters. Posters advertise voyages to New York on SS Atlas, which was nearing the end of its life at the time, having served the company since the early 1860s. Oriel Chambers is shown in its original street context and looks so well 'bedded in' that it is difficult to understand the criticism its architect, Peter Ellis, received from a hostile press.

I am fascinated by the enigma of Ellis. Why is so little known about his subsequent career? Did he really only design two buildings (Oriel Chambers and 16 Cook Street)?

MIDDLETON BUILDINGS
CUNARD EMIGRATION OFFICE
1, RUMFORD-STREET, ROUND THE CORNER.
CUNARD LINE.
ROYAL MAIL STEAMERS
For NEW YORK and BOSTON.
CUNARD LINE.
CUNARD EMIGRATION OFFICE
BOSTON.
NEW YORK

THE SAILORS' HOME, 1860.

For years I have planned to write a photographic history of Liverpool. The problem is that although there are numerous text references to the earliest period (from 1840 to 1870), there is a distinct lack of images to substantiate the city's undoubted photographic activity. I still hope that a hidden cache of photographs will emerge – either in a public archive or private collection – so the hunt goes on. The idea of my blog was to pose questions and widen the research into the way Liverpool has been represented in photographs and, hopefully, others might have knowledge of early images.

This is one of the earliest images in my collection – a photograph of the Sailors' Home in 1860, just after a catastrophic fire had destroyed its interior, apparently caused by a disgruntled lodger. John Cunningham, the architect, had a bit of a disaster with his two important Liverpool buildings. The Sailors' Home was opened in 1846 and was rebuilt after the fire to serve generations of seamen. With its cast-iron galleries housing 'cabins' for its inhabitants, it was scandalously demolished in 1974 to make way for a speculative development that never happened. A major loss to the city's architectural heritage, its site is now occupied by John Lewis's store in Liverpool One. Cunningham's other major building, the original Philharmonic Hall on Hope Street, opened in 1849. Greatly admired for its acoustics, it too suffered a major fire in 1933. Fortunately, its replacement, by arguably Liverpool's greatest twentieth century architect, Herbert Rowse, is a magnificent addition to the city's heritage.

SAILORS' HOME, 1973.

In 1973, I spent the summer working in a warehouse in Manesty's Lane, off Hanover Street and was fortunate enough to grab a last view of the interior of the Sailors' Home. It was a sad sight; abandoned and neglected, waiting for demolition. The building had been deemed a serious risk under the strict fire regulations, which insisted on a 30-minute fire safety limit between the floors of a building. This was understandable after the horrendous fire at Henderson's store in 1960, in nearby Church Street, when 11 people lost their lives. Fire regulations were tightened up but the Sailors' Home was an open void and any attempt to fire-proof it would have posed an intolerable financial burden for a building that no longer served its original function. At the same time, the plot was sold in anticipation of a government department relocating to Liverpool. That did not materialise but demolition had already been completed and the end result was a hole in the ground for the next thirty years. Here, for the record, are two photographs of what was lost.

ACQUIRED
FOR
REDEVELOPMENT

PLEASANT HILL STREET, 1918.

Two fascinating photographs from WW1. The factory of James Troop, a brass foundry, on Pleasant Hill Street (off Sefton Street), had evidently been turned into an aircraft factory. Although women had worked in factories and mines from the start of the Industrial Revolution, the necessity to recruit women as part of the war effort was to give the Suffragette Movement the momentum required to gain the vote (in 1918 for women over 30 but 1928 before they gained the same rights as men).

TROLLOPE & COLLS LTD
IVERPOOL
K-1743

SCENES FROM LIVERPOOL LIFE, c1895.

The above two photographs are from a set of lantern slides, which I purchased from Frank Lenhan (whose own photographs I published in *My Liverpool: The Photographs of Frank Lenhan*). Frank explained that he had inherited them from his father, who was a friend of the photographer N. Stephen, and that they had been used in temperance meetings to highlight the evils of drink. Frank remembered helping his father project the slides at meetings in the 1930s when he was a young boy.

By coincidence, I was recently researching the educational uses of lantern slides and came across a reference to the Church of England Temperance Society. Apparently the Society had commissioned hundreds of photographs (to be turned into lantern slides) of children in the streets with jars of alcohol – all taken in Liverpool. I have tried to locate these slides, but to no avail so far. Perhaps these photographs taken by Stephen around Scotland Road c1895 (I have about 20) were part of that collection – or does anyone have any further information that can help 'rediscover' these important images of Liverpool's social history?

IMPORTERS AND BONDERS OF

ALKER S.
SALT & Co's
PALE ALE

LIME STREET STATION, c1890.

Watching Michael Portillo's programme Great British Railway Journeys, it struck me how often it is outsiders who make the most of Liverpool's heritage. In this instance, Portillo was enthusing about the unique place Lime Street Station held in the history of the railway. His first impression – the magnificent canyon cut out of rock as you approach the station – was exactly the same as mine on my first visit to Liverpool in 1965. He marvelled at the station, but was somewhat bemused by the statues of Ken Dodd and Bessie Braddock. I too am puzzled. With no disrespect to either local personality, why isn't British Rail shouting from the rooftops that this was where the greatest transport revolution in history started. Thousands of strangers arrive at Lime Street each year, and most will not have a clue who Ken Dodd or Bessie Braddock are, but they would certainly appreciate the fact that they are standing in one of the oldest working railway stations in the world (I suppose Crown Street comes first). So why not install something eye-catching to celebrate our great claim to fame, instead of a couple of, for me, dull statues that have little to do with the great age of steam that transformed the world.

## HOW THE OLYMPIC MOVEMENT STARTED IN LIVERPOOL.

With all the fuss about London's 2012 Olympics, it is worth remembering Liverpool's pivotal role in the Olympic movement. The two main protagonists were Charles Melly (an ancestor of George Melly), a wealthy philanthropist, and John Hulley. Charles Melly attended Rugby school at the same time as Thomas Hughes, author of Tom Brown's Schooldays.

Like Hughes, Hulley was a firm believer in sporting competition and the idea of Muscular Christianity. Born in Liverpool in 1832, he attended Liverpool Collegiate and later trained under Louis Huguenin, a famous French gymnast living in Liverpool.

Melly and Hulley joined forces to form Liverpool Athletic Club in 1861 and, in 1862, held the first Grand Olympic Festival on the Parade Ground at Mount Vernon. Over 10,000 people turned up to watch a programme including running, walking, high jump, boxing, wrestling, fencing and gymnastics – a list of events that was very similar to that of the first Modern Olympics held in Athens in 1896.

Further Olympic Festivals were held, with increasing popularity, and Melly and Hulley raised the funds to open Liverpool Gymnasium on Myrtle Street (opposite: photographed c1870). Following its opening on 6 November 1865, the first meeting of the National Olympics Association was held there, with Hulley on the committee. The NOA defined Olympism long before the foundation of the International Olympic Committee, and its ideas were to have a profound influence on a young Pierre de Coubertin.

Hulley was buried at Smithdown Road cemetery. As a result of the work of a group of enthusiasts, a damaged gravestone bearing the motto mens sana in corpore sano (a healthy mind in a healthy body) was repaired and rededicated in June 2009. Thanks to their efforts, the huge, global impact of both Hulley and Melly can be more fully recognised.

LIVERPOOL
GYMNASIUM

CHORLEY COURT, c1925.

Which Liverpool-born person had the greatest effect on the world? The Beatles must be candidates, having launched a cultural revolution that still resonates fifty years on. From the nineteenth century, we have William Ewart Gladstone (1809-1898), four times Prime Minister and champion of Home Rule for Ireland. From the generation before, we have William Roscoe (1753-1831), a self-made banker and anti-slavery campaigner, whose love of the Italian Renaissance and the Medici's city state of Florence helped define the concept of a cultured city in which merchants' wealth was not an end in itself but the means to enlightenment.

What is remarkable about all of these is that their homes are still part of the city's fabric. However, one of the most influential of all Liverpudlians is not honoured at all and all traces of his birthplace have long been obliterated.

Robert Morris (1734-1806) was born into poverty in Chorley Court, which was at the foot of Dale Street by the Queensway Tunnel entrance. At the age of 13, he left for America, helping out on his father's tobacco farm. By the age of 18, he was a banker and shipping merchant in Philadelphia. Rapidly acquiring wealth, he put his weight behind the fight for independence from Britain, effectively bankrolling George Washington's army. Responsible for establishing the financial and banking systems of the newly independent country, Morris was one of only two people to sign the three significant founding documents of the United States, the Declaration of Independence, the Articles of Confederation, and the US Constitution.

Perhaps because of our ambivalent relationship with the USA, Liverpool failed to recognise the significance of Chorley Court and it was pulled down in the early 1930s to make way for the Blackburn Assurance building (later Stanley Leisure).

BILLIARD
BILLIAR

NEW BRIGHTON 1890s.

Here are two photographs of a day out at New Brighton. I know my blog is about Liverpool but New Brighton was so much a part of people's lives that I will make an exception. For many people, it was as near to a holiday that they got and must have been an amazing place on a hot summer?s day.

The two photographs were both taken by N. Stephen, who also photographed the children carrying beer mugs in an earlier post. I have had difficulty pinpointing any real details about Stephen. The only match in Gore's Directory (1910) is of a Nathan Stephen of 22 Russian Drive, Stoneycroft. Stephen is listed as a County Court officer, so was presumably relatively well-paid. Hand-held cameras had just been introduced in the late 1880s, so Stephen was an early exponent. The advent of hand-held cameras and roll film were to democratise photography. Even so, it still wasn't a cheap hobby and it would take a further ten years or more before it became a truly mass medium.

If anyone has more information on Stephen, I would be grateful. It is good to give credit when due, however belatedly.

MA EGERTON.

There cannot be many pubs in Liverpool named in honour of their landlord/landlady. Peter Kavanagh's in Egerton Street is one and Ma Egerton's on Pudsey Street is another. Dublin-born Mary Egerton came to Liverpool in the 1890s and managed the American Bar in Lime Street before taking over The Eagle in Pudsey Street, behind the Empire Theatre. Her bar became the favourite haunt of the performers and she made friends with many of them, including Charlie Chaplin, Laurel and Hardy and, later, Judy Garland.

One of her claims to fame is that her observation led to the arrest of the infamous Dr Crippen, but first to the photographs. The bottom image is of an older Ma enjoying the company of visiting sailors. The top photograph is of her in the company of visiting performers including her friend Marie Lloyd (seated wearing a black dress and pearls. Ma is standing next to her). Marie was a superstar of her time, a bawdy singer whose use of double-entendre thrilled audiences, yet shocked the moralists. A typical song line 'I sits among the cabbages and peas' outraged her critics, so she agreed to change the line to 'I sits among the cabbages and leeks' to even greater audience approval. A strong supporter of workers' rights, she was at the forefront of a strike by theatre workers for better pay. Picketing outside a London theatre, her attention was drawn to a young actress, Belle Elmore, crossing the strike line. 'Don't worry about her ... she will empty the theatres faster than us,' Marie shouted, and here the story of the top photograph unfolds.

Belle Elmore was married to Dr Crippen and less than three years later was murdered and dismembered by her husband, who took up with his lover, Ethel le Neve. At some point after the murder, Ma Egerton visited London, where she came across Crippen, who was an old friend. She noticed that le Neve was wearing Belle's jewellery and, her suspicions aroused, contacted the police. Crippen, realising that he was under threat of being exposed, fled to Belgium with le Neve, where they boarded *SS Montrose* that was bound for Canada. To cover their tracks, le Neve dressed as a young man. Unfortunately for the pair, *Montrose* was one of the first ships to have the newly invented Marconi wireless installed and the ship's captain, suspicious of the couple, who had been seen holding hands, contacted his base, who in turn called in Scotland Yard. Crippen was arrested on arrival and returned to Britain, where he was tried and hanged. So there is a bit of criminal history encapsulated in this one photograph.

EVERTON TOFFEE SHOP, c1880.

Liverpool has made an invaluable contribution to the cause of the dental profession, through two of its great industries: tobacco and confectionary. They both have a long history, although little remains of either. Liverpool, as a major importer of sugar, was well placed to benefit from the spin-offs and, in the late eighteenth century, an Everton woman, Molly Bushell, decided to increase her income by using recipes from her local doctor to make toffee.

The business boomed and others started up in competition, including Mary Cooper in 1810. Trading from a cottage in Browside, her Everton toffee achieved national fame. In a local rhyme of the time:

*Everton Toffee! Ever dear to lass and lad:*
*More certain cure than balm of Gilead.*
*Come friends, come buy – your pennies give.*
*While you keep sucking you'll be sure to live!*

Balm of Gilead referred to 'cures' of snake-oil salesman, Dr Solomon of Liverpool, who made a fortune out of his patent medicines. At least toffees gave a burst of welcome glucose!

The memory of this small local industry lives on in the nickname of Everton Football Club. I am not sure when the cottages on Browside disappeared, although I have seen a late nineteenth century photograph of them in disrepair. The photograph above was probably taken in the early 1880s. The cottage was in the vernacular Lancashire style that was gradually replaced by Georgian and, later, Victorian terraces.

COOPER

BEN JONSON STREET, c1890.

The courts and back streets of Liverpool's slums were private places where few outsiders ventured. In 1856, the journalist Hugh Shimmin railed against: ... "*the old, dilapidated courthouses, with their fetid air and small squalid rooms' which 'still form the only dwellings which are supposed to be within the means of the labouring and casually employed poor ... the Liverpool courts present scenes of social degredation and misery which it will be almost hopeless to induce people who have no practical acquaintances with the habits of the people to believe.*"

In 1883, *Liverpool Daily Post* published a series of articles under the heading Squalid Liverpool. Ben Jonson Street gets a special mention: "*Our next visit was to Ben Jonson Street. The good priest who guided us through by day asserted it was the "worst street in the city". Our escort now fully corroborated this opinion. "I could not pick out for you," said one of our protectors, "six men who work for a living in this street. There is not another honest man here; the rest are all thieves and vagabonds. The women, at least such as are not too old, are ... you know what." This is a street which, counting its courts, must contain a population of more than a thousand persons. We made our way into one of the lodging-houses. As we pushed open the door of the kitchen, a dozen drunken men and hideous prostitutes jumped up and regarded us with silent alarm.*"

GOOD ACCOMODATION
FOR
TRAVELERS

Photographers tended to avoid the slums, probably with good reason. The hand-held camera allowed some anonymity, but most amateurs stuck to the street scenes around Pier Head and St John's Market. You will not find Ben Jonson Street (rather inappropriately named after the dramatist and poet contemporary of Shakespeare) in Gore's Directory because it is not listed (along with all the other surrounding courts and backstreets. The population was so numerous and transient that there was little value adding the current occupants to its list). This view of the street, which connected Comus Street and Scotland Road, is particularly interesting in that the raised viewpoint has captured a candid scene that contrasts with the later photographs of the City Engineer's Department, where a plate camera was used at street level. My immediate thought is that the photographer must have been sitting on the upper deck of an omnibus as it passed along Scotland Road.

The doss-house with its sign 'good accomodation for travellers' (sic) reminds me of the ubiquitous sign outside public houses offering good food and fine ales. When did you ever see a sign offering bad food or bad accommodation? Bearing in mind the above quote from *Squalid Liverpool*, the thought of a night in such a place does not bear thinking about.

THE GOREE, c1890.

The sight of sheep and cattle being driven through the streets of Liverpool is unthinkable today but even into the early years of the twentieth century, it was the only way of transporting livestock to the abattoir. Liverpool was a major port for the import of meat – and fortunes were made supplying the needs of the exploding urban populations. Two Liverpool brothers, in particular, made their mark. The Vestey family had been local butchers for several generations but William and Edmund were to transform the business by taking advantage of Liverpool's links with South America. Buying land and ranches in Brazil, Uruguay and Argentina, they began supplying meat in wholesale quantities. Using their wealth to start their own Blue Star shipping line, they were the first company to use refrigeration to transport meat.

Never far from controversy, they bought their peerages from the Lloyd George government and then fell out spectacularly over demands for exemption from income tax (nothing is new in politics) and moved abroad as tax exiles.

The Vestey Company was better known for its Dewhurst chain of butchers – which ceased trading in 1996. An interesting fact I picked up in researching this piece is that Dewhurst's were the first butchers to install glass windows in their shops, rather than have open displays. The Vesteys were also responsible for funding the tower of Liverpool's Anglican Cathedral (still known as the Vestey Tower).

The livestock in the photographs would have come from fairly local sources – possibly North Wales or Ireland. The top photograph (probably in the early 1890s) shows cattle being driven along the Goree, with Princes Dock in the background. The bottom image is of livestock on Prescot Road on the way to Stanley Abattoir.

THEATRE ROYAL, c1965.

My photograph of the interior of the Sailors' Home (page 19) created a great response – it would appear that it is the only colour image that anyone has seen. I used to have passionate discussions (in the past rather than now) with photographers who believed that black and white brought out the true 'sense' of a place and that colour was a distraction. I was never of that school of thought, although I could always appreciate the graphic qualities of a good monochrome image.

That said, this photograph is also a rarity – one of the last taken of John Foster's Theatre Royal in Williamson Square before it was demolished in 1970. By that time, it was owned by the Union Cold Storage Company (a Vestey company), who used it to store meat to service St John's Market. The theatre opened in 1803 and staged both plays and opera. For years it held a monopoly in Liverpool, until a government act of 1843 introduced competition. In the face of new theatres opening, including the Star – now the Playhouse – across the square, the Theatre Royal went into decline and by 1890 it was acquired for use as a cold store.

I rank the loss of the theatre amongst Liverpool's most preventable. Georgian theatres are extremely rare – as are surviving John Foster buildings. The Council announced back in 2008 that Williamson Square was a 'world-class square', following its pointless refurbishment. With a 'tin-roofed' shopping block, that you can see in any run-down city centre anywhere, in the place where the Theatre Royal once stood, and an insipid open space with a couple of bedraggled market stores, it really makes one wonder whether those responsible had ever been to Rome, Prague, Paris or Barcelona, to name just four places where the expression 'world-class' might have some validity.

UNION COLD STORAGE
ICE
QUINNS

ROE STREET, 1964.

When people talk about 'lost' Liverpool, it is individual buildings that usually come to mind – such as the Custom House or Sailors' Home. Their loss is relatively easy to assess in terms of their architectural and historical merits. The Theatre Royal is one such building but it also illustrates precisely what was possibly an even greater tragedy – the destruction of the mainly Georgian context of which it formed a key part. The whole area around St John's Market, through Williamson Square and across to Queen Square remarkably survived serious war damage. Here were dozens of small businesses, pubs and shops – with very active markets spilling out into the surrounding streets. Their loss – for a soulless 1960s shopping mall – ripped out the character of an area which, had it survived could have been the Covent Garden of the North.

T.J. POUPART (NORTHERN) LTD
CHARLES WHITE

UPPER DAWSON STREET

ST JOHN'S MARKET, 1963.

I have just returned from a few days in the North East, including a day spent wandering around Newcastle. Walking past Eldon Square, once one of Europe's finest squares, it seems inconceivable that a magnificent Georgian townscape could be so ruthlessly destroyed for a concrete replacement. Much of the town centre was the work of architect John Dobson, the Newcastle equivalent of the Fosters (father and son) who dominated Liverpool's emerging townscape in the first half of the nineteenth century. The Fosters had similar grandiose plans to reshape Liverpool and were responsible for many of the public buildings including the Custom House, the School for the Blind, the Oratory and St James's Cemetery, St Luke's Church, St Andrew's (Rodney Street) and St John's Market. The Market, regarded by the much-travelled artist James Audobon as the finest he had seen, was widely admired for its fine Classical detail, advanced lighting and engineering. Sadly, its fate was, like Eldon Square, to be replaced by an ugly concrete shopping centre that, like its Newcastle equivalent, had nothing in keeping with its surroundings. Although, in Liverpool's case, they went one step further and obliterated the surroundings over the next decade.

W
BRABIN&C
MEAT
PURVEYOR
ROBERT ISAAC LTD
ROSS
W. D. BRABIN & Co
WRIGHTS
Fishlocks

LIVERPOOL OVERHEAD RAILWAY, 1957.

A depressing image for anyone who cares about Liverpool's history; the Overhead Railway officially closed on 30 December 1956. Subsequent rescues failed and, in September 1957, the dismantlers moved in. The photograph was probably taken at the beginning of the demolition process – although it might have been as late as 1958.

The cigarette booth is still trading but the scene is a melancholy one, with the Goree Piazzas in the background awaiting their fate. The closure of the Railway was probably inevitable. Its original function of servicing the docks was no longer viable when set against the rapid growth of car ownership. Tourism was not an option and the cost of repairing the whole line was prohibitive. The 1950s was not a time for sentiment – the vision was of a shiny new city of concrete and steel with rapid transit road systems based on the American model. The Overhead was the past and although the campaign to save it was vociferous, no solution other than demolition could be found.

BUNNEY'S, c1955.

I do not have much information about Bunney's store. Henry Greenwood, the outfitters, apparently bought the site (if not the business) in the late 1950s. Their new store was opened on the site in 1958, so the photograph was taken some time before that. Bunney's building was slightly eccentric – a bit of Edwardian baroque in the high street. The 1950s building that replaced it is one of our better post-War buildings, although I imagine most readers will feel more strongly about the more characterful original.

Bunney's
Hope Brothers
Greenwood

ST GEORGE'S PLACE, c1964.

Two photographs – a before and after; the first was taken in about 1964 and shows a lively St George's Place with the famous Guinness Clock. The architecture may not be first-rate but the setting has lived long in the memory of many I have talked to. This is where a lot of people had their first Chinese meal (at the Empress on the far right of the block). The two hotels – the Washington and Imperial – were landmarks, which brightened up the entrance to Lime Street station.

The second photograph, taken about a year later, captures the last moments of a much-loved corner, as the building of the new St John's Market gets underway. It is interesting to see the old Lime Street station approach before its demolition to make way for the recently demolished tower block and shopping arcade. At least there are some grounds for optimism – the new station entrance, completed in 2010, gives, at last, an appropriate setting for St George's Hall and William Brown Street.

MARTELL
SCHWEPPES
TONIC TONIC TONIC

Heinz

RANELAGH STREET, 1965.

In my list of Liverpool 'grot spots', this corner of Ranelagh Street would be near the top (along with the rest of the block along Lime Street). My reaction, though, is generated by the lack of care and maintenance rather than the intrinsic quality of the architecture. In fact, considering how the building looked when it first opened, as Peter Robinson's new store, one can see the boldness and brightness of the architect's vision. Concrete is not a material that ages well, but the addition of strong colour gives a cohesion and life to the building that is sadly lacking today.

Post-War architecture is slowly coming back into fashion as a new, younger generation looks at it with different eyes. Just as Georgian architecture fell out of favour with the Victorians and Victorian architecture, in turn, was disliked until the 1970s, the Modernist movement of the 1950s and 60s has had its years in the shadows. Much that was built in the rush to reconstruct after the War was substandard but there are gems that should be appreciated. I would not go so far as to include this building in Ranelagh Street, but it would certainly look much better if restored to its original colour scheme.

PETER ROBINSON

## DOES LIVERPOOL HAVE MORE GEORGIAN BUILDINGS THAN BATH?

In a discussion with Mike Chitty of the Wavertree Society, two old chestnuts came up. The first, that Liverpool has more listed buildings than any other city outside of London, simply is not true, according to Mike. That honour goes to Bradford – and he has checked it up on the Department of Environment lists. I must admit to being surprised by his revelation – but the information is there in black and white.

The other much-quoted statement is that Liverpool has more Georgian buildings than Bath. The source for this was Micky King, Conservation Officer for Liverpool in the 1970s, who, when asked in a press interview why Liverpool's architecture was so special, replied with a soundbite he knew would catch their interest – but without any grounding in fact. I have always had this in the back of my mind, having visited Bath fairly regularly over the years. Bath is solidly Georgian (true Georgian – not Regency or early Victorian buildings in the Georgian style like much of Liverpool). Mike Chitty argued that Liverpool might have the edge – it was a much larger city than Bath which had a population of 34,000 in 1801 against Liverpool's 77,000. By 1851, Bath had grown slightly to 43,000 but Liverpool had exploded to 376,000. So the issue is still unresolved. I reckon that Bath probably scrapes ahead – although that would not have been the case in the 1960s, when fine terraces such as this one in the photograph were routinely pulled down. In the case of Bedford Street North, it was to make way for the University Sports Centre – which I am sure could have easily have been built on a less sensitive site. The aerial photograph of the University precinct area in the mid-1930s, gives some indication of the extent of Georgian Liverpool before the 1960s clearance. The Victoria Building, top left, faces the Students' Union building. Opposite them is the huge Workhouse, soon to be cleared for the Metropolitan Cathedral. Bedford Street North is the road just above the Students' Union, just one of many Georgian/Early Victorian terraced streets that have since disappeared.

## WHERE ARE THEY NOW?

When I started off my *Streets of Liverpool* blog, one of my main aims was to highlight the amazing number of photographs about Liverpool that were in private and public collections. These range from documentation of local authority work (such as the City Engineer's Department), the outright commercial (Francis Frith and other companies) to the personal work of photographers just looking for an interesting shot.

I hoped to stimulate discussion on issues such as access, the whereabouts of 'unknown' collections and the history of photography in Liverpool. Above all, it was meant to bring previously unseen images to public attention and, hopefully, stimulate discussions about the city and its history. This image is another gem from 1953 of a house in Liverpool, with three generations posing for the photographer. Like my first ever post – of three young boys – this photograph of three girls, who would all be in their mid-60s now, begs the same questions – who are they and how did their lives turn out?

## THE SWAN, LONDON ROAD, 1969.

Here is an image from 1969 that should raise a smile or two. The Swan was pulled down a few years back for road improvements but I don't think it ranks highly on the list of lost buildings. As for the mini skirts, they were amongst the last to be seen for a while, with long, flowing skirts and loon pants taking over. The police, as always, are on the lookout for crime on the streets.

## ORANGE PARADE, LONDON ROAD, 1969.

I had not come across the annual Orange marches until I came to Liverpool. My first experience was when I worked in Seel Street, in 1974, and heard an incredible thumping of drums and the wail of bagpipes. Rushing up to Berry Street, I was mesmerised by a long procession of pipers, drummers, baton carriers and serious-looking men and women, all marching in time to different bands. Above all was the sight of numerous King Billys (all female and dressed up with flowing wigs) with their consort, Queen Mary, alongside them.

This was the Dingle contingent marching to catch the train to Southport and, in the early 1970s, they made up a sizeable crowd.

Sectarianism is one of those unspoken aspects of Liverpool's history and the violent riots of the early twentieth century have been pushed back from memory. However one views its historical past, it is surprising that the annual parades have not been better documented. They are a fascinating part of local history and, judging by recent thinly attended parades, might eventually follow Judas burning and other once common ceremonies into folklore. Photographs like this are not about partisanship, but about recording for posterity – although I am not sure whether the three girls in their orange costumes would be quite as keen to be reminded of their fashion faux pas.

MARCEL

SALE
TIMPSON

DOCK RAILWAY, PIER HEAD, 1953.

Most people over 40 know about the Overhead Railway but are often surprised to discover there was a railway line that ran beneath it. The line serviced the docks and was operated by British Rail. The locomotive is a 0-4-0 saddle tank shunter, nicknamed a 'Pug'. Their short wheelbase made them ideal for the sharp curves of the dockland lines. Imagine, today, allowing a train to run freely where pedestrians could cross without any barriers or restrictions.

SAY CWS
AND SAVE
GENTLEMEN

SATURDAY MATINEE, THE GAUMONT, 1953.

I suppose you have to be of a certain age, but back in the 1950s and early 60s, the Saturday morning film show aimed at children was a fantastic institution. The films usually had a Hollywood B movie feel to them, with a preponderance of 'cowboys and indians'. For adults, the 1950s were, at the start, difficult years, as the country adjusted to post-War life, but talk to most of those (now 50+) who were kids at the time and a different picture emerges – of freedom to roam, and play in the streets and be your own age.

The Gaumont chain had a number of cinemas in Liverpool. I thought this photograph was taken in Camden Street, off London Road, but this caused a storm of responses, none of them decisive. I think the Savoy on Brougham Terrace was the most popular suggestion. As for the Gaumont, Camden Street, it was originally named the Trocadero, but renamed the Gaumont in 1950 and was the first cinema in Liverpool to install CinemaScope with stereophonic sound (in 1954). Its close proximity to the Odeon on London Road was its undoing; the final straw coming when the Odeon converted to a multi-screen (four screens by 1973). The Gaumont limped on until its final performance in May 1974. It had a brief life as a snooker hall but was demolished in 1996. It may have gone, but for a generation of kids it was a magical place, like many other cinemas, for a few hours every Saturday morning.

A GAUMONT THEATRE
The Critics Cheer New Boy Star...
AN OUTSTANDING BRITISH FILM
The KIDNAPPERS
STEPHEN McNALLY
JULIA ADAMS
THE STAND AT
APACHE RIVER
TODAY

THE NORTHERN HOSPITAL, 1963.

The history of hospitals in Liverpool is one of constant change and renewal. The building photographed here was the third Northern – the first opening in 1834 in Leeds Street. The influx of Irish immigrants into the area soon put it under pressure and the badly overcrowded hospital was replaced by a new hospital in Great Howard Street, on the site of the old Pig Market, in 1844. The architect was Edward Welch, whose best known building is Birmingham Town Hall.

The opening coincided with another huge influx of Irish escaping famine. Ninety thousand entered Liverpool in the first three months of 1846 alone, and 300,000 in the following twelve months. No town in England was so densely populated and unhealthy and, again, the hospital struggled to cope. Finally, in 1902, a new hospital opened on a site bounded by Old Hall Street, Bath Street, Sutton Street and Brook Street. The architect was CW Harvey – an outsider – much to the annoyance of local architects. The closure of the Northern in 1978 brought to an end nearly 150 years of medical care for the impoverished neighbourhoods of Vauxhall and surrounding areas.

One tragic story was the murder of a young nurse, Alice Jones. An American soldier, Joseph Hutty, had enlisted in The Canadian Expeditionary Force, and had been admitted to the Northern suffering from shell-shock. He became infatuated with Nurse Jones but, on her rejection, shot her dead outside the hospital entrance. He was found guilty but the jury recommended mercy on the grounds of his acute mental condition. Sentenced to death, Hutty was finally reprieved after a petition signed by the Lord Mayor, amongst others, persuaded the Home Secretary to commute the sentence.

GOING TO THE MATCH, ANFIELD, 1953.

One event that anyone interested in football always remembers is his or her first football match. I was a late starter, being 13 before I went along to watch the famous Spurs double team of 1961 play Sheffield United. The match passed by in a blur, but my abiding memory was of being jostled by a huge crowd – mainly flat-capped men all smoking their Woodbines or Park Drives. There were the old wooden rattles and handbells – all creating an atmosphere that got me hooked for life.

Once I arrived in Liverpool, I did the unforgiveable, and switched allegiance – not a bad move since the last major honour won by a Sheffield club was back in 1935!

What I like about the photograph is that it captures the spirit of a typical Saturday afternoon match day. I can never understand why so few photographers film that aspect of the sport, rather than what is happening on the pitch. Football is such an important part of our culture and needs a better photographic record.

1'9
1'9
1'9
STAND 4'6

ELDON STREET, 1964.

John Alexander Brodie (1858-1934) deserves a chapter to himself in the story of Liverpool's growth as a city. The City Engineer, he had a creative mind – responsible for 'inventing' goal nets to stop the disputes that broke out when there were just goalposts and a crossbar – he was also the man who created a modern road network in Liverpool that is the envy of cities across the country. A visionary, he foresaw the need to accommodate the motorcar at a time when car ownership was restricted to a few wealthy enthusiasts, himself included. Through a cunning strategy of buying up outlying plots of greenfield land, he was able to steer through the construction of Queen's Drive and the radial roads into the city centre. The magnificent dual carriageways, many now tree-lined, are part of his legacy, along with such initiatives as creating a photographic record of his department's work (now in the Liverpool Records Office) and the use of pre-cast concrete as a building material.

Historically, he should be better recognised, He realised that the need to provide low-cost housing to replace the appalling slums of Liverpool required a fresh approach – and came up with the concept of casting panels of concrete which could be quickly erected in situ. His first experimental houses were in Eldon Street in 1903. The photographs opposite, of the front and rear elevations, were taken in 1964, just prior to demolition. There is one surviving example – Walton stables – on the corner of Rice Lane and Queens Drive; although modified, the block is very much intact. Sadly for Brodie, and Liverpool, the system of using factory-produced panels failed because of trade union opposition. Other countries were less resistant to change – and in the 1960s Liverpool was importing panels from France, made under the Camus system to construct the Shiel Park flats.

Looking at the photographs, the result is interesting but not convincing. They personify the worst aspects of concrete as a building material – somewhat crude, with a tendency to discolour and stain in an unattractive way. Whether they were pleasant places to live in is another matter – but the photographs are a final record of an innovation which Liverpool could have developed and pioneered.

ST ANNE STREET, 1975.

The last blog was about Liverpool pioneering pre-cast concrete. This one is about the city's role in pioneering the uses of cast-iron for structural purposes in buildings. It is often said, incorrectly, that Ironbridge, near Telford, was where the Industrial Revolution started – following Abraham Darby's construction of the cast-iron bridge that still stands today as a major tourist draw. The bridge was constructed in 1779 – some seven years after iron was used for structural purposes in St Anne's Church on St Anne Street (now demolished). Two years later, iron pillars were used in the construction of St James Church, on Upper Parliament Street, making it the oldest surviving use of structural cast-iron in Britain.

The photograph is of a later building, the Export Carriage and Wheelworks that stood on St Anne Street until the 1990s before it burned down. Ironically, the Fire Station is now on its site. With its facade reminiscent of the Southern States of the USA, it was highly regarded by Picton as being: *among the very handsome buildings which Liverpool contains. This must be considered one of the ornaments of the town. The interior is arranged at the front of the building with large, commodious and very light showrooms, wherein are on view very handsome and first-class carriages of every description.*

The building was opened in 1859 – some five years before Peter Ellis's bold use of cast-iron in the construction of Oriel Chambers. Liverpool's history of innovation with the material can still be seen in the two magnificent cast-iron churches of St George's Everton (1812-14) and St Michael in the Hamlet (1814-15), as well as the magnificent facade of Greenbank House (c1815). What a great shame it is that the Carriage Works and the Sailors' Home have not survived to add to the list.

owen
owen
WELSH FOR 3 PIECE

WAPPING AND THE BALTIC FLEET, 1929.

Here is a wonderfully, moody shot of a carter heading west along Wapping in the early morning. To his left is the Overhead Railway and in the shadows is The Baltic Fleet, a remarkable survivor of the many pubs that once lined the Dock Road. The photograph was taken in 1929, by John Newburn, a member of The Photographic Circle, based in Birkenhead. Judging by the label on the back of the print, it was a submission to *The Amateur Photographer* magazine's Advanced Workers' Competition. I hope it won; it really does capture the place and time. Perhaps more attention should be paid to the work of amateur photographic societies. For decades they were the standard bearers of photography in Liverpool but their efforts are often overlooked because of that dreaded word 'amateur'. In truth, many of the photographers were highly skilled and dedicated and more than happy to pursue photography as a hobby. Commercial photography places different demands – working to commissions rather than having the freedom to just enjoy taking a shot, simply for the sake of a pleasing picture.

PIER HEAD, AS YOU WILL NEVER SEE IT AGAIN.

This was without doubt the post that attracted the biggest response to my blog – all in support of my assertion that this development is an unmitigated disaster for the city.

It is easy to cast oneself as yet another moaner who is always finding fault with any changes. I'd like to think I have a positive attitude to change and I have welcomed many of the recent developments that have transformed the city. I am a big fan of the new Museum of Liverpool and see it as a graceful addition to the waterfront, along with the Arena. However, the destruction of one of the best cityscapes in the country makes my blood boil.

The waterfront has always been restricted to the people of Liverpool and the first view, taken in 1911, shows a scene that would have been enclosed by storage sheds along the Dock Road. However, the opening up of the vista, particularly from 1984 with the landscaping around Albert Dock, created a magnificent view that lifted the spirits as you walked or drove past. The view through the arch became a favourite photo opportunity – framing the Pier Head in all its glory. My view, taken in 2000, captures a scene that must have impressed any visitor to the city. (I used a similar shot for the cover of Quentin Hughes' *Liverpool City of Architecture* to highlight the best view in the

HARLEY &
MILLER Ltd

city). So what have they done? Taken away an iconic view that sold the city, for the sake of three blocks of black glass-faced speculative development that has changed the waterfront for generations (or at least until they pull them down). Why there? Why black? when virtually every building in Liverpool is either brick or white stone? We talk about listing buildings. The space around Mann Island should have been declared public open space and landscaped accordingly.

The public are treated with derision by decision-makers. Remember the Fourth Grace fiasco when the public were asked for an opinion and then completely ignored? The obsession with filling every space with commercial buildings is wrong-minded and damages the city's heritage. We need more open space not less. We need space to view our great buildings – not hem them in as if they did not matter. Shame on all those who voted for this development, which apparently only got through on a casting vote.

HOUGHTON STREET, c1963.

Houghton Street was once a busy street connecting Williamson Square and Clayton Square. It is still there, but one side is now taken up by St John's Market, and the other by what were George Henry Lee's and Owen Owens. This is an interesting colour photograph taken just before the buildings were demolished to make way for the new market. There is not a lot I can add to my previous comments about the destruction of this area.

I can remember that when the precinct caught fire (sometime in the 1980s – my memory fails me), architects gathered at their club in Bluecoat Chambers and toasted its demise. They celebrated too soon. Unfortunately, the fire damage was repairable and the Market continued to trade. There are a few other buildings I would raise a glass to if they were to be consumed by fire (no casualties of course): the black glass buildings on Mann Island and St John's Market topping the list.

GOLDEN PHOENIX
Restaurant
Yards and Yards

SQUEAKING JIMMY, CHURCH STREET, 1890s.

My apologies for the quality of this photograph, an 1890s lantern slide, which has deteriorated over the years. Nevertheless, it is a great image of street life taken with a hand-held camera. In my book on Charles Frederick Inston, I outlined the way in which camera technology became more portable and film became faster and easier to use once roll-film came into use. Naturally this changed the way photographers worked and candid street photography became a fashion that was reflected in the competition categories amongst amateur photographic societies. Within a short period of time, photography shifted from being a rich man's pursuit to a popular medium within the pockets of working men and women.

The photograph is captioned 'Squeaking Jimmy, Church Street'. The building in the background is Russell's Building, which was bombed during the War and later replaced by Littlewoods (now Primark). As for Squeaking Jimmy, I can only guess that he was selling those little toy whistles that imitate bird noises or something similar, unless there is a more sinister interpretation to his name.

MARKET STREET, 1890s.

While researching yesterday's post about Squeaking Jimmy, I dug out my copies of Horne and Maund's seminal five-book series *Liverpool Transport*. A lifetime's work – these are often described as books for 'anoraks' by those with only a passing interest in transport. To me, they belong to a fine tradition of writing about Liverpool that I believe is unrivalled in any other city.

Over the last 40 plus years, the number of books keeps rising, including many seminal works such as Quentin Hughes's *Seaport* – which had a profound effect on all who read it – and the Pevsner series, recently brilliantly revised in two volumes by Richard Pollard and Joseph Sharples. There have been many other important books – including English Heritage's six-volume series published for Capital of Culture Year. I have published approaching 200 titles as Bluecoat Press and yet I have turned down five times as many, because there is a limit to what I can do. The result of all this effort is a deep awareness of Liverpool's rich history – quite astonishing for such a 'young' city. Go to Manchester, Newcastle, Leeds or any other city and you will find nothing like the same breadth or depth of titles.

Publishing is at an interesting crossroads and I hope my blog helps bridge the gap in the inevitable transition from paper to digital. These photographs are a case in point: two previously unpublished images of market life in the 1890s. Both are captioned 'Back o' the Market'. This is life in the raw as hawkers try to make a few pennies from selling rags, broken crockery, or whatever else can make them a precarious living.

MARKET
STREET

THE
Butter
Place

TATE AND LYLE, 1960.

Who would have believed 50 years ago that there would be no Tate and Lyle in Liverpool and that the company would no longer be in the sugar business? Last year's news that the sugar business had been sold brings to an end a company history that started in Liverpool in 1859, when Henry Tate became a partner of a small sugar refinery in Manesty's Lane (just off Hanover Street). My own business career started back in 1973, in a warehouse owned by Tate and Lyle on the site of the original refiners, although the warehouse was built in the 1870s and demolished in the 1980s.

The history of sugar in Liverpool will, I imagine, be likely to cause more than a few readers to stifle a yawn – but it really is an interesting part of the city's history. Along with tobacco and cotton, the wealth of the city was built on the import of goods from the New World. Sugar had its own spin-offs. The famous Everton toffee mentioned in an earlier post was the fledgling start of a much bigger confectionary industry (Barker and Dobson amongst others) as well as providing the basic ingredient for the massive Hartley's jam business.

The Love Lane Refinery was completed in 1873 and in its time employed thousands from the surrounding Vauxhall district. Other local refineries such as Farrie's and Macfie's could not compete with Tate's and were absorbed into the sugar empire. Henry Tate himself was a benefactor on a significant scale – building the Hahnemann Hospital on Hope Street, providing the funds for Liverpool University's library block, as well as giving generous donations to the Royal Infirmary and Liverpool Institute. His biggest gift was to found the Tate Gallery in London – now with its Liverpool offshoot. Ironically, the opening of Tate Liverpool came only a few years after the closure of Love Lane, in that brutal period in the early 1980s which also saw other great names, including British American Tobacco, pull the plug on their Liverpool bases.

In a recent discussion with an ex-union convenor at Fords, he referred to Tate and Lyle as an exemplar in employee relations. It treated its staff with great fairness and dignity, unlike his experiences in the motor trade.

TATE & LYLE Ltd

THE BLITZ, 1940.

Watching BBC News, I was reminded that September 2010 marked the 70th anniversary of the start of the Blitz. As always, the focus was on London, with just an incidental mention that other places in the country were also affected. I was going to post these photographs in November, to mark the Durning Road tragedy, but the news item made me reconsider the timing. The direct hit on the large underground shelter in Durning Road, Edge Hill, was the worst single incident in the Liverpool Blitz as regards loss of life.

In the early hours of 29 November 1940, during the heaviest air raid to date, a parachute mine hit the Junior Instruction Centre in Durning Road, collapsing into the shelter below and crushing many of its 300 occupants. Boiling water from the central heating system, and gas from the fractured mains, poured in. Raging fires overhead also made rescue work extremely dangerous. In all, 166 men, women and children were killed. Many more were badly injured. Joe Lucas lost two brothers and two sisters in the tragedy and recalled that his traumatised mother did not speak for six months.

We are not very good at marking such events, but Liverpool did have the highest number of casualties of any city outside of London and it is important that there is proper recognition of such suffering.

RAG DAY, 1936.

Colin McIndoe emailed me in reply to one of my blogs and reminisced about his Liverpool schooldays, remembering a short verse he had gleaned from the 1962 Sphinx – that slightly risqué Panto magazine that students sold as part of their Rag Week charity drive.

*I wandered lonely as a cloud*
*That floats on high o'er hills and vales*
*When all at once I met this lad,*
*A Scouser who had dirty nails.*

It got me thinking as to what had happened to Rag Week. Has it just disappeared? I remember the parades they used to have in Sheffield, with dozens of decorated floats parading through town with students holding out buckets to catch the (old and heavy) pennies that were thrown at them, often with deliberate intention to maim. It was a week in which substantial amounts were raised for charities and was one of the few occasions when gown met town.

The press photograph is of a 1936 Rag stunt in Church Street. The caption reads: 'A happy band of the students playing 'Ring-a-Roses' round a traffic policeman in Church Street'. I had always thought that Rag Week was a post-War phenomenon. Does anyone know its history and what has happened to it? Surely with ten times as many students today, it could make a dramatic revival.

6A
CASTLE ST
WOOLDRIDGE REMOVES RHEUMATISM FOR 2/-
2/- BOTTLE SUFFICES OF ALL CHEMISTS 80 YEARS REPUTATION ALSO CURES GOUT
115

NETHERFIELD ROAD, 1927.

I have deliberately avoided selecting photographs from well-known sources, such as the City Engineer's Collection in the Liverpool Record Office. Today's selection does come courtesy of LRO but I hope I can add an additional dimension to what is my favourite photograph in the whole CE archive.

The role of the CE photographers was to document their department's work. They did not see themselves as artists but they were nevertheless skilled at using the plate cameras, as well as being able to deal with the attention their presence would always attract. Setting up a camera would take enough time for all the kids in the neighbourhood to appear – it was an event and they wanted to be part of it. Fortunately for us, the CE photographers clearly realised that it was easier to humour the crowds and include them in the photographs, rather than spend futile time chasing them away. As a result, their earlier photographs (until the 1940s when they had largely switched to 35mm), are full of animation.

JACOB'S
CREAM
CRACKERS
L.BARKER
RED SEAL TOFFEE
GENERAL L.BARKER STORES
RED SEAL TOFFEE
HOME MADE ICES
HOME MADE ICES

Why I specifically like the Netherfield Road photograph, is because it has three distinct areas of interest:

BELOW What a fabulous image of Ms Barker's shop, with the boys looking enviously at the sweets on display. Isolated from the main photograph, it stands up as a brilliant image in its own right.

OPPOSITE TOP Here we have those strange landings, leading to Everton Terrace at the back, with a group of children gathered to have their photos taken.

OPPOSITE BOTTOM Finally, and possibly the weakest image, but fascinating nevertheless, is of this other group, standing watching the proceedings, and of the small boy who follows his mate up to the first landing. How much do you want in one photograph!

JACOB'S
CREAM
CRACKERS
L.BARKER
RED SEAL TOFFEE
GENERAL
L.BARKER
STORES
RED SEAL TOFFEE
HOME MADE ICES
HOME MADE ICES
ICES

CUSTOM HOUSE c1875.

Two photographs taken from the same collection, taken in the 1870s. Frustratingly, I cannot identify the photographer, although there is a barely visible blind stamp on one photograph. The presence of the blind stamp suggests a professional photographer – and there were a number in Liverpool at that time making a living selling local views. There are 36 photographs in total – showing both familiar and unfamiliar Liverpool landmarks, but all taken from slightly unusual vantage points. The two of the Custom House are cases in point – for the focus seems to be the Pump House to the Albert Dock, which of course survives. The bottom photograph gives a clear idea of the height line of the buildings along the dock road – with the prominent spire of St George's Church standing high above the surrounding warehouses. The rows of barrels along the quayside have markings – but nothing clear enough to identify their contents.

Are there any other collections out there from this period? I have a rare copy of Francis Frith's album of a similar period, but surely there are other collections of photographs pre-1875. I have stereo views and the odd individual image going back to the 1860s but I still think that there must be images out there that will bridge the gap from c1850 to 1875, which would add significantly to our knowledge of how Liverpool looked at the height of its economic power.

COMPTON HOUSE, CHURCH STREET, c1880.

When Liverpool's most important buildings are discussed, it is surprising how often retailing is left out. In Quentin Hughes's *City of Architecture*, not a single shop features in his selection – a surprising omission. Cripp's on Bold Street (now Waterstones), what was until recently GH Lee on Basnett Street, Lewis's (one of the better post-war buildings) and Premier Buildings (on the corner of Church Street and Hanover Street) were all worthy of inclusion. However, the shop that should have been in for both architectural and historical significance is Compton House – now home to Marks and Spencer. Joseph Sharples, in his essential book about Liverpool architecture, describes it as majestic and of international significance because it was one of the earliest, if not the first, purpose-built department store, finished five years before Bon Marché in Paris.

The store replaced an earlier building destroyed by fire in 1865. Two brothers, William and JR Jeffrey financed a new building, which opened in 1867. In James Picton's words, tragedy struck again:
*Mr William Jeffrey, the brother and right hand of the principal, was cut off suddenly by apoplexy and JR Jeffrey was left to fight his battle alone. The battle was a losing one. The receipts of the new shop never met the outgoings and, in March 1871, the shutters came down for the last time.*

The photograph shows its later reincarnation as Compton Hotel, with William Russell as proprietor. On the ground floor, the shops are Lilly Addinsell (hatter and hosier), JR Cramer & Co, William Hay & Co and, on the right hand side, Watts & Co, drapers.

RUSSELL'S
COMPTON
HOTEL

## THE OLDEST PHOTOGRAPH OF LIVERPOOL, 1850.

This was a special post – my 100th. When I started in January 2010, I had a reasonably clear idea of what I wanted to do, which was to highlight the importance of photography in our understanding of the history of Liverpool. What has been a passion of mine has found focus in my blog, which gives me the flexibility to move from subject to subject and place to place within a fairly loose structure.

What I could not predict was how my blog would be received and whether it would have the legs to carry on for any length of time. In fact, I have been overwhelmed by the response, which, thanks to the Internet, has come from all over the world.

This post is, possibly, the most exceptional one I have made. It is the earliest photograph of Liverpool I have discovered in 30 years of searching. It is a copy, taken from a lantern slide of the original print. I found the slide hidden away in a drawer in the Liverpool Record Office and I suspect it has not been seen for many years.

Why is the photograph so important? There are newspaper accounts of photographs taken in Liverpool but I have never discovered any physical evidence. There were a number of amateur photographers in Liverpool, including Francis Frith who, with others, started the Liverpool Amateur Photographic Association in 1853. However, it is not until the 1860s that any images of the city begin to surface in any number (and not many at that).

St George's Hall is, not surprisingly, the subject matter. Most of us are familiar with Victorian photographs of the Hall but here it is still in construction with the original pillars being constructed along the plateau. What really strikes me is what the building must have meant to the people of the time. Its scale is so huge that it must have overwhelmed everyone that saw it. It was ambition on a fantastic scale. Today we may be more blasé about it – after all it has been around for 160 years – but the photograph gives us a window in time to its scale and original setting.

Now the pressure is on to find earlier images ... I am certain they exist somewhere.

PREESON'S ROW, c1905.

The street is initially hard to place – but there at the bottom of James Street can be seen the newly-built White Star building and, above it, James Street station, with its hydraulic tower, which was destroyed by enemy bombing. So the view we are looking at is from Derby Square, from the statue of Queen Victoria. Preeson's Row is still there, in theory. It was a street that ran along the river side of Derby Square, along the line of the old castle ditch. Picton's indispensible *Memorials of Liverpool* is, as so often, my guide to its history. Back in the seventeenth century, it was called Tarlton's field. Alderman Thomas Preeson built the first houses, living himself on the opposite side, fronting the castle fosse. A stone in front of the house was dated 1660. In about 1721, the buildings of the castle were removed and a small square, Derby Square, was formed for a new market.

So what has happened to these old streets such as Sea Brow, Prison Weint, Redcross Street, Benns Gardens and Preeson's Row, which were all part of the history of Liverpool? Occasionally, as in Redcross Street, the name survives in a meaningless context but the rest have been swept away and an association with the old town lost forever.

The pub on the corner, in the photograph, is the Queen's Hotel, which was destroyed during the War, and then rebuilt. It has had a name change recently but, no doubt, will resurface as the Queens again sometime in the future, as is the trend, (remember the Brookhouse, on Smithdown Road, which was painted a shocking yellow and renamed The Scream before the pub chain came to its senses).

INE & BRANDY
WAREHOUSE
WINE & SPIRIT
MALT & HOP
MERCHANTS
WINES & SPIRITS
C.P.R

CASTLE STREET, 1875.

Two photographs of Castle Street. The first is largely unchanged – although the block of offices on the left had been replaced by the turn of the century. The main area of interest is the horse-drawn omnibus alongside the row of carriages. To the right, the old Exchange building can be seen, behind the Town Hall.

The view of South Castle Street is a Frith photograph of about the same time. The ghostly spire of St George's Church can be seen above the buildings on the left. In the foreground are the shops of Thomas Ogden (presumably the Ogden's tobacco magnate), who also had shops in St James Street, Mill Street, Green Lane, Park Lane and Cornwallis Street according to my 1874 Gore's Directory. On the other corner, at 61 Castle Street, is J. Sewill's, Watch and Chronometer Maker, which is still trading from its current shop in the Albert Dock.

Ogden's building on the left, and much of its terrace, survived wartime bombing – but was swept away in the early 1970s to make way for the monstrous Canning Place development. It had survived for over 125 years, whereas its concrete replacement managed only 25 years. Enough said.

Francis Frith made his fortune in Liverpool before devoting his life to photography and becoming one of the great topographical photographers of the nineteenth century, particularly through his amazing photographs of Egypt and Sinai. His commercial enterprise covered the country but he was particularly strong on Liverpool, taking hundreds of photographs of buildings and ships. I am particularly interested in finding out more about Frith and would welcome any information about his time in Liverpool and of any photographs he took, especially earlier ones. He deserves a book – but I need to dig out a few more facts first!

CHRONOMETER WATCH & NAUTICAL INSTRUMENT CORRECTO
MANUFACTURER TO HER MAJESTY'S ROYAL NAVY COMPASSE

LIMEKILN LANE, c1900.

It is now over ten years since I published Freddy O'Connor's *Pubs on Every Corner* series (four in all). What astonished me then, was the incredible number of pubs – many of them faithfully documented by the brewery – in both cases here by Peter Walker's. Liverpool was the first city to embrace brewery-managed pubs. In most other places, the pubs were either owned by landlords, or run by tenants. Walker changed all that and introduced an efficient pub system with strict rules laid down by the brewery. The result was that the Walker family grew very rich but, also, Liverpool inherited brewery-built pubs like the Philharmonic that had few equals.

Both the pubs shown here were more modest. The Langsdale Street pub was managed by Catharine Kip, who stands proudly outside the entrance, while one of her customers is leaving with a jug of ale from the other door. Langsdale Street ran down off Shaw Street.

Both photographs come from the Walker archive, now in Liverpool Record Office. The brewery photographed all its pubs for licensing purposes and stuck the photographs in large ledgers labelled with the address of each one. Other breweries, such as Higsons, did the same – but unfortunately their archives have not been kept intact, although there are quite a few in private hands, as I discovered when I put together the books with Freddy. What we really do need is a collaborative effort to bring such photos into the public arena. They are part of Liverpool's history and add to our understanding of how the city grew. The internet opens up a fantastic opportunity to share images without sacrificing ownership and I hope my blog will encourage like-minded collectors to join in.

MYERS PLACE
WARRINGTON

LANGDALE STREET
WALKER'S WARRINGTON ALES.
WALKER'S WARRINGTON ALES
LICENSED TO SELL BY RETAIL ALE & PORTER TO BE CONSUMED EITHER ON OR OFF THE PREMISES & DEALER IN TOBACCO
BURTON NOTED MILD ALES
BURTON NOTED

LIVERPOOL DOCKERS, c1910.

Early photographs of dockers at work are quite rare, which is surprising considering their contribution to the growth of Liverpool. They were a tough breed, surviving on casual labour, which rarely offered more than a day's work at a time. The second photograph shows dockers 'on the stand' at Alexandra Docks, going through the ritual of being picked by a foreman for a day's work.

I have just finished reading a new book, *Our Liverpool*, by Piers Dudgeon, which gives a marvellous oral history of the people of the city and their memories of work, the war, community and life in general. Piers quotes ex-docker, Bill Smathers about his days on the docks: *"You had to 'get on the stand', and if your face fitted, you got a job. You had to form a stand inside the dock gates then. The boss would come out and put his hand on your shoulder. Well, when he done that, you were employed. You might get half a day's work, a day's work, or you might get a week's work, which was very, very seldom. Only the bosses, like the office staff, were employed permanent. The ordinary dockers were all casual workers. You got eight shillings a day. That's all and you had to work very hard for it. You had no mechanical gear. Everything was hand-balled … you worked any kind of cargo that came along … grain, hides, sugar, tea, cotton, asbestos, carbon-black. You were glad to do the day's work to get the money."*

This is just one of many such sharp insights into the Liverpudlian character and is the real story behind these photographs. Without the oral accounts, they are diminished in meaning. The words bring history to life.

BERESFORD ROAD, c1890.

Old photographs of the South End are, strangely, less common than those of Everton, Kirkdale and the North End in general. In fact, in some kind of perverse reversal, the better off the area, the fewer old photographs, particularly of street life. With camera ownership being very much restricted to the better-off in the 1890s, I would have expected that most photographers would have been keener on recording their own areas – although a regular category in amateur photographic society competitions was for street characters/scenes.

The street scene is of Beresford Road as it crosses Mill Street. The church on the corner is St Cleopas, with St Cleopas School next to it. Judging by the number of children in the street, school is out. The photograph shows a well-ordered neighbourhood with the children generally smartly dressed – although there are two bare-footed boys just behind the two girls in the foreground. Although the image lacks sharpness, the shop on the corner is owned by William Needs, greengrocer.

PARK HILL ROAD, c1910.

Another image by the same photographer, the focus of this shot appears to be the shop of Ann Young, confectioner and wholesaler of crumpets and muffins, at 64 Park Hill Road, with a young delivery boy in the doorway. The street looks prosperous and ordered, clearly a respectable neighbourhood.

It is great to have 'ordinary' streets of areas such as the Dingle captured for posterity. The prevailing opinion that such districts were all poverty-stricken was clearly not the case. These are streets outside of the inner-ring of courts and tenements and my 1910 *Gore's Directory* lists the next-door neighbours as John Rathbone, police constable (number 66) and Park Hill Higher Grade School (44-62). Other occupations on the street include joiners, a printer, pawnbroker, engine driver, teacher of music and coppersmith – a real solid mix of working-class trades.

KARDOMAH
TEA TEA

KENT SQUARE, c1930.

These images were all taken by Father d'Andria, the parish priest of St Peter's Church, in Seel Street. His small collection of photographs is in the Liverpool Record Office collection.

The area around Kent Street and Pitt Street was the centre of Liverpool's Chinatown. Kent Square was once a very fashionable place in which to live and even into the early twentieth century it held its charm. Charles Reilly, the University's dynamic Professor of Architecture, described it as: "... *one of the most charming things in Liverpool, it is a tiny square, not really a square but an oblong, with a single narrow street entering the middle of each of the two shorter sides ... it is like a Cambridge court, rather than a square, only it is Georgian, with all the elegance that implies. The houses are small and refined. The doorways are in pairs, raised above the ground, and giving on to a stone landing, each doorway is pedimented and the entablatures have varying motifs modelled on them: some rams' heads, some urns, some flowers. Many of the doors – neat six-panel doors with raised panels – have even their Georgian knockers left.*

*It is altogether charming. At present, one wise decorator lives in it and some Chinamen. If anyone, however, wants to found a settlement, and at the same time preserve a beautiful thing, let him buy these houses.*"

Sadly, no such visionary came forward to preserve the square for, within little more than a decade, the area was demolished to make way for council tenements, which lasted little more than fifty years before they too were reduced to dust.

CLAYTON STREET, NUMBER 3 COURT, c1930.

Here is another fascinating photograph of a Liverpool court, which demands a storyline. The young man with his caged bird standing between two grim-faced women suggests impending eviction. Certainly, it was around the time that the street, which backed on to the Walker Art Gallery and the Museum, was demolished in the 1930s slum clearance programme, which saw Gerard Gardens spring up nearby. What tough lives are etched in all their faces! Everything about their demeanour suggests resignation and defeat – but perhaps there was a different storyline – although I don't think they had just won the Pools!

BYROM TERRACE, c1930.

The media's fascination with Liverpool is not a recent phenomenon. It used to really annoy me back in the 1980s when London-based newspapers continually featured pictures of Liverpool to illustrate urban deprivation in Britain. I particularly remember *The Sunday Times* leading with a photograph of the Pier Head shot from Birkenhead. In the foreground was a car breakage yard – the cheap headline being 'Liverpool on the scrapheap'.

For years, Liverpool was the target of television and newspaper features seemingly revelling in the spiral of decline the city was facing – but then, in 2008, it all started to disappear as the realisation dawned that it was no longer such a soft target. However, one interesting legacy is that future generations will have no shortage of images to illustrate those hard years. In a similar way, the city attracted press coverage in the 1930s and the photograph of Byrom Terrace was used to illustrate an article in the *Daily Herald* with the caption: 'The terrible conditions under which people live in the slum areas of Liverpool are strikingly illustrated by this picture of Byrom Terrace.'

No doubt the image annoyed many people in the city – who maybe felt such photographs gave a distorted view of Liverpool, and I would have been amongst them, had I been around at the time. But you cannot have it both ways – and the photograph is a valuable reflection of what life was like for a sizeable number of citizens back in the 1930s. Poverty is poverty and pretending Liverpool is just about fine buildings and great tourist attractions is no real answer.

CANTERBURY STREET, 1946.

The first reaction might be that this is another photograph of Liverpool in the 1930s but the young mother's dress is the giveaway. The year is 1946 and the press caption on the reverse states: Tenements in Canterbury Street, Liverpool, are being demolished while they are still occupied. Mrs Rossiter, of No. 41, in the doorway of her scullery.

Whatever happened to Mrs Rossiter and her daughter, who would now be about 65? A decade later, Harold Macmillan announced, 'Let us be frank about it ... most of our people have never had it so good.' For those that were left behind, nothing much changed. Hopefully, Mrs Rossiter's life improved as the austerity years moved into the prosperity years – now that would be an interesting story.

EDGE LANE, 1939.

At first glimpse, just a photograph of a Liverpool tobacconist – in this case 426 Edge Lane. Without the caption on the back, this press photograph would simply be a record of a shop advertising the joy of smoking (For your throat's sake – smoke Craven A). The only clue to another storyline is the man with his back to the camera. Surely, if he were the proud shop owner he would be facing the photographer!

The caption reveals all, or nearly all, because I am missing the conclusion. The date is 24 January 1939: 'A member of Liverpool CID locking up the premises of 426 Edge Lane yesterday. The tobacconist occupier, Thomas Edward Kelly, aged 32, was arrested and charged at Liverpool yesterday with having in his possession four kegs of potassium chlorate. He was remanded in custody.'

On 16 January, the IRA launched a campaign of bombing and sabotage directed at government targets such as post offices, bridges and railway stations. The object was material damage, not civilian deaths, although a number of people were injured. Much of the campaign was targeted on London, although Birmingham and Manchester were affected. In the same year, 17-year-old Brendan Behan, a runner for the IRA, was arrested in Liverpool following bombing in Coventry. He was sentenced to three years in Borstal – an experience he used in writing *Borstal Boy*.

Once again, there is a fascinating story behind the photograph. Sadly, too often, all we are left with is an image with no obvious thread to follow. A lesson to us all – always caption photographs for future generations.

Postscript: Kelly was charged, along with eight other Liverpool men, with possessing explosives, weapons and ammunition with intent to endanger life and cause destruction of property. Kelly was later accused of being the adjutant of an IRA cell. Five of the men stood trial at Manchester Assizes charged with conspiracy to cause explosions. One, Hannon, was found guilty and sentenced to seven years penal servitude. The rest, including Kelly, were found not guilty and discharged.

Number 426 Edge Lane stood one along from the corner of Binns Road, going towards town and just opposite The Barbers.

Player's Navy Cut
TOBACCO & CIGARETTES.
PICCADILLY
VIRGINIA CIGARETTES
10 FOR 4D
For your throats sake smoke
CRAVEN A
426
For your throat's sake – smoke
CRAVEN "A"
Cadbury's Chocolates
For your throat's sake-smoke
CRAVEN "A"
WILLS'S CAPSTAN
NAVY CUT CIGARETTES

SEFTON PARK, 1890s.

The scene is little changed today, although the boathouse has been replaced by an impressive modern cafe.

I need a clothing expert to date these three photographs. My suspicion is that they are late 1890s / early 1900s but they could be earlier. The December of 1890 was the coldest on record until December 2010, so possibly the photographer's intention was to record that severe winter. The lake is well and truly frozen over – with no Health and Safety worries for the dozens of skaters taking advantage. I particularly like the photograph of the young girls letting their hair down.

Clearly, from the warm outfits, this was mainly a middle-class day out. It is shocking to think that there were thousands of children walking around with bare feet only a few miles away, but Liverpool really was a tale of two cities.

LIME STREET, 1931.

A busy view of Ranelagh Place and Lime Street in 1931. The building, partly shown, on the direct left, is the original Lewis's department store which was bombed in May 1941. Nearby Blackler's store, and the facing block on the corner of Lime Street (the building with the strange observation tower in the top photograph) were no less fortunate. The Palais de Luxe, whose awning can be seen just beyond the second tram, was also badly damaged but reopened only a month later. After a further fire in 1951, it was modernised again, only to close for the final time in 1959 to make way for the modern development that is still with us (photograph page 55).

Looking at the 1930s photograph, it makes sense of the ostentatious and somewhat unnecessary tower on The Vines public house. It looks as if the architect was trying to balance the streetscape. Against today's 1960s modern development, it looks more eccentric than it would have done in its original setting.

In the top photograph, the corner block housed John Tyler (shoes and boots), The Fifty Shilling Taylors, Meeson's (confectioners) and Finlay & Co (tobacconists). Looking at my 1932 *Gore's Directory*, it is surprising how many creative industries, as we now call them, were concentrated in Lime Street. Apart from the four cinemas (the Forum, Scala, Palais de Luxe and Futurist) along with The Empire Theatre, there were all manner of small businesses including photographers (Dorondo Mills and Carbonora), Jazon & Montgomery (theatrical agents), the Variety Artists Federation (agent Ma Egerton), the Cinema Publicity Supply Company (poster writers), Liverpool Press Club (and sundry press photographers), Radio Pictures Ltd (film renters), Walturdaw Cinema Supply Company and North Western Film Booking Agency.

It is sad to contemplate Lime Street today; this lively mix of businesses has been replaced by a very dead and degraded thoroughfare. True, the buildings on the right hand side have all survived, but they look uncared for and are an ugly mix of empty shops and cinemas and fast food outlets. A facelift is long overdue to restore some of the street's grandeur. As for the facing 1960s block, the less said the better. The marvellous new panorama of Lime Street that has been gained from removing the blocks fronting Lime Street Station is sadly framed by an eyesore, which will probably remain for years given current public sector funding. A great shame that it missed out on the spending spree of the last decade.

HILLING TAILORS
FINLAY & Co
NO ENTRY
MY 2550

BUSY CLEANING WINDOWS, 1953.

This photograph marked the completion of my first year's blogging. Like the photograph that was my first post in January 2010, this image is by that talented American photographer, Frank Dugan, who was here for such a short time at the beginning of the 1950s. It captures a lost world – the once-familiar sight of a proud housewife rather precariously cleaning her windows.

BARTHOLOMEW'S
POCKET
ATLAS AND GUIDE
TO
LIVERPOOL
ONE SHILLING NET

# BARTHOLOMEW'S

## POCKET

# ATLAS AND GUIDE

## TO

# LIVERPOOL AND BIRKENHEAD

DEUS NOBIS HÆC OTIA FECIT

*Printed and Published in Great Britain by*

JOHN BARTHOLOMEW & SON, LTD.

THE GEOGRAPHICAL INSTITUTE

DUNCAN STREET, EDINBURGH

1928

# POCKET GUIDE

TO

# LIVERPOOL AND BIRKENHEAD.

| | |
|---|---|
| **Area of City and County Borough of Liverpool** | **21,242 acres** |
| **Population in 1921 of City and County Borough** | **802,940** |
| **Area of County Borough of Bootle** | **1,947 acres** |
| **Population in 1921 of County Borough of Bootle** | **76,487** |
| **Area of County Borough of Birkenhead** | **3,909 acres** |
| **Population in 1921 of County Borough of Birkenhead** | **145,577** |
| **Area of County Borough of Wallasey** | **3,324 acres** |
| **Population in 1921 of County Borough of Wallasey** | **90,809** |

## PRINCIPAL RAILWAY STATIONS

| | | | |
|---|---|---|---|
| **Central** (Cheshire Lines; Mersey Railway, Underground) | 32 | **Q** | **10** |
| **Exchange** (London Midland and Scottish) | 31 | **N** | **11** |
| **James Street** (Mersey Railway; Overhead Railway) | 32 | **P** | **12** |
| **Lime Street** (London Midland and Scottish) | 32 | **P** | **9** |
| **Riverside** (London Midland and Scottish) | 31 | **O** | **13** |

There are also numerous Suburban Stations.

## HOTELS

| | | | |
|---|---|---|---|
| **Adelphi,** Ranelagh Place | 32 | **P** | **9** |
| **Angel,** 22 Dale Street | 32 | **O** | **11** |
| **Antrim,** 73 Mount Pleasant | 32 | **Q** | **9** |
| **Bradford,** 53 Tithebarn Street | 31 | **O** | **11** |
| **Burleigh,** Berry Street | 33 | **R** | **10** |
| **Childwall Abbey,** 4½ miles south-east by Car or Railway. | | | |
| **Continental,** 33 Mount Pleasant | 32 | **Q** | **9** |
| **Cook's Mona,** St John's Lane | 32 | **P** | **10** |
| **Exchange Station,** Tithebarn Street | 31 | **O** | **11** |
| **Hanover,** 62 Hanover Street | 32 | **Q** | **10** |
| **Hotel Victoria,** Heswall, 7 miles south-west of Birkenhead. | | | |
| **Hunt's Hotel** (Temperance), 52 Mount Pleasant | 32 | **Q** | **9** |
| **Imperial,** 20 Lime Street | 32 | **P** | **10** |
| **Lawrence,** 75 Mount Pleasant | 33 | **Q** | **9** |
| **Lime Street Station Hotel** (North-Western) | 32 | **P** | **10** |
| **Mellifont,** 117 Mount Pleasant | 33 | **Q** | **9** |
| **Mitre,** Dale Street | 32 | **O** | **11** |
| **Queen's,** Birkenhead Park | 36 | **B** | **2** |
| **St John's,** 18 St John's Lane | 32 | **P** | **10** |
| **Shaftesbury** (Temperance), 28 Mount Pleasant | 32 | **Q** | **9** |
| **Stork,** 2 Queen Square | 32 | **P** | **10** |
| **Victoria,** 21 St John's Lane | 32 | **P** | **10** |
| **Woodside,** 2 Chester Street, Birkenhead | 37 | **C** | **2** |

## RESTAURANTS AND TEA ROOMS

**Angel Hotel,** 22 Dale Street.
**Bear's Paw,** 53 Lord Street.
**Berkley Cafe,** 71 Church Street.
**Cafe Parisien,** 176-180 London Road.
**Carlton,** 8 Eberle Street.
**Connolly's** (Oyster Rooms), 29 Basnett Street.
**Cooper's Stores,** Church Street.
**Cottle's Cafés,** Bold Street; Dale Street; Church Street; Elliot Street; Lord Street; N. John Street; Oldhall Street; Paradise Street; and Ranelagh Street.
**Creewood,** 17 Brunswick Street.
**Crocodile,** 54 Cable Street.
**Crooked Billet,** 28 Exchange Street East.
**Duffrey's** (Oyster Rooms), Lime Street.
**Fullers,** Dale Street; Bold Street; and Ranelagh Street.

Restaurants and Tea Rooms—*continued.*

**Kardomah Cafés,** 37 Castle Street; 32 Church Street; 40 Dale Street; and 14 Redcross Street.

**Kirkland,** 11 Lord Street and 13 Hardman Street.

**J. Lyons & Co., Ltd., State Café,** Dale Street; 14 Cook Street; 87 Lord Street; 53 London Road; 23 Old Haymarket; 59 Church Street; and 10 James Street.

**Mecca Cafés,** Exchange Buildings; Drury Lane; Old Hall Street.

**Reece's Cafés,** 1a Bold Street; 14 Castle Street; 29 Dale Street; 3 Deane Street; 40 Great Charlotte Street; Parker Street; and 7 Queen Avenue.

**Ridgeway's,** India Buildings, Water Street; Royal Liver Buildings, Pierhead; and 7 Whitechapel.

**Sainsbury's,** Exchange Street East; Exchange Flags; and Brunswick Street.

**Silver Grill,** 106 Dale Street.

**State,** 14 Dale Street.

**Stork,** 2 Queen Square.

**Strand,** Strand, near Water Street; 26 Brunswick Street.

**Swiss Café,** 57 Bold Street.

**Vegetarian Cafés,** 54 Whitechapel; and 24 Dale Street.

**Yamen Café,** 65 Bold Street.

## BATHS

**Corporation Baths,** Burrough's Gardens; Cornwallis Street; Lister Drive; Lodge Lane; Margaret Street; Queen's Drive; Picton Road; Speke Road; Steble Street; Westminster Road; and Woolton.

**Birkenhead Corporation Baths,** Livingstone Street; Argyle Street South.

**Bootle Corporation Baths,** Balliol Road.

**Turkish Baths,** Duke Street; Eberle Street.

**Vapour Baths,** at several of the Corporation Baths.

## THEATRES

| | | | |
|---|---|---|---|
| **Empire,** Lime Street | 32 | **P** | **9** |
| **Metropole,** Stanley Road, Bootle. | | | |
| **Pavilion,** Lodge Lane | 24 | **T** | **6** |
| **Playhouse,** Williamson Square | 32 | **P** | **10** |
| **Rotunda,** Stanley Road | 20 | **K** | **8** |
| **Royal Court,** Great Charlotte Street | 32 | **P** | **10** |
| **Royal Hippodrome and Theatre of Varieties,** West Derby Road | 22 | **O** | **6** |
| **Shakespeare,** Fraser Street | 32 | **O** | **9** |

## CINEMATOGRAPH THEATRES

**Futurist**; **Scala**; and **Palais de Luxe,** Lime Street. **Majestic,** Daulby Street. **Olympia,** West Derby Road. **Liverpool Picture House,** Clayton Square. **Rialto,** Upper Parliament Street. **Trocadero,** Camden Street.

## MUSEUMS, ART GALLERIES AND LIBRARIES

| | | | |
|---|---|---|---|
| **Public Reference Library** (Picton Reading Room, Hugh Frederick Hornby Library, Patents and Newspaper Department), William Brown Street | 32 | **O** | **10** |
| With 17 Branch Libraries and Reading Rooms. | | | |
| **Central Lending Library,** William Brown Street | 32 | **O** | **10** |
| **Museums** (including Lord Derby Natural History Museum and Mayer Museum of Archaeology and Ethnography), William Brown Street | 32 | **O** | **10** |
| **Walker Art Gallery,** William Brown Street | 32 | **O** | **10** |

## MONUMENTS

| | | | |
|---|---|---|---|
| **Balfour, Alexander,** St John's Gardens | 32 | **O** | **10** |
| **Beaconsfield,** St George's Hall | 32 | **O** | **10** |
| **Canning,** in Town Hall | 32 | **O** | **12** |
| **Cenotaph,** St George's Plateau | 32 | **O** | **10** |
| **Earle, Major-General,** St George's Hall | 32 | **O** | **10** |
| **Edward VII.,** Pierhead | 32 | **P** | **12** |
| **Edward VII.,** Stanley Gardens, Bootle | 17 | **E** | **7** |
| **Engine Room Heroes' Memorial,** St Nicholas Place | 31 | **O** | **12** |
| **Forwood,** St John's Gardens | 32 | **O** | **10** |
| **George III.,** London Road | 22 | **P** | **8** |
| **Gladstone,** St John's Gardens | 32 | **O** | **10** |
| **Huskisson,** St James' Cemetery, S 9, and at Custom House | 32 | **Q** | **12** |
| **Jones, Sir Alfred,** Pierhead | 32 | **O** | **12** |

**Monuments**—*continued.*

| | | | |
|---|---|---|---|
| **King's Liverpool Regiment Memorial,** St John's Gardens | 32 | O | 10 |
| **Laird, John,** Hamilton Square, Birkenhead | 37 | C | 2 |
| **Lestor, Canon,** St John's Gardens | 32 | O | 10 |
| **Nelson,** Exchange Flags | 32 | O | 12 |
| **Nightingale, Florence,** Princes Road | 24 | T | 9 |
| **Nugent, Monsignor,** St John's Gardens | 32 | O | 10 |
| **Prince Albert,** St George's Hall | 32 | O | 10 |
| **Queen Victoria,** St George's Hall | 32 | O | 10 |
| **Queen Victoria Memorial,** Lord Street | 32 | P | 12 |
| **Rathbone, William,** St John's Gardens; also Sefton Park | 32 | O | 10 |
| **Wellington,** Commutation Row | 32 | O | 9 |

## PUBLIC BUILDINGS

| | | | |
|---|---|---|---|
| **Blind, School for the,** Hardman Street | 33 | R | 9 |
| **Blue Coat Hospital and School,** Wavertree | 15 | W | 1 |
| **Cathedral, The,** St James' Road | 33 | S | 10 |
| **Central Hall (Garrett Memorial),** Renshaw Street | 32 | Q | 10 |
| **Collegiate School,** Shaw Street | 22 | O | 7 |
| **Corn Exchange,** Brunswick Street | 32 | P | 12 |
| **Cotton Exchange,** Old Hall Street | 31 | O | 12 |
| **County Sessions House,** William Brown Street | 32 | O | 9 |
| **Cunard Buildings,** Pierhead | 32 | P | 12 |
| **Custom House,** Canning Place | 32 | Q | 12 |
| **Education Offices,** Sir Thomas Street | 32 | O | 11 |
| **Exchange Buildings,** Castle Street | 32 | O | 12 |
| **General Post Office,** Victoria Street | 32 | P | 11 |
| **Gladstone's Birthplace,** 62 Rodney Street | 33 | R | 9 |
| **Inland Revenue Offices,** Victoria Street | 32 | O | 11 |
| **Liverpool Institute,** Mount Street | 33 | R | 9 |
| **Municipal Offices,** Dale Street | 32 | O | 11 |
| **Philharmonic Hall,** Myrtle Street | 33 | R | 9 |
| **Produce Exchange,** Victoria Street | 32 | O | 10 |
| **Roman Catholic Pro-Cathedral** (St Nicholas), Hawke Street | 32 | P | 9 |
| **Royal Infirmary,** Pembroke Place | 22 | P | 8 |
| **Royal Institution,** 22 Colquitt Street | 33 | R | 10 |
| **Royal Insurance Buildings,** Dale Street | 32 | O | 11 |
| **Royal Liver Building,** Pierhead | 32 | O | 12 |
| **Sailors' Home,** Paradise Street | 33 | Q | 11 |
| **St George's Hall,** Lime Street | 32 | O | 10 |
| **St John's Market,** Elliot Street | 32 | P | 10 |
| **School of Art,** Hope Street | 23 | R | 9 |
| **Technical School, Central,** Byrom Street | 32 | O | 10 |
| **Town Hall,** Dale Street | 32 | O | 12 |
| **University,** Brownlow Hill | 22 | Q | 8 |
| **Y.M.C.A.,** Mount Pleasant | 22 | Q | 8 |

## PRINCIPAL PARKS, Etc.

| | | | |
|---|---|---|---|
| **Aintree Race Course,** 5 miles north from Exchange Station. | | | |
| **Allerton Estate** (150 acres) } 6 miles south-east from Lime Street Station. | | | |
| **Allerton Tower Estate** (78 acres) } 6 miles south-east from Lime Street Station. | | | |
| **Birkenhead Park** (190 acres). | | | |
| **Botanic Gardens** (11 acres) | 13 | R | 4 |
| **Bowring Park** (100 acres), Roby, 5 miles east from Town Hall. | | | |
| **Calderstones Estate** (94 acres), 4 miles east-south-east from Town Hall. | | | |
| **Camp Hill Estate** (18¾ acres). | | | |
| **Clarke Gardens** (41½ acres). | | | |
| **Clubmoor Recreation Ground** (24½ acres) | 10 | K | 1 |
| **Greenbank Estate** (14 acres), Greenbank Road | 15 | X | 3 |
| **Hart Hill Estate** (32½ acres). | | | |
| **Kensington Gardens** (18½ acres) | 22 | Q | 5 |
| **Long Lane Recreation Ground** (35 acres), Garston. | | | |
| **Lower Breck Road Recreation Ground** (22½ acres) | 11 | M | 3 |
| **Newsham Park** and **Sheil Park** (149½ acres) | 11 | O | 2 and 4 |
| **Princes Park** (44½ acres) | 25 | V | 8 |
| **Rice Lane Recreation Ground** (24½ acres) | 7 | C | 2 |
| **Sefton Park** (269 acres) | 25 | X | 5 |
| **Sherwood's Lane Recreation Ground** (10½ acres). | | | |
| **Sparrow Hall Estate** (30 acres). | | | |
| **Springfield Park** (21¾ acres). | | | |
| **Springwood Gardens, etc.** (22½ acres). | | | |
| **Stanley Park** (100 acres) | 9 | H | 5 |
| **Walton Hall Estate** (130½ acres). | | | |
| **Wavertree Park** (32½ acres) | 13 | R | 4 |
| **Wavertree Playground** (108 acres) | 15 | V | 2 |
| **Woolton Wood Estate** (62 acres). | | | |

# INDEX TO STREETS AND OTHER PLACES.

The figure immediately following the name indicates the page of the Atlas, and the succeeding letter and figure the square on that page in which the name will be found. Thus, Abbey Rd. will be found on page 10 in the square under the top marginal letter **L** and along from the side marginal figure **3.**


Abattoir, The, Trowbridge St. 22 **Q** 9
Abattoir, Tranmere . 37 **C** 3
Abbey Rd. . 10 **L** 3
Abbey St. . 21 **M** 7
Abbot St. . 20 **L** 6
Aber St. . 21 **O** 6
Aber St., Bootle . 16 **B** 9
Abercromby Sq. . 23 **R** 8
Aberdeen St. . 35 **W** 9
Abingdon Rd. . 8 **G** 1
Abram St. . 20 **M** 7
Abyssinia St. . 14 **U** 3
Acton St. . 14 **T** 5
Adam St. . 20 **K** 5
Addison St. . 31 **N** 10
Adelaide Pl. . 20 **M** 8
Adelaide Rd. . 22 **Q** 6
Adelaide St. . 20 **K** 7
Adelphi Hotel . 32 **P** 9
Adlington St. . 31 **N** 10
Admiral Grove . 25 **V** 8
Admiral Place . 35 **V** 9
Admiral St. . 35 **V** 9
Afghan St. . 20 **K** 6
Agate St. . 21 **M** 5
Agnes St. . 23 **R** 5
Agricultural Show Ground, B'head 38 **A** 4
Aigburth Drive . 25 **X** 6
Aigburth Rd. . 25 **X** 8
Aigburth St. . 24 **S** 6
Aiken St. . 35 **W** 10
Ainsworth St. . 32 **P** 9
Aintree Rd. . 16 **B** 5
Aintree St. . 20 **K** 9
Airdale Rd. . 15 **W** 3
Airlie Grove . 11 **M** 1
Ajax St. . 18 **F** 8
Albany Rd. . 22 **P** 6
Albany Rd., Tranmere . 36 **B** 4
Albany St. . 17 **C** 8
Albert Dock . 32 **Q** 12
Albert Drive . 6 **A** 3
Albert Parade . 32 **Q** 13
Albert Rd. . 14 **T** 4
Albert Rd., Tue Brook . 11 **M** 1
Albert St. . 23 **Q** 7
Albert Ter. . 23 **S** 6
Albert Edward Rd. 22 **P** 6
Albion St. . 20 **K** 7
Albion St., New Brighton . 38 **B** 1
Aldams Grove . 18 **F** 6
Alder St. . 35 **V** 9
Alderson Rd. . 14 **T** 3
Alderville Rd. . 8 **G** 1
Alexander St. . 19 **H** 5
Alexander Pope St. 31 **N** 10
Alexandra Docks 27 **B** 11
Alexandra Drive . 25 **X** 8
Alexandra Drive, Walton . 6 **A** 3
Alexandra Rd. . 14 **T** 4
Alexandra Ter. . 24 **T** 9
Alexandra & Canada Goods Stn. 28 **E** 10
Alexandra & Langton Docks Goods Station . 26 **A** 10
Alexandra Dock Stations . 27 **C** 10
Alfonso Rd. . 18 **G** 7
Alford St. . 13 **R** 2
Alfred Dock, Wallasey . 39 **C** 4
Alfred Pl. . 35 **W** 9
Alfred St., Great George St. . 33 **S** 10
Alfred St., Picton Rd. . 14 **T** 4
Alice St. . 23 **Q** 7
Allen St. . 11 **M** 4
All Saints Church, Bentley Rd. . 24 **V** 7
All Saints Church, Gt. Nelson St. . 21 **M** 9
All Souls' Church, Eaton St. . 31 **M** 11
Alma St. . 21 **O** 7
Almond St. . 23 **S** 7
Alroy Rd. . 9 **I** 5
Alt St. . 23 **T** 7
Altcar Av. . 14 **U** 4
Althorp St. . 35 **X** 10
Alton Rd. . 11 **N** 2
Amber St. . 23 **Q** 7
Amberley St. . 24 **T** 8
Ambrose Pl. . 30 **L** 9
Ambrose St. . 22 **P** 7
Amersham Rd. . 9 **G** 1
Amity St. . 35 **V** 9
Amos St. . 20 **M** 7
Anderson St. . 20 **K** 8
Andrew St. . 18 **G** 5
Anfield Park Cem. 9 **G** 3
Anfield Rd. . 10 **L** 4
Angel Hotel . 32 **O** 11
Angela St. . 23 **S** 6
Anglesea Rd. . 7 **E** 3
Anglesea St. . 35 **W** 10
Annerley St. . 14 **T** 4
Annesley Rd., Seacombe . 38 **B** 3
Ansdell St. . 32 **Q** 12
Anson Pl. . 22 **P** 8
Anson St. . 22 **P** 8
Anthony St. . 20 **L** 8
Antonio St. . 18 **E** 6
Apollo St. . 11 **M** 4
Apothecaries Hall, Wood St. . 33 **Q** 10
April Grove . 11 **N** 2
Arcade, The . 32 **P** 11
Archer St. . 19 **I** 7
Architecture, School of . 32 **P** 11
Arctic Rd. . 27 **B** 10
Argos Rd. . 18 **F** 7
Argyle Rd. . 10 **L** 3
Argyle St. . 35 **Q** 11
Argyle St. South, Tranmere . 36 **B** 3
Ariel St. . 18 **F** 8
Arkles Lane . 10 **K** 4
Arkles Rd. . 10 **K** 4
Arkwright St. . 20 **L** 8
Arley St. . 31 **M** 10
Arlington Av. . 15 **X** 3
Arlington St. . 30 **I** 9
Armley Rd. . 10 **K** 3
Arno Rd., Oxton . 36 **A** 3
Arnold St. . 24 **U** 8
Arnot St. . 18 **F** 5
Arnside Rd. . 23 **R** 5
Arrad St. . 23 **R** 8
Arrow St. . 23 **S** 5
Art Gallery, Colquitt St. . 33 **R** 10
Art, School of, Wallasey . 38 **B** 3
Arthur St. . 35 **X** 10
Arthur St., Walton 7 **D** 4
Arundel Av. . 25 **V** 5
Arundel St. . 24 **U** 8
Arundel St., County Rd. . 18 **F** 5
Asbridge St. . 24 **U** 7
Ascot St. . 30 **K** 9
Ash Grove, Linton St. . 11 **O** 4
Ash Grove, Picton Rd. . 14 **T** 3
Ash St., Bootle . 16 **B** 7
Ash St., Wavertree Rd. . 23 **S** 5
Ashburton Rd., Oxton . 36 **A** 2
Ashcroft St. . 17 **C** 9
Ashdale Rd. . 7 **C** 1
Ashfield, Picton Rd. . 14 **T** 3
Ashfield St. . 30 **L** 10
Ashleigh . 10 **L** 4
Ashley St. . 22 **P** 7
Ashton Hall, Ashton St. . 22 **Q** 8
Ashton St. . 22 **Q** 8
Ashville Rd., Birkenhead Park . 36 **A** 2
Ashwell St. . 34 **T** 10
Ashworth St. . 13 **S** 1
Askew St. . 8 **G** 5
Aspen Grove . 24 **U** 6
Aspinall St. . 19 **I** 9
Assembly Rooms, Walton . 19 **H** 5
Astor St. . 8 **E** 4
Atheldene Rd. . 8 **G** 1

| | | | |
|---|---|---|---|
| Athenaeum | 32 | P | 10 |
| Atherton St. | 32 | P | 11 |
| Atherton St., New Brighton | 38 | B | 1 |
| Athol St. | 30 | K | 10 |
| Atlantic Rd. | 27 | B | 9 |
| Atlas Rd. | 26 | B | 9 |
| Atlas St. | 30 | L | 11 |
| Attwood St. | 19 | I | 5 |
| Atwell St. | 21 | N | 5 |
| Aubrey St. | 21 | N | 6 |
| Audley St. | 22 | P | 8 |
| Audley St., Bootle | 16 | B | 8 |
| Aughton St. | 20 | K | 8 |
| August Rd. | 11 | M | 2 |
| August St. | 16 | A | 7 |
| Avison St. | 34 | T | 9 |
| Avon St. | 11 | M | 4 |
| Avondale Rd. | 15 | V | 3 |
| Back Boundary St. | 20 | K | 8 |
| Back Bridport St. | 32 | P | 9 |
| Back Canning St. | 33 | S | 9 |
| Back Chatham Pl. | 23 | R | 6 |
| Back Clare St. | 32 | O | 9 |
| Back Compton St. | 21 | N | 5 |
| Back Falkner St. | 23 | S | 8 |
| Back Falkner St. East | 23 | S | 7 |
| Back Field St. | 21 | N | 8 |
| Back Gibson St. | 24 | T | 9 |
| Back Gill St. | 22 | P | 8 |
| Back Grafton St. | 34 | T | 11 |
| Back Goree | 32 | P | 12 |
| Back Great Mersey St. | 19 | I | 8 |
| Back Guildford St. | 21 | N | 7 |
| Back Huskisson St. | 23 | S | 8 |
| Back Irvine St. | 23 | Q | 6 |
| Back Kelvin Grove | 25 | V | 8 |
| Back Langham St. | 19 | H | 5 |
| Back Leeds St. | 31 | N | 12 |
| Back Molyneux Rd. | 22 | P | 5 |
| Back Newlands St. | 21 | M | 6 |
| Back Nile St. | 33 | S | 10 |
| Back Parkfield Rd. | 25 | X | 7 |
| Back Parliament St. | 34 | S | 10 |
| Back Percy St. | 33 | S | 9 |
| Back Portland St. | 30 | L | 10 |
| Back Queen Anne St. | 21 | O | 8 |
| Back Roscommon St. | | M | 8 |
| Back St James' Mount | 33 | S | 9 |
| Back Salisbury St. | 21 | N | 8 |
| Back Stanley St. | 32 | O | 11 |
| Badminton St. | 35 | X | 10 |
| Bagnall St. | 20 | K | 5 |
| Bagot St. | 14 | U | 3 |
| Bailey St. | 33 | R | 10 |
| Baines Pl. | 21 | M | 6 |
| Baker St. | 22 | O | 6 |
| Bala St. | 10 | L | 4 |
| Bala St., Bootle | 16 | B | 9 |
| Balfour Institute | 24 | U | 5 |
| Balfour St. | 19 | I | 5 |
| Balliol Rd. | 17 | D | 8 |
| Balliol Rd. Stn. | 17 | D | 9 |
| Balls Rd., B'head | 36 | A | 3 |
| Balm St. | 22 | Q | 5 |
| Balmoral Rd., Prescot Rd. | 12 | P | 3 |
| Balmoral Rd.. Walton | 6 | B | 2 |
| Baltic Rd. | 27 | B | 9 |
| Baltic St. | 20 | K | 5 |
| Baltimore St. | 33 | Q | 9 |
| Bamber St. | 23 | Q | 7 |
| Banastre St. | 31 | N | 10 |
| Bangor St. | 16 | B | 8 |
| Bank Rd. | 16 | C | 8 |
| Bankfield St. | 28 | G | 10 |
| Bankfield & Canada Dock Goods Station | 28 | F | 10 |
| Bank Hall Lane | 29 | G | 9 |
| Bank Hall Stn. | 18 | G | 8 |
| Bank Hall St. | 18 | G | 9 |
| Banner St. | 14 | U | 3 |
| Bannerman St. | 14 | T | 4 |
| Baptist St. | 31 | O | 9 |
| Barbara St. | 35 | V | 11 |
| Barclay St. | 35 | W | 10 |
| Bardsay Rd. | 8 | G | 4 |
| Barlow Lane | 19 | G | 6 |
| Barlow St. | 19 | H | 6 |
| Barmouth St. | 30 | K | 10 |
| Barnes St. | 21 | M | 5 |
| Barnet St. | 24 | T | 5 |
| Barnhill Rd. | 15 | X | 1 |
| Barnsbury Rd. | 8 | G | 1 |
| Barnston Rd. | 6 | A | 1 |
| Barr St. | 29 | G | 9 |
| Barrington Rd. | 15 | V | 3 |
| Barry St. | 19 | I | 6 |
| Barter St. | 35 | W | 9 |
| Bartlett St. | 14 | U | 3 |
| Barton Rd. | 7 | D | 3 |
| Barton St. | 31 | M | 12 |
| Basnett St. | 32 | P | 10 |
| Batchelor St. | 32 | O | 11 |
| Bath Lane, Bath St. | 31 | N | 12 |
| Bath St. | 31 | N | 12 |
| Baths, Beckett St. | 21 | N | 8 |
| Baths, Bevington Bush | 21 | M | 10 |
| Baths, Bootle | 17 | D | 8 |
| Baths, Cornwallis St. | 33 | R | 10 |
| Baths, Lime Kiln Lane | 31 | M | 9 |
| Baths, Lister Drv. | 21 | O | 1 |
| Baths, Lodge Lane | 24 | T | 6 |
| Baths, Margaret St. | 21 | N | 6 |
| Baths, Marsh La. | 16 | A | 8 |
| Baths, Picton Rd. | 14 | U | 2 |
| Baths, Steble St. | 35 | V | 10 |
| Baths, Walton | 8 | E | 4 |
| Baths, Westminster Rd. | 19 | I | 7 |
| Battenberg St. | 22 | Q | 6 |
| Battery St. | 28 | F | 10 |
| Bay Horse Lane | 22 | P | 8 |
| Baythorne Rd. | 8 | F | 1 |
| Beacon Lane | 20 | K | 6 |
| Beacon St. | 29 | I | 10 |
| Beaconsfield Rd. | 7 | D | 3 |
| Beaconsfield Stat. | 32 | P | 9 |
| Beaconsfield St. | 24 | U | 7 |
| Beamish St. | 35 | V | 10 |
| Beatrice St., Bootle | 18 | E | 7 |
| Beatrice St., Great Homer St. | 20 | L | 8 |
| Beau Lane | 21 | N | 8 |
| Beau St. | 21 | N | 8 |
| Beaufort Rd., Birkenhead | 38 | A | 4 |
| Beaufort St. | 34 | T | 11 |
| Beaumaris St. | 28 | F | 9 |
| Beaumont St. | 24 | T | 7 |
| Beaver Grove | 6 | A | 1 |
| Bebington Rd., Tranmere | 36 | B | 4 |
| Becket St. | 19 | H | 8 |
| Beckett St. | 21 | N | 8 |
| Beckwith St. | 33 | Q | 11 |
| Beckwith St., Birkenhead | 36 | B | 2 |
| Becky St. | 11 | M | 4 |
| Bective St. | 14 | T | 4 |
| Bedford Av., Rock Ferry | 36 | B | 4 |
| Bedford Dr., Rock Ferry | 36 | B | 4 |
| Bedford Pl. | 27 | E | 9 |
| Bedford Rd. | 18 | E | 5 |
| Bedford Rd., Rock Ferry | 37 | C | 4 |
| Bedford St. North | 23 | Q | 8 |
| Bedford St. South | 23 | R | 8 |
| Beech Rd. | 8 | F | 3 |
| Beech St., Bootle | 16 | B | 7 |
| Beech St., Kensington | 12 | Q | 4 |
| Beech Bank Rd. | 15 | X | 3 |
| Beechdene Rd. | 10 | K | 3 |
| Beeston St. | 18 | G | 6 |
| Belgrave St. | 22 | O | 7 |
| Bell Rd., Seacombe | 39 | C | 3 |
| Bellamy Rd. | 18 | E | 5 |
| Belle Vue | 14 | T | 3 |
| Belmont Drive | 11 | N | 2 |
| Belmont Grove | 11 | N | 3 |
| Belmont Rd. | 11 | M | 4 |
| Beloe St. | 35 | X | 10 |
| Belvidere Rd. | 25 | W | 8 |
| Belvidere Rd., Liscard | 38 | B | 2 |
| Bembridge St. | 35 | W | 10 |
| Benbow St. | 27 | D | 10 |
| Benedict St. | 18 | E | 7 |
| Bengel St. | 22 | Q | 7 |
| Ben Johnson St. | 31 | N | 9 |
| Benledi St. | 30 | L | 9 |
| Benns Gdns. | 32 | P | 12 |
| Benson St. | 32 | Q | 9 |
| Bent St. | 31 | N | 9 |
| Bentinck St. | 30 | K | 11 |
| Bentinck St., Birkenhead | 36 | B | 2 |
| Bentley Rd. | 24 | V | 7 |
| Beresford Rd. | 35 | W | 10 |
| Beresford St. | 21 | M | 8 |
| Berkley St. | 34 | T | 9 |
| Berry St. | 33 | R | 10 |
| Berry St., Bootle | 17 | C | 9 |
| Bertram Rd. | 25 | X | 7 |
| Berwick St. | 11 | O | 4 |
| Bessemer St. | 35 | W | 10 |
| Beverley Rd. | 15 | W | 1 |
| Bevington Bush | 31 | N | 9 |
| Bevington Hill | 31 | M | 9 |
| Bevington St. | 31 | M | 10 |
| Bewley St. | 19 | I | 8 |
| Bianca St. | 18 | E | 8 |
| Bibby Lane | 16 | A | 9 |
| Bidder St. | 22 | O | 8 |
| Bidston Av. | 9 | I | 2 |
| Bidston Av., Birkenhead | 36 | A | 2 |
| Bidston Hill, Bidston | 38 | A | 4 |
| Bidston Moss, Bidston | 38 | A | 3 |
| Bidston Rd., Oxton | 36 | A | 2 |
| Bigham Rd. | 12 | P | 4 |
| Bingley Rd. | 10 | K | 3 |
| Binney St. | 22 | P | 7 |
| Binns Rd. | 13 | R | 1 |
| Birch St. | 30 | K | 11 |
| Birchall St. | 29 | H | 9 |
| Birchdale Rd. | 7 | D | 2 |
| Birchfield Rd. | 13 | R | 2 |
| Birchfield Rd., Walton | 8 | F | 3 |

| | | | |
|---|---|---|---|
| Birchfield St. | 22 | O | 8 |
| Bird St. | 24 | U | 5 |
| Birkenhead Bor. Hospital | 36 | B | 2 |
| Birkenhead Park, Birkenhead | 36 | A | 2 |
| Birkenhead Park Stn., Birkenh'd | 36 | B | 2 |
| Birkenhead Rd., Seacombe | 39 | C | 4 |
| Birkenhead Union Workhouse | 36 | B | 3 |
| Birkett St. | 31 | N | 9 |
| Birstall Rd. | 22 | P | 5 |
| Bishop Rd. | 10 | L | 2 |
| Bishopgate St. | 14 | T | 3 |
| Bishops Palace, Abercromby Sq. | 23 | R | 8 |
| Bismarck St. | 20 | L | 6 |
| Bispham St. | 31 | N | 10 |
| Bittern St. | 23 | Q | 9 |
| Bixteth St. | 31 | O | 11 |
| Black Bull Lane | 19 | I | 7 |
| Blackburn Grove | 26 | A | 9 |
| Blackburne Pl. | 33 | R | 9 |
| Black Diamond St. | 30 | L | 10 |
| Blackfield St. | 19 | I | 8 |
| Black Horse Hotel | 8 | F | 4 |
| Blackstock St. | 31 | M | 10 |
| Blackstone St. | 29 | I | 11 |
| Blair St. | 34 | T | 10 |
| Blake St. | 32 | P | 9 |
| Blake St., Bootle | 27 | D | 9 |
| Blanche St. | 23 | R | 7 |
| Blantyre Rd. | 15 | V | 3 |
| Blenheim Rd. | 15 | X | 2 |
| Blenheim St. | 30 | L | 10 |
| Blessington Rd. | 19 | I | 5 |
| Bligh St. | 14 | U | 3 |
| Blind Asylum, Brunswick Rd. | 22 | O | 7 |
| Blind School, Hardman St. | 33 | R | 9 |
| Bloom St. | 23 | S | 7 |
| Blossom St. | 16 | A | 7 |
| Blucher St. | 23 | R | 7 |
| Blue Coat School, Wavertree | 15 | W | 1 |
| Blundell St. | 33 | R | 11 |
| Blythe St. | 21 | M | 6 |
| Boaler St. | 22 | O | 5 |
| Bodley St. | 19 | I | 6 |
| Bodmin Rd. | 8 | G | 4 |
| Bold Pl. | 33 | R | 9 |
| Bold St. | 32 | Q | 10 |
| Bolt Hill, Tranmere | 36 | B | 3 |
| Bolton St. | 32 | P | 10 |
| Bon Marche | 32 | P | 10 |
| Bond St. | 31 | M | 10 |
| Bootle Baths | 16 | A | 8 |
| Bootle C'nty Hall | 17 | D | 8 |
| Bootle Football & Cricket Ground | 18 | E | 6 |
| Bootle Free Lib'ry | 16 | A | 8 |
| Bootle Free Lib'ry | 17 | D | 8 |
| Bootle Hospital | 27 | D | 9 |
| Bootle Station | 17 | D | 8 |
| Bootle Town Hall | 17 | D | 8 |
| Boreland St. | 16 | B | 8 |
| Borough Rd., Birkenhead | 36 | B | 2 |
| Borrowdale Rd. | 15 | W | 3 |
| Bostock St. | 20 | L | 8 |
| Boston St. | 17 | C | 8 |
| Boswell St., Bootle | 26 | A | 9 |
| Boswell St., Lodge Lane | 24 | U | 6 |
| Botanic Gardens, Edge Lane | 13 | R | 4 |
| Botanic Grove | 13 | R | 4 |
| Botanic Pl. | 13 | Q | 4 |
| Botanic Rd. | 13 | R | 4 |
| Botanic St. | 13 | S | 5 |
| Boundary Lane | 21 | N | 5 |
| Boundary Pl. | 22 | P | 7 |
| Boundary Rd., Bidston | 36 | A | 2 |
| Boundary St. | 29 | I | 10 |
| Boundary St. East | 20 | K | 8 |
| Bourne St. | 22 | O | 5 |
| Bousfield St. | 19 | I | 7 |
| Bouverie St. | 35 | V | 9 |
| Bower St. | 29 | I | 10 |
| Bowman St. | 35 | V | 10 |
| Bowood St. | 35 | X | 10 |
| Bowring St. | 35 | W | 9 |
| Boyd St. | 20 | L | 7 |
| Boyton St. | 24 | T | 5 |
| Bradewell St. | 19 | H | 6 |
| Bradfield St. | 13 | Q | 4 |
| Brae St. | 23 | Q | 5 |
| Braemar St. | 18 | F | 7 |
| Brainerd St. | 11 | O | 1 |
| Bramberton Pl. | 9 | H | 1 |
| Bramberton Rd. | 9 | H | 1 |
| Bramley St. | 13 | S | 1 |
| Bramleymoore Dock | 29 | I | 12 |
| Bran St. | 35 | V | 10 |
| Brandon St. | 20 | K | 6 |
| Brasenose Rd. | 18 | E | 9 |
| Brassey St. | 34 | T | 10 |
| Brassey St., Birkenhead | 36 | B | 1 |
| Breck Grove | 21 | M | 6 |
| Breck House | 10 | L | 2 |
| Breck Pl. | 21 | M | 6 |
| Breck Rd. | 10 | M | 4 |
| Breck Rd., Poulton | 38 | A | 3 |
| Breckfield Rd. No. | 20 | L | 6 |
| Breckfield Rd. So. | 21 | M | 5 |
| Breck Rd. Station | 10 | K | 1 |
| Breckside Park | 11 | M | 2 |
| Breeze Hill | 17 | D | 6 |
| Breeze Hill House | 17 | D | 5 |
| Breeze Lane | 7 | E | 4 |
| Bremner St. | 13 | R | 4 |
| Brenton St. | 35 | W | 9 |
| Brereton Av. | 15 | W | 1 |
| Brewster St. | 18 | F | 6 |
| Briar St. | 19 | H | 8 |
| Brick St. | 33 | S | 11 |
| Brickfield Cottages | 10 | I | 1 |
| Bridewell | 30 | K | 9 |
| Bridge Rd. | 13 | S | 4 |
| Bridge St. | 17 | D | 9 |
| Bridge St., Birkenhead | 37 | C | 2 |
| Bridgewater St. | 33 | S | 11 |
| Bridport St. | 32 | P | 9 |
| Brierfield Rd. | 15 | W | 2 |
| Bright St. | 21 | O | 6 |
| Brighton St. | 34 | T | 9 |
| Brighton St., Seacombe | 39 | C | 3 |
| Brindley St. | 33 | S | 11 |
| Brisbane St. | 19 | I | 8 |
| Bristol Rd. | 15 | W | 1 |
| Britannia Av. | 14 | U | 4 |
| Britton St. | 34 | T | 11 |
| Broadwood St. | 14 | U | 3 |
| Brock St. | 19 | H | 7 |
| Brockenhurst Rd. | 6 | B | 2 |
| Brocklebank Dock | 27 | D | 11 |
| Brocklebank Dock Station | 27 | D | 10 |
| Brocklebank Graving Dock | 27 | E | 10 |
| Brocklebank St. | 27 | D | 10 |
| Brompton Av. | 25 | V | 5 |
| Brompton Rd. | 13 | R | 2 |
| Bronte St. | 22 | P | 9 |
| Brook Rd., Bootle | 16 | B | 9 |
| Brook Rd., Walton | 7 | C | 2 |
| Brook St. | 31 | N | 12 |
| Brook St., Birkenhead | 37 | C | 2 |
| Brookdale Rd. | 15 | V | 3 |
| Brookhill Rd. | 16 | B | 6 |
| Broomfield Rd. | 6 | B | 3 |
| Browne St. | 17 | C | 9 |
| Browning St. | 26 | A | 9 |
| Brownlow Hill | 22 | Q | 9 |
| Brownlow St. | 22 | P | 8 |
| Browside | 21 | N | 7 |
| Broxton St. | 14 | U | 2 |
| Brunel St. | 21 | M | 6 |
| Brunsw ck Dock | 34 | T | 12 |
| Brunswick Dock Station | 34 | T | 12 |
| Brunswick Pl. | 28 | F | 10 |
| Brunswick Rd. | 22 | O | 7 |
| Brunswick Sq. | 19 | G | 6 |
| Brunswick St. | 32 | P | 12 |
| Brunswick Goods Station | 34 | U | 11 |
| Brunswick Half Tide Dock | 34 | T | 12 |
| Bryan St. | 34 | U | 10 |
| Brydges St. | 23 | R | 6 |
| Brythen St. | 32 | P | 10 |
| Buchanan Rd. | 7 | E | 4 |
| Buchanan Rd., Seacombe | 39 | C | 3 |
| Buckingham Av. | 25 | W | 5 |
| Buckingham Rd., Tue Brook | 11 | M | 1 |
| Buckingham Rd., Walton | 6 | A | 1 |
| Buckingham St. | 20 | L | 8 |
| Bull Lane | 6 | A | 2 |
| Bullens Rd. | 9 | G | 4 |
| Bullens Ter. | 16 | B | 8 |
| Bulwer St. | 20 | M | 5 |
| Bunyan St. | 22 | P | 7 |
| Burke St. | 11 | O | 4 |
| Burleigh Rd. No. | 20 | K | 5 |
| Burleigh Rd. So. | 20 | K | 5 |
| Burlington St. | 30 | M | 10 |
| Burnand St. | 19 | I | 5 |
| Burnet St. | 30 | K | 9 |
| Burnley St. | 21 | N | 5 |
| Burns St. | 26 | A | 9 |
| Burrell St. | 19 | H | 5 |
| Burroughs Green | 31 | M | 9 |
| Burton St. | 29 | I | 10 |
| Burwen Drive | 6 | A | 2 |
| Bushey Rd. | 8 | G | 1 |
| Bute St. | 21 | N | 8 |
| Butler St. | 12 | O | 5 |
| Butterfield St. | 19 | I | 6 |
| Button St. | 32 | P | 11 |
| Byford St. | 13 | R | 5 |
| Byles St. | 25 | W | 9 |
| Byng St. | 27 | D | 9 |
| Byrom St. | 31 | O | 10 |
| Byron St. | 26 | A | 9 |
| Cable St. | 32 | P | 11 |
| Cadmus St. | 21 | M | 7 |
| Cadogan St., Rosebery St. | 24 | T | 7 |
| Cadogan St., Spofforth Rd. | 14 | T | 4 |
| Caird St. | 21 | O | 6 |
| Cairns St. | 24 | U | 7 |
| Cairo St. | 18 | F | 6 |
| Caithness Drive, Liscard | 38 | B | 2 |
| Calder St. | 20 | K | 6 |

| | | | |
|---|---|---|---|
| Calderfield Rd. | 6 | A | 3 |
| Caldy Rd. | 6 | A | 1 |
| Caledonia St. | 23 | R | 9 |
| Callander Rd. | 12 | P | 2 |
| Callow Rd. | 14 | U | 4 |
| Cam St. | 24 | T | 7 |
| Cambria St. | 12 | O | 4 |
| Cambridge Rd. | 18 | E | 6 |
| Cambridge St., Arrad St. | 23 | R | 8 |
| Cambridge St., Wavertree | 14 | T | 4 |
| Camden St. | 32 | O | 9 |
| Camden Street, Bootle | 17 | E | 9 |
| Cameron St. | 12 | Q | 4 |
| Campbell St., Bootle | 27 | C | 9 |
| Campbell St., Duke St. | 32 | Q | 11 |
| Canada Basin | 27 | E | 11 |
| Canada Branch Dock No. 3 | 27 | E | 10 |
| Canada Dock | 27 | F | 11 |
| Canada Dock Gds. Station | 28 | G | 10 |
| Canada Dock Stn. | 27 | G | 10 |
| Canada Graving Dock | 27 | F | 10 |
| Canada Lock | 27 | E | 11 |
| Canada St. | 27 | E | 10 |
| Canal St. | 17 | D | 9 |
| Candia St. | 20 | K | 8 |
| Candlish St. | 21 | M | 5 |
| Canning Dock | 32 | P | 12 |
| Canning Graving Docks | 32 | P | 12 |
| Canning Half Tide Dock | 32 | Q | 12 |
| Canning Pl. | 32 | Q | 11 |
| Canning St. | 33 | S | 9 |
| Canning St., Birkenhead | 37 | C | 2 |
| Canon Rd. | 10 | L | 2 |
| Canova St. | 13 | R | 5 |
| Canterbury St. | 21 | O | 8 |
| Canton St. | 21 | O | 6 |
| Cantsfield St. | 24 | T | 5 |
| Cardigan St. | 14 | T | 4 |
| Cardwell St. | 23 | R | 7 |
| Carisbrooke Rd. | 18 | F | 6 |
| Carlingford St. | 24 | T | 7 |
| Carlisle St. | 23 | S | 6 |
| Carlton Hill | 35 | V | 9 |
| Carlton St. | 30 | L | 12 |
| Carlyle St. | 14 | T | 4 |
| Carmel St. | 20 | K | 6 |
| Carnarvon Rd. | 7 | E | 3 |
| Carnarvon St. | 19 | I | 7 |
| Carno St. | 14 | U | 2 |
| Carolina St. | 17 | C | 8 |
| Caros St. | 20 | L | 7 |
| Carriers Dock | 27 | E | 10 |
| Carrington St. | 24 | T | 8 |
| Carruthers St. | 31 | M | 11 |
| Carson St. | 21 | M | 8 |
| Carstairs Rd. | 12 | O | 3 |
| Carter St. | 24 | T | 9 |
| Carver St. | 22 | O | 8 |
| Caryl St. | 34 | T | 11 |
| Cases St. | 32 | P | 10 |
| Casterton St. | 14 | T | 4 |
| Castle St. | 32 | O | 12 |
| Castor St. | 11 | M | 4 |
| Catacombs, Anfield Park Cemetery | 9 | H | 3 |
| Catharine St. | 23 | S | 9 |
| Cathcart St. | 13 | S | 3 |
| Cathcart St., Birkenhead | 36 | B | 2 |
| Cathedral, Saint James Road | 33 | S | 10 |
| Cathedral Rd. | 10 | L | 3 |
| Cattle Station | 30 | K | 11 |
| Cattle Station | 12 | P | 1 |
| Cavendish Rd. | 7 | D | 3 |
| Cavendish St. | 31 | N | 10 |
| Cavendish St., Birkenhead | 36 | B | 1 |
| Cawdor St. | 24 | U | 8 |
| Cazneau St. | 21 | M | 9 |
| Cearns Rd., Oxton | 36 | A | 3 |
| Cecil St., Hardwick St. | 22 | P | 7 |
| Cecil St., Picton Rd. | 14 | T | 4 |
| Cedar Grove | 24 | U | 6 |
| Cedar Rd. | 6 | A | 1 |
| Cedar St. | 16 | B | 7 |
| Cedardale Rd. | 7 | D | 2 |
| Celia St. | 18 | F | 8 |
| Celt St. | 11 | N | 4 |
| Celtic St. | 24 | U | 8 |
| Cemeas St. | 30 | K | 10 |
| Central Corporation Yard | 23 | R | 7 |
| Central Hall, Wesleyan | 32 | Q | 10 |
| Central Pk., Egremont | 38 | B | 3 |
| Central Station | 32 | Q | 10 |
| Central Station, Birkenhead | 36 | B | 2 |
| Ceres St. | 18 | F | 9 |
| Chadwick St. | 31 | M | 11 |
| Chalmers St. | 23 | S | 6 |
| Chaloner St. | 33 | S | 12 |
| Chambers St. | 20 | K | 6 |
| Chancel St. | 19 | H | 7 |
| Chandos St. | 23 | S | 5 |
| Channell Rd. | 12 | P | 4 |
| Chantrey St. | 13 | R | 5 |
| Chapel Av. | 6 | B | 1 |
| Chapel Gdns. | 20 | L | 8 |
| Chapel Lane | 32 | Q | 9 |
| Chapel Pl. | 22 | O | 7 |
| Chapel Rd. | 10 | L | 3 |
| Chapel St. | 32 | O | 12 |
| Chapel St., Bootle | 27 | C | 9 |
| Chapman St. | 34 | T | 11 |
| Charlecote St. | 35 | X | 10 |
| Charles St. | 32 | P | 10 |
| Charles Berrington Rd. | 15 | X | 1 |
| Charters St. | 31 | M | 11 |
| Chatham Pl. | 23 | R | 6 |
| Chatham St. | 23 | R | 8 |
| Chatsworth Av. | 6 | A | 3 |
| Chatsworth St. | 23 | S | 6 |
| Chaucer St. | 31 | N | 9 |
| Chaucer Street, Bootle | 16 | A | 9 |
| Cheapside | 31 | O | 11 |
| Chelmsford St. | 18 | H | 8 |
| Chelsea Rd. | 6 | A | 1 |
| Cheltenham Av. | 25 | W | 5 |
| Chepstow St. | 18 | F | 5 |
| Cherry Av. | 9 | G | 2 |
| Cherry Lane | 31 | N | 10 |
| Cherry Lane, Walton | 9 | H | 2 |
| Cheshire Lines, Cattle & Goods Station | 14 | T | 3 |
| Chesnut Gr., Bootle | 16 | A | 8 |
| Chesnut Grove, Wavertree | 14 | U | 1 |
| Chesnut St. | 23 | R | 8 |
| Chester Rd. | 11 | N | 1 |
| Chester St. | 34 | T | 10 |
| Chester St., Birkenhead | 37 | C | 2 |
| Chesterfield St. | 34 | T | 10 |
| Chevin Rd. | 6 | B | 2 |
| Chichester St. | 14 | T | 4 |
| Children's Infirmary, Myrtle St. | 23 | R | 8 |
| Childwall Av. | 14 | U | 4 |
| China St. | 21 | M | 8 |
| Chipping St. | 35 | V | 9 |
| Chirkdale St. | 18 | F | 6 |
| Chisenhale St. | 31 | M | 11 |
| Chiswell St. | 12 | Q | 4 |
| Chorley St. | 31 | O | 10 |
| Christchurch, Gt. Homer St. | 20 | K | 8 |
| Christ Church, Hunter St. | 32 | O | 9 |
| Christ Church, Kensington | 22 | P | 5 |
| Christ Church, Linnet Lane | 25 | X | 7 |
| Christian St. | 31 | O | 9 |
| Christopher St. | 19 | H | 6 |
| Church House, Lord St. | 32 | P | 11 |
| Church Lane | 32 | P | 11 |
| Church Mount | 23 | R | 6 |
| Church Rd., Stanley | 13 | R | 1 |
| Church Rd., Wavertree | 15 | W | 1 |
| Church Rd., Seacombe | 39 | C | 3 |
| Church Rd., Tranmere | 36 | B | 3 |
| Church Rd. West, Walton | 8 | F | 4 |
| Church St. | 32 | P | 11 |
| Church St., Birkenhead | 37 | C | 2 |
| Church St., Bootle | 27 | C | 9 |
| Church St., Egremont | 39 | C | 3 |
| Church View | 17 | C | 9 |
| Churchill St. | 24 | U | 8 |
| Churnet St. | 19 | H | 6 |
| Cicely St. | 23 | R | 6 |
| Cicero Ter. | 20 | K | 7 |
| Circus St. | 31 | O | 9 |
| City Rd. | 8 | G | 4 |
| City Engineer's Depot, Edge Lane. | 13 | R | 3 |
| City Hospital for Infect. Diseases | 34 | U | 11 |
| Clapham Rd. | 10 | K | 3 |
| Clare Rd. | 18 | E | 6 |
| Clare St. | 31 | O | 9 |
| Claremont Rd. | 15 | V | 3 |
| Claremount, Wallasey | 38 | A | 2 |
| Claremount Rd., Wallasey | 38 | A | 2 |
| Clarence Dock | 30 | L | 12 |
| Clarence Dock Stn. | 30 | K | 12 |
| Clarence Graving Docks | 30 | K | 12 |
| Clarence Grove | 20 | L | 6 |
| Clarence Half Tide Dock | 30 | L | 12 |
| Clarence Pier Head | 30 | L | 13 |
| Clarence St. | 32 | Q | 9 |
| Clarendon Rd. | 10 | L | 3 |
| Clarendon Rd., Seacombe | 39 | C | 3 |
| Clarendon St. | 24 | T | 6 |
| Claribel St. | 24 | U | 8 |
| Clarke St. | 34 | T | 10 |
| Claude Rd. | 10 | L | 2 |
| Claudia St. | 9 | G | 4 |

| | | | |
|---|---|---|---|
| Claughton, Birkenhead | 36 | A | 2 |
| Claughton Rd., Birkenhead | 36 | B | 2 |
| Clay St. | 30 | L | 11 |
| Claypole St. | 24 | T | 5 |
| Clayton Sq. | 32 | P | 10 |
| Clayton St. | 32 | O | 10 |
| Clement St. | 31 | M | 11 |
| Cleopas St. | 35 | W | 10 |
| Clevedon St. | 35 | W | 9 |
| Cleveland Sq. | 32 | Q | 11 |
| Cleveland Street, Birkenhead | 36 | B | 1 |
| Cliff St. | 13 | Q | 4 |
| Clifford St., Bootle | 16 | B | 8 |
| Clifford St., Islington | 22 | O | 9 |
| Clifton Pk., Birkenhead | 36 | B | 2 |
| Clifton Rd. | 11 | N | 2 |
| Clifton Rd., Birkenhead | 36 | B | 3 |
| Clifton Rd. East | 11 | M | 1 |
| Clifton St. | 21 | M | 8 |
| Clint Rd. | 13 | R | 5 |
| Clive St. | 34 | U | 11 |
| Clock Tower, Wavertree | 14 | V | 1 |
| Clovelly Rd. | 10 | L | 3 |
| Clubmoor Recreation Ground | 10 | K | 1 |
| Clyde Rd. | 13 | R | 1 |
| Clyde St. | 28 | F | 9 |
| Cobbs Quarry | 20 | K | 6 |
| Cobden St. | 21 | O | 6 |
| Cobham Av. | 6 | A | 3 |
| Coburg Dock | 34 | T | 12 |
| Coburg Granary | 34 | T | 12 |
| Cochrane St. | 20 | M | 7 |
| Cockburn St. | 35 | W | 10 |
| Cockerell St. | 19 | H | 6 |
| Cockspur St. | 31 | N | 11 |
| Coleridge Street, Bootle | 26 | A | 9 |
| Coleridge Street, Kensington | 12 | P | 5 |
| Colinton St. | 14 | T | 2 |
| College, Carver St. | 22 | O | 8 |
| College Lane | 32 | P | 11 |
| College St. North | 22 | O | 7 |
| College St. South | 22 | O | 7 |
| College View | 17 | D | 8 |
| Collegiate Institution, Shaw St. | 22 | O | 7 |
| Collingwood Dock | 30 | K | 12 |
| Collingwood St. | 21 | M | 9 |
| Collins St. | 35 | V | 9 |
| Colquitt St. | 33 | Q | 10 |
| Coltart Rd. | 24 | U | 7 |
| Coltman St. | 22 | P | 5 |
| Columbia Rd. | 8 | F | 3 |
| Colville St. | 14 | U | 2 |
| Colvin St. | 30 | K | 9 |
| Combermere St., Mill St. | 34 | U | 10 |
| Combermere St., Picton Rd. | 13 | S | 3 |
| Commercial Rd. | 19 | H | 8 |
| Commutation Row | 32 | O | 9 |
| Compton Hotel | 32 | P | 10 |
| Compton St. | 21 | N | 5 |
| Comus St. | 31 | N | 9 |
| Concert St. | 32 | Q | 10 |
| Concord St. | 17 | C | 8 |
| Congreve St. | 31 | N | 12 |
| Coningsby Rd. | 19 | I | 5 |
| Coniston St. | 10 | M | 5 |
| Connaught Rd. | 22 | Q | 6 |
| Constance St. | 22 | P | 8 |
| Consumption Hos., Mt. Pleasant | 33 | Q | 9 |
| Conway St., Bootle | 16 | B | 8 |
| Conway St., Great Homer St. | 20 | L | 8 |
| Conway St., Birkenhead | 36 | B | 2 |
| Conyers St. | 20 | K | 7 |
| Cook St. | 32 | P | 11 |
| Cookson St. | 33 | S | 10 |
| Cooper Row | 32 | Q | 11 |
| Copeland St. | 21 | M | 7 |
| Copenhagen Rd. | 14 | S | 5 |
| Copley St. | 21 | M | 6 |
| Copperas Hill | 32 | P | 9 |
| Copperfield St. | 34 | U | 9 |
| Corless St. | 19 | I | 6 |
| Corlett St. | 23 | S | 7 |
| Corn Exchange, Brunswick St. | 32 | P | 12 |
| Corn St. | 35 | V | 10 |
| Corney St. | 24 | T | 5 |
| Cornhill | 33 | R | 11 |
| Cornwall Street, Bootle | 17 | C | 6 |
| Cornwall Street, Clifton St. | 21 | M | 8 |
| Cornwallis St. | 33 | R | 10 |
| Coronation Av. | 12 | P | 3 |
| Corporation Road, Birkenhead | 36 | B | 1 |
| Corporation Works Depot, Wallasey | 38 | B | 3 |
| Corsewall St. | 14 | T | 4 |
| Costain St. | 19 | G | 9 |
| Cotswold St. | 22 | Q | 5 |
| Cottenham St. | 12 | P | 5 |
| Cotter St. | 34 | T | 10 |
| Cotton Exchange, Old Hall St. | 31 | O | 12 |
| Cotton St. | 30 | L | 12 |
| County Rd. | 18 | G | 5 |
| County Sessions House, Islington | 32 | O | 9 |
| Courthope Rd. | 8 | G | 2 |
| Covent Garden | 32 | O | 12 |
| Coventry Rd. | 15 | X | 1 |
| Cow Lane | 31 | O | 10 |
| Cowl St. | 20 | L | 6 |
| Cowley Rd. | 8 | G | 4 |
| Cowper St. | 26 | A | 9 |
| Cranborne Rd. | 14 | T | 4 |
| Cranbourne St. | 23 | Q | 7 |
| Cranehurst Rd. | 8 | G | 2 |
| Cranmer St. | 30 | K | 9 |
| Cranworth St. | 26 | A | 10 |
| Craven St. | 22 | O | 8 |
| Craven St., Birkenhead | 36 | B | 2 |
| Crawford Av. | 15 | X | 2 |
| Crealock St. | 19 | I | 8 |
| Credington St. | 35 | X | 9 |
| Credworth St. | 24 | T | 6 |
| Crematorium, Anfield Park Cem. | 9 | I | 4 |
| Crescent Rd. | 7 | D | 1 |
| Cresswell St. | 21 | N | 6 |
| Creswick St. | 21 | M | 6 |
| Cretan Rd. | 14 | U | 4 |
| Crete St. | 20 | K | 7 |
| Crete St., Bootle | 16 | B | 7 |
| Crocus St. | 19 | H | 8 |
| Crooked Lane | 32 | P | 12 |
| Cropper St. | 33 | Q | 10 |
| Crosfield Rd. | 23 | R | 5 |
| Crosgrove Rd. | 9 | H | 2 |
| Cross St. | 14 | T | 4 |
| Crosshall St. | 32 | O | 10 |
| Crow St. | 34 | T | 11 |
| Crown Pl., Crown St. | 23 | Q | 7 |
| Crown St. | 23 | Q | 7 |
| Crown St. Depot, L.M.S. | 23 | R | 7 |
| Croxteth Drive | 25 | W | 5 |
| Croxteth Gate | 25 | W | 6 |
| Croxteth Grove | 25 | V | 6 |
| Croxteth Road, Bootle | 16 | A | 7 |
| Croxteth Road, Prince's Park | 25 | V | 6 |
| Croxton St. | 19 | H | 7 |
| Croylands St. | 19 | G | 6 |
| Crump St. | 33 | S | 10 |
| Cubbin St. | 20 | K | 8 |
| Cullen St. | 24 | T | 5 |
| Cumberland Av. | 15 | W | 4 |
| Cumberland St. | 32 | O | 11 |
| Cunard Building | 32 | P | 12 |
| Cupid St. | 11 | M | 4 |
| Curate Rd. | 10 | L | 2 |
| Currie St. | 31 | M | 9 |
| Curtis Rd. | 9 | H | 1 |
| Curzon St., Brompton Rd. | 13 | R | 2 |
| Curzon St., Mount Vernon St. | 22 | P | 7 |
| Custom House | 32 | Q | 12 |
| Custom House Stn. | 32 | Q | 12 |
| Customs Baggage Shed, Prince's Parade | 31 | O | 13 |
| Cypress St. | 23 | R | 8 |
| Cyprus Rd. | 16 | B | 7 |
| Dacre Hill, Rock Ferry | 37 | C | 4 |
| Dacre St. | 24 | T | 5 |
| Dacre St., Bootle | 28 | E | 10 |
| Dacy Rd. | 20 | L | 5 |
| Daisy Grove | 23 | R | 5 |
| Daisy St. | 19 | H | 8 |
| Dale St. | 32 | O | 11 |
| Dalkeith St. | 24 | T | 7 |
| Dallas Grove | 6 | A | 1 |
| Dalmorton Road, New Brighton | 38 | B | 1 |
| Dalrymple St. | 20 | K | 8 |
| Dalton St. | 22 | P | 7 |
| Danby St. | 20 | M | 6 |
| Dane St. | 18 | G | 5 |
| Dansie St. | 22 | P | 8 |
| Danube St. | 24 | T | 6 |
| Darling St. | 14 | T | 4 |
| Darnley St. | 34 | U | 10 |
| Darrel St. | 24 | T | 6 |
| Dart St. | 19 | H | 7 |
| Darwen St. | 30 | I | 10 |
| Date St. | 23 | S | 7 |
| Daulby St. | 22 | P | 8 |
| David St. | 35 | W | 9 |
| David Lewis Hostel | 34 | S | 10 |
| David Lewis Nor. Hospital, Great Howard St. | 31 | N | 12 |
| Davies St., Bootle | 17 | C | 7 |
| Davies St., Dale St. | 32 | O | 11 |
| Davy St. | 20 | K | 5 |
| Dawber St. | 21 | N | 5 |
| Dawson Grove | 21 | M | 7 |
| Dawson St. | 32 | P | 10 |
| Deacon St. | 21 | O | 6 |
| Deaf and Dumb Institute | 23 | R | 7 |
| Deane Rd. | 12 | Q | 4 |
| Deane St. | 32 | P | 10 |
| Dee St. | 21 | O | 5 |
| Deepfield Rd. | 15 | X | 2 |
| Delamore St. | 18 | F | 6 |
| Delaware St. | 16 | B | 7 |

| | | | |
|---|---|---|---|
| Dell St. | 12 | Q | 4 |
| Demesne St., Seacombe | 39 | C | 3 |
| Denbigh Rd. | 7 | E | 4 |
| Denbigh St., Bootle | 16 | B | 8 |
| Denbigh St., Great Howard St. | 30 | K | 11 |
| Denebank Rd. | 10 | K | 3 |
| Denison St. | 31 | N | 12 |
| Denman Drive | 11 | N | 3 |
| Denman St. | 12 | P | 5 |
| Dental Hospital | 32 | Q | 9 |
| Dental Hospital | 22 | P | 7 |
| Denton Grove | 11 | N | 3 |
| Denton St. | 35 | V | 10 |
| Dentwood St. | 35 | X | 9 |
| Derby Park | 17 | C | 5 |
| Derby Park, Rock Ferry | 37 | C | 4 |
| Derby Pl. | 13 | R | 1 |
| Derby Rd., Bootle | 27 | C | 9 |
| Derby Rd., Tranmere | 36 | B | 3 |
| Desmond St. | 21 | M | 6 |
| Destructor, Hodder St. | 20 | K | 6 |
| Deveraux Drive, Seacombe | 38 | B | 3 |
| Devon St., Bootle | 17 | C | 6 |
| Devon St., Stafford St. | 22 | O | 8 |
| Devonfield Rd. | 6 | A | 3 |
| Devonport St. | 34 | U | 10 |
| Devonshire Pl. | 20 | I | 7 |
| Devonshire Rd. | 25 | V | 8 |
| Dewsbury St. | 10 | K | 3 |
| Dexter St. | 34 | T | 10 |
| Dial St. | 12 | Q | 4 |
| Diana St. | 9 | H | 4 |
| Dickens St. | 34 | U | 9 |
| Dickinson St. | 33 | R | 11 |
| Dickson St. | 30 | L | 12 |
| Dido St. | 21 | N | 7 |
| Digby St. | 35 | W | 9 |
| Dingle Grove | 35 | X | 9 |
| Dingle Hill | 35 | X | 9 |
| Dingle Mount | 35 | X | 9 |
| Dingle Station | 35 | X | 9 |
| Dingle Ter. | 35 | X | 9 |
| Dingley Av. | 6 | A | 3 |
| Dinorben St. | 24 | S | 7 |
| Dinorwic Rd. | 10 | L | 4 |
| Dobson St. | 21 | M | 6 |
| Dock Board Offices | 32 | P | 12 |
| Dock Rd., Seacombe | 38 | B | 4 |
| Docks Station, Birkenhead | 38 | A | 4 |
| Doddridge St. | 22 | P | 7 |
| Dodge St. | 23 | R | 5 |
| Dombey St. | 34 | U | 10 |
| Dominion St. | 11 | N | 3 |
| Donaldson St. | 20 | K | 5 |
| Doncaster St. | 30 | K | 9 |
| Doon St. | 19 | G | 7 |
| Dora St. | 23 | R | 5 |
| Dorans Lane | 32 | P | 11 |
| Dorothy St. | 23 | R | 5 |
| Dorrington St. | 20 | M | 8 |
| Dorrit St. | 34 | U | 10 |
| Dorset Av. | 14 | U | 4 |
| Dorset Rd. | 11 | N | 1 |
| Dorset St. | 17 | C | 6 |
| Douglas Rd. | 10 | L | 3 |
| Douro Pl. | 13 | S | 1 |
| Douro St. | 21 | N | 8 |
| Dove Rd. | 6 | A | 3 |
| Dove St. | 24 | T | 6 |
| Dovey St. | 25 | V | 9 |
| Downe St. | 31 | N | 9 |
| Downham Road, Tranmere | 36 | B | 3 |
| Downing Rd. | 18 | E | 6 |
| Downing St. | 20 | L | 6 |
| Draycott St. | 35 | X | 10 |
| Drayton Rd. | 8 | F | 3 |
| Drayton St. | 20 | K | 6 |
| Drinkwater Gdns. | 21 | N | 8 |
| Drummond Rd. | 9 | H | 1 |
| Drury Lane | 32 | O | 12 |
| Dryburgh St. | 19 | H | 6 |
| Dryden Rd. | 13 | R | 2 |
| Dryden St. | 20 | M | 9 |
| Drysdale St. | 35 | W | 9 |
| Dublin St. | 30 | L | 12 |
| Ducie St. | 24 | U | 7 |
| Duckinfield St. | 22 | Q | 8 |
| Dudley Rd. | 15 | X | 2 |
| Duke St. | 32 | Q | 11 |
| Duke St., Birkenhead | 36 | B | 2 |
| Duke St. Wharf, Birkenhead | 36 | B | 1 |
| Duke's Dock | 32 | R | 12 |
| Duke's Rd. | 20 | K | 7 |
| Duke's Yard | 32 | R | 12 |
| Dumbarton St. | 18 | G | 5 |
| Dunbar St. | 8 | F | 4 |
| Duncan St. | 33 | S | 10 |
| Duncan St., Bootle | 18 | E | 9 |
| Dundee St. | 31 | M | 12 |
| Dunkeld St. | 21 | O | 6 |
| Dunluce St. | 18 | F | 5 |
| Dunmore Rd. | 12 | Q | 1 |
| Dunnet St. | 28 | F | 10 |
| Dunstan St. | 14 | U | 2 |
| Durban Rd., Liscard | 38 | B | 2 |
| Durden St. | 24 | T | 5 |
| Durning Rd. | 23 | R | 5 |
| Dutton St. | 31 | N | 12 |
| Dwerryhouse St. | 34 | S | 11 |
| Dyke St. | 21 | M | 5 |
| Dyson St. | 8 | F | 4 |
| Earle Rd. | 24 | T | 5 |
| Earle St. | 31 | N | 12 |
| Earl's Rd. | 17 | C | 6 |
| Earlsfield Rd. | 15 | X | 1 |
| Earlston Rd., Liscard | 38 | B | 2 |
| Easby Rd. | 19 | H | 8 |
| East St. | 31 | N | 12 |
| East St., Seacombe | 39 | C | 4 |
| East Albert Rd. | 25 | X | 7 |
| Eastbourne St. | 21 | N | 7 |
| Eastdale Rd. | 14 | U | 1 |
| Eastern Dist. P.O. | 22 | P | 6 |
| Eastlake St. | 21 | M | 6 |
| Easton Rd., New Ferry | 37 | C | 4 |
| East Waterloo Dk. | 31 | M | 12 |
| Eastwood St. | 13 | R | 4 |
| Eaton Pl. | 21 | M | 6 |
| Eaton St. | 31 | M | 11 |
| Eberle St. | 32 | O | 11 |
| Eccles St. | 31 | M | 11 |
| Eccleston Rd. | 6 | A | 2 |
| Eden St. | 24 | U | 7 |
| Edenfield Rd. | 15 | W | 2 |
| Edensor Ter. | 21 | M | 5 |
| Edgar St. | 31 | N | 10 |
| Edge Grove | 13 | Q | 2 |
| Edge Lane | 13 | Q | 3 |
| Edge Lane Station | 13 | R | 1 |
| Edge Mount | 23 | Q | 6 |
| Edge Vale | 23 | S | 7 |
| Edgehill Station | 23 | S | 5 |
| Edgeley Gdns. | 6 | A | 2 |
| Edgeware St. | 23 | S | 5 |
| Edinburgh Rd. | 22 | P | 6 |
| Edinburgh St. | 20 | L | 8 |
| Edington St. | 14 | T | 2 |
| Edith Rd. | 10 | K | 4 |
| Edmond St. | 31 | O | 12 |
| Edward St. | 32 | Q | 9 |
| Effingham St. | 27 | D | 9 |
| Egerton Dock, Birkenhead | 37 | C | 2 |
| Egerton Pk., Rock Ferry | 36 | B | 4 |
| Egerton Rd. | 14 | U | 4 |
| Egerton Road, Claughton | 36 | A | 2 |
| Egerton St. | 23 | S | 9 |
| Egerton St., New Brighton | 38 | B | 1 |
| Egremont, Wallasey | 39 | C | 2 |
| Egremont Prom., Wallasey | 39 | C | 2 |
| Elaine St. | 24 | U | 9 |
| Elcho St. | 12 | Q | 5 |
| Elderdale Rd. | 10 | K | 3 |
| Eldon Pl. | 31 | M | 10 |
| Eldon St. | 31 | M | 10 |
| Eldon St., Birkenhead | 36 | B | 2 |
| Eleanor St. | 28 | F | 9 |
| Elgin Dr., Liscard | 38 | B | 2 |
| Elias St. | 20 | L | 8 |
| Elizabeth St. | 22 | Q | 7 |
| Ellel Grove | 11 | N | 3 |
| Ellenboro St. | 31 | M | 9 |
| Ellerslie Rd. | 11 | M | 1 |
| Ellesmere St. | 22 | P | 7 |
| Elliot St. | 32 | P | 10 |
| Ellison St. | 20 | K | 8 |
| Elm Grove | 23 | Q | 7 |
| Elm Rd., Walton | 8 | F | 3 |
| Elm Rd., W. Derby St. | 22 | Q | 7 |
| Elm St. | 22 | Q | 7 |
| Elm Vale | 12 | P | 3 |
| Elm Bank Rd. | 15 | X | 3 |
| Elmdale Rd. | 7 | D | 2 |
| Elmfield Rd. | 6 | B | 2 |
| Elmore St. | 21 | M | 6 |
| Elmswood Road, Tranmere | 36 | B | 3 |
| Elphin Grove | 8 | F | 4 |
| Elsie Rd. | 10 | L | 4 |
| Elstow St. | 19 | H | 8 |
| Elstree Rd. | 12 | P | 3 |
| Elswick St. | 35 | X | 10 |
| Eltham St. | 13 | R | 2 |
| Elton St. | 8 | E | 4 |
| Elwy St. | 25 | V | 9 |
| Embledon St. | 24 | T | 6 |
| Emerald St. | 35 | X | 10 |
| Emery St. | 8 | F | 4 |
| Emley St. | 27 | E | 9 |
| Emlyn St. | 22 | O | 6 |
| Emmanuel Church, Derby Rd. | 22 | O | 6 |
| Empire St. | 22 | O | 5 |
| Empire Theatre, Lime St. | 32 | P | 9 |
| Empress Rd., Kensington | 22 | Q | 6 |
| Empress Road, Townsend Lane | 10 | L | 2 |
| Endborne Rd. | 6 | A | 2 |
| Endsleigh Rd. | 12 | Q | 1 |
| Enid St. | 24 | U | 9 |
| Ennerdale St. | 31 | M | 9 |
| Ensor St. | 28 | E | 9 |
| Epsom St. | 30 | K | 9 |
| Epworth St. | 22 | P | 7 |
| Eridge St. | 35 | X | 9 |
| Erith St. | 25 | W | 9 |

| | | | |
|---|---|---|---|
| Ermine St. | 20 | L | 6 |
| Ernest St. | 35 | W | 9 |
| Errington St. | 29 | H | 10 |
| Erskine St. | 22 | P | 7 |
| Esher Rd. | 12 | P | 4 |
| Esk St. | 28 | F | 9 |
| Eskdale Rd. | 6 | B | 2 |
| Esmond St. | 11 | M | 4 |
| Espin St. | 8 | G | 5 |
| Esplanade, Rock Ferry | 37 | C | 4 |
| Essex St. | 34 | U | 10 |
| Essex St., Bootle | 17 | C | 6 |
| Eton St. | 18 | G | 5 |
| Ettington Rd. | 10 | K | 3 |
| Eustace St. | 22 | Q | 7 |
| Euston St. | 8 | E | 4 |
| Evelyn St. | 19 | I | 9 |
| Evered Av. | 7 | C | 1 |
| Eversley St. | 24 | U | 8 |
| Everton Brow | 21 | N | 7 |
| Everton Cres. | 21 | N | 8 |
| Everton Football Ground | 9 | G | 5 |
| Everton Rd. | 21 | N | 7 |
| Everton Ter. | 21 | M | 7 |
| Everton Vale | 19 | I | 7 |
| Everton View | 27 | D | 9 |
| Every St. | 11 | O | 5 |
| Ewart St. | 23 | S | 6 |
| Ewbank St. | 20 | L | 7 |
| Exchange Bldgs., Town Hall | 32 | O | 12 |
| Exchange Station, L.M.S. | 31 | N | 11 |
| Exchange St. | 32 | O | 11 |
| Exe St. | 24 | T | 7 |
| Exeter Rd. | 17 | E | 8 |
| Exeter St. | 35 | V | 11 |
| Exley St. | 22 | O | 5 |
| Exmouth St. | 21 | N | 7 |
| Exmouth St., Birkenhead | 36 | B | 2 |
| Eye Hosp., Myrtle St. | 23 | R | 9 |
| Eyes St. | 20 | K | 7 |
| Eyrie, The, Wallasey | 38 | A | 3 |
| Fairbank St. | 14 | U | 2 |
| Fairclough Lane | 22 | P | 7 |
| Fairfield Cres. | 12 | P | 2 |
| Fairfield St. | 12 | Q | 2 |
| Fairhurst St. | 31 | O | 11 |
| Fairview Pl. | 35 | W | 9 |
| Fairview Rd., Oxton | 36 | B | 3 |
| Fairy St. | 20 | L | 7 |
| Falkland Rd., Seacombe | 39 | C | 3 |
| Falkland St. | 22 | O | 8 |
| Falkner Sq. | 23 | S | 8 |
| Falkner St. | 23 | S | 8 |
| Fallowfield Rd. | 15 | X | 1 |
| Falstaff St. | 18 | F | 8 |
| Faraday St. | 21 | M | 5 |
| Farnworth St. | 22 | O | 5 |
| Faveham Rd. | 12 | Q | 3 |
| Fazakerley | 7 | C | 1 |
| Fazakerley Rd. | 7 | C | 1 |
| Fazakerley St. | 31 | O | 12 |
| Fearnside St. | 14 | T | 5 |
| Fedora St. | 11 | O | 4 |
| Fell St. | 22 | Q | 5 |
| Feltwell Rd. | 10 | L | 3 |
| Female Penitent'y | 23 | S | 8 |
| Fenwick St. | 32 | P | 12 |
| Fern Grove | 25 | V | 6 |
| Ferndale Rd. | 15 | W | 3 |
| Fernhill Rd. | 17 | C | 5 |
| Fern Hill St. | 24 | U | 8 |
| Fernie St. | 34 | U | 10 |
| Ferry Rd., New Ferry | 37 | D | 4 |
| Fever Hospital, Birkenhead | 38 | A | 4 |
| Field Rd., New Brighton | 38 | B | 1 |
| Field St. | 21 | N | 8 |
| Fielding St. | 22 | P | 6 |
| Finborough Rd. | 8 | G | 1 |
| Finchley Rd. | 10 | K | 3 |
| Fingland Rd. | 15 | V | 3 |
| Finlay St. | 12 | P | 4 |
| Fir Lane | 15 | W | 1 |
| Firdale Rd. | 7 | D | 2 |
| Fire and Police Offices | 31 | O | 11 |
| Fire Station, Bootle | 27 | C | 9 |
| Fish Market | 32 | P | 10 |
| Fisher St. | 34 | T | 11 |
| Fishguard St. | 21 | M | 6 |
| Fitzclarence St. | 21 | N | 7 |
| Fitzroy St. | 22 | O | 6 |
| Flaxman St. | 13 | R | 4 |
| Fleet St. | 32 | Q | 10 |
| Fletcher Grove | 13 | R | 1 |
| Fletcher St. | 34 | T | 9 |
| Flinders St. | 19 | I | 9 |
| Flint St. | 33 | S | 11 |
| Flint St., Bootle | 16 | B | 8 |
| Floating Bridge | 32 | O | 13 |
| Florence Institute | 35 | W | 10 |
| Florence Rd. | 7 | D | 4 |
| Florence St. | 19 | H | 6 |
| Florida St. | 17 | C | 8 |
| Foley St. | 19 | I | 7 |
| Fontenoy St. | 31 | N | 10 |
| Fonthill Rd. | 18 | G | 7 |
| Forbes St. | 23 | S | 6 |
| Ford St. | 31 | M | 10 |
| Fordham St. | 19 | H | 6 |
| Forge St. | 28 | F | 9 |
| Formby St. | 31 | M | 12 |
| Forrest St. | 33 | Q | 11 |
| Fortescue St. | 22 | P | 7 |
| Forth St. | 28 | F | 9 |
| Foster St. | 29 | H | 9 |
| Fountains Rd. | 19 | H | 7 |
| Fowler St. | 20 | M | 5 |
| Fox St. | 21 | N | 8 |
| Fox Hill St. | 24 | U | 8 |
| Frank St. | 34 | U | 11 |
| Franklin Pl. | 11 | M | 4 |
| Fraser St. | 32 | O | 9 |
| Frederick St. | 32 | Q | 11 |
| Free Lib., William Brown St. | 32 | O | 10 |
| Freehold St. | 12 | Q | 2 |
| Freeland St. | 19 | H | 6 |
| Freeman St. | 14 | T | 4 |
| Freemasons Row | 31 | N | 10 |
| Freshfield Rd. | 15 | W | 2 |
| Friar St. | 20 | L | 6 |
| Friends' Meeting House | 31 | O | 9 |
| Frith St. | 18 | F | 8 |
| Frodsham St. | 8 | G | 4 |
| Frogmore Rd. | 12 | Q | 1 |
| Frost St. | 13 | Q | 4 |
| Fruit Exchange | 32 | O | 11 |
| Fruit Station, Edgehill | 23 | S | 5 |
| Fulford St. | 20 | K | 8 |
| Fulton St. | 29 | I | 11 |
| Furlong St. | 30 | L | 9 |
| Furness St. | 19 | H | 7 |
| Gadsby St. | 21 | N | 8 |
| Gaerwen St. | 22 | P | 5 |
| Gainsborough Rd. | 15 | V | 3 |
| Galloway St. | 14 | T | 4 |
| Galton St. | 31 | M | 12 |
| Gambier Ter. | 33 | S | 9 |
| Gannock St. | 13 | Q | 4 |
| Garden Lane | 17 | C | 7 |
| Garden St. | 23 | Q | 7 |
| Gardner's Drive | 12 | O | 3 |
| Gardner's Row | 31 | N | 10 |
| Garfield St. | 16 | B | 7 |
| Garibaldi St. | 21 | M | 7 |
| Garmoyle Rd. | 15 | V | 3 |
| Garnett Av. | 19 | G | 7 |
| Garrick St. | 24 | U | 5 |
| Gas Works, Bootle | 16 | A | 6 |
| Gas Works, Lightbody St. | 30 | K | 10 |
| Gascoyne St. | 31 | N | 11 |
| Gaskell St. | 34 | U | 10 |
| Gautby Rd., Bidston | 38 | A | 4 |
| Gay St. | 31 | N | 9 |
| Gayton St. | 13 | R | 2 |
| Gelling St. | 34 | U | 10 |
| General Post Office | 32 | P | 11 |
| General Post Office, Birkenhead | 36 | B | 2 |
| Geneva Rd. | 12 | P | 3 |
| George St. | 31 | O | 11 |
| George III. Statue | 22 | P | 8 |
| George's Dock Way | 32 | P | 12 |
| George's Landing Stage | 32 | O | 13 |
| George's Parade | 32 | P | 13 |
| George's Pierhead | 32 | P | 13 |
| George's Rd. | 11 | N | 4 |
| Geraint St. | 24 | U | 9 |
| Gerald St. | 22 | O | 7 |
| Gerard Bridge | 30 | L | 10 |
| Gerard St. | 31 | O | 9 |
| Gertrude Rd. | 10 | K | 4 |
| Gibb St. | 20 | K | 6 |
| Gibralter Row | 31 | N | 12 |
| Gibson St. | 24 | T | 9 |
| Giffen St. | 14 | T | 4 |
| Gilbert St. | 33 | Q | 11 |
| Gildart Gdns. | 31 | M | 10 |
| Gildart St. | 22 | O | 8 |
| Gilead St. | 12 | Q | 5 |
| Gilfillan St. | 25 | N | 5 |
| Gill St. | 22 | P | 8 |
| Gilman St. | 20 | K | 5 |
| Gilpin St. | 35 | W | 9 |
| Gilroy Rd. | 12 | O | 4 |
| Gladstone Docks | 26 | A | 11 |
| Gladstone Dock Station | 26 | A | 10 |
| Gladstone Rd. | 23 | R | 5 |
| Gladstone Road, Walton | 7 | E | 3 |
| Glaisher St. | 20 | K | 5 |
| Glamis Rd. | 11 | M | 1 |
| Gleave St. | 21 | N | 6 |
| Gledmore Rd. | 12 | Q | 1 |
| Glegg St. | 30 | L | 11 |
| Glendower St. | 18 | F | 8 |
| Glenfield Rd. | 15 | W | 1 |
| Glenvale St. | 21 | M | 6 |
| Globe Rd. | 16 | B | 9 |
| Globe St. | 19 | I | 6 |
| Gloucester Pl. | 22 | P | 6 |
| Gloucester Road, Bootle | 16 | B | 6 |
| Gloucester Road, W. Derby Rd. | 11 | N | 1 |
| Glover St. | 34 | T | 11 |
| Glynn St. | 14 | U | 2 |
| Godfrey St. | 21 | N | 6 |
| Golden Grove | 8 | G | 4 |
| Goldie St. | 19 | I | 6 |
| Goldsmith St. | 22 | O | 5 |

| | | | |
|---|---|---|---|
| Goldsmith Street, Bootle | 26 | A | 9 |
| Gomer St. | 21 | O | 8 |
| Gondover Av. | 6 | A | 3 |
| Gonville Rd. | 18 | E | 6 |
| Goodall Pl. | 18 | G | 6 |
| Goodall St. | 18 | G | 6 |
| Goodison Av. | 19 | H | 5 |
| Goodison Rd. | 8 | G | 5 |
| Goodwood St. | 30 | K | 9 |
| Gordon St., Great Homer St. | 20 | L | 8 |
| Gordon St., Wavertree | 14 | U | 3 |
| Gordon Working Lads' Institute | 19 | H | 8 |
| Gore St. | 34 | T | 10 |
| Goree Piazzas | 32 | P | 12 |
| Goring St. | 34 | V | 10 |
| Gorsebank Rd. | 15 | X | 3 |
| Gorsefield Rd. | 6 | A | 3 |
| Gorsehill Rd., New Brighton | 38 | B | 1 |
| Gorsey La., Poulton | 38 | B | 3 |
| Gorst St. | 19 | I | 5 |
| Goschen St. | 20 | K | 6 |
| Gosford St. | 35 | W | 10 |
| Goswell St. | 14 | U | 2 |
| Goth St. | 11 | N | 4 |
| Goulden St. | 23 | R | 6 |
| Government Bldgs., Victoria St. | 32 | O | 11 |
| Gower St. | 33 | Q | 12 |
| Grace St. | 35 | W | 10 |
| Gradwell St. | 32 | Q | 11 |
| Grafton St. | 34 | T | 11 |
| Graham St. | 25 | W | 8 |
| Grain St. | 35 | V | 10 |
| Grampian Rd. | 13 | R | 1 |
| Granby St. | 24 | T | 7 |
| Grand Hotel | 32 | P | 10 |
| Grange Rd., Birkenhead | 36 | B | 2 |
| Grange Rd. West, Birkenhead | 36 | B | 2 |
| Grange St. | 11 | N | 2 |
| Grange Ter. | 14 | U | 1 |
| Grant Av. | 15 | W | 2 |
| Grant St. | 23 | R | 7 |
| Grantham St. | 12 | P | 4 |
| Granton Rd. | 20 | L | 5 |
| Granville Rd. | 14 | U | 4 |
| Grasmere St. | 10 | L | 4 |
| Graving Docks | 27 | D | 10 |
| Graylands Pl. | 9 | G | 2 |
| Graylands Rd. | 8 | G | 2 |
| Grayson St. | 33 | R | 11 |
| Gt. Charlotte St. | 32 | P | 10 |
| Gt. Crosshall St. | 31 | O | 10 |
| Great Float East, Birkenhead | 39 | C | 4 |
| Great Float West, Birkenhead | 38 | B | 4 |
| Gt. George Pl. | 33 | S | 10 |
| Gt. George Sq. | 33 | R | 10 |
| Gt. George St. | 33 | R | 10 |
| Gt. Homer St. | 20 | L | 8 |
| Gt. Howard St. | 30 | K | 11 |
| Gt. Mersey St. | 19 | I | 9 |
| Gt. Nelson St. | 21 | M | 9 |
| Gt. Newton St. | 22 | P | 8 |
| Gt. Orford St. | 22 | Q | 8 |
| Gt. Richmond St. | 21 | N | 8 |
| Greaves St. | 35 | V | 10 |
| Grecian Ter. | 20 | L | 7 |
| Greek Church | 34 | T | 9 |
| Greek St. | 22 | P | 8 |
| Greenbank Drive | 15 | W | 4 |
| Greenbank Road, Tranmere | 36 | B | 3 |
| Green Bank Rd. | 15 | X | 3 |
| Green Heys Rd. | 25 | V | 7 |
| Greenland St. | 33 | S | 11 |
| Green La., Egremont | 38 | B | 2 |
| Green La., Wallasey | 38 | A | 2 |
| Green La. Stn., Tranmere | 37 | C | 3 |
| Greenleaf St. | 24 | U | 5 |
| Greenside, Brunswick Rd. | 22 | O | 7 |
| Greenwood St. | 21 | N | 5 |
| Greetham St. | 33 | R | 11 |
| Gregson St. | 21 | O | 7 |
| Greig St. | 35 | W | 10 |
| Grenville Street South | 33 | R | 10 |
| Gresford Av. | 15 | W | 4 |
| Gresham St. | 13 | R | 2 |
| Greta St. | 35 | V | 9 |
| Grey Rd. | 7 | D | 3 |
| Grey St. | 34 | T | 9 |
| Grey Rock St. | 21 | N | 5 |
| Grierson St. | 24 | T | 6 |
| Grindison Rd. | 9 | G | 1 |
| Grinfield St. | 23 | R | 7 |
| Grins Hill St. | 24 | V | 8 |
| Grist St. | 18 | F | 6 |
| Grosvenor Rd. | 9 | H | 2 |
| Grosvenor Rd. | 14 | U | 3 |
| Grosvenor Road, Claughton | 36 | A | 2 |
| Grosvenor Road, New Brighton | 38 | B | 1 |
| Grosvenor St. | 31 | N | 9 |
| Grosvenor St., Liscard | 38 | B | 2 |
| Grove Park | 25 | V | 6 |
| Grove Pl. | 19 | H | 7 |
| Grove Rd. | 12 | P | 3 |
| Grove Rd., Wallasey | 38 | A | 2 |
| Grove St., Bootle | 26 | A | 10 |
| Grove St., Crown St. | 23 | R | 7 |
| Grove St., Wavertree | 14 | U | 1 |
| Grove, The, Seacombe | 38 | B | 3 |
| Grundy St. | 29 | I | 10 |
| Guelph St. | 22 | P | 6 |
| Guest St. | 35 | V | 11 |
| Guildhall Rd. | 6 | A | 1 |
| Guildford St. | 21 | N | 7 |
| Guion St. | 12 | O | 4 |
| Gurnall St. | 19 | I | 5 |
| Guthrie St. | 22 | O | 5 |
| Gwendoline St. | 24 | U | 9 |
| Gwenfron Rd. | 22 | P | 5 |
| Gwent St. | 24 | U | 8 |
| Gwladys St. | 9 | G | 4 |
| Gwydir St. | 25 | V | 8 |
| Hackins Hey | 32 | O | 11 |
| Haddock St. | 28 | F | 9 |
| Haddon Av. | 6 | A | 3 |
| Haddon St. | 21 | M | 8 |
| Haggerston Rd. | 8 | F | 3 |
| Hahnemann Rd. | 18 | F | 5 |
| Haigh St. | 21 | N | 7 |
| Haldane Rd. | 8 | F | 4 |
| Hale Rd. | 18 | F | 5 |
| Hale St. | 32 | O | 11 |
| Haliburton St. | 35 | V | 9 |
| Halkyn Av. | 15 | W | 4 |
| Halkyn St. | 21 | M | 5 |
| Hall Lane | 22 | P | 6 |
| Hallam St. | 13 | R | 5 |
| Halsbury Rd. | 12 | P | 4 |
| Hamilton Rd. | 20 | M | 6 |
| Hamilton Rd., New Brighton | 38 | B | 1 |
| Hamilton Square, Birkenhead | 37 | C | 2 |
| Hamilton Sq. Stn., Birkenhead | 37 | C | 2 |
| Hamilton Street, Birkenhead | 37 | C | 2 |
| Hamlet St. | 18 | F | 8 |
| Hampden St. | 8 | F | 4 |
| Hampson St. | 11 | N | 2 |
| Hampstead Rd. | 12 | O | 3 |
| Hampton St. | 34 | T | 9 |
| Handel St. | 24 | U | 7 |
| Handfield St. | 20 | L | 5 |
| Hanford Av. | 6 | A | 3 |
| Hankin St. | 30 | K | 9 |
| Hannan Rd. | 12 | P | 4 |
| Hanover St. | 32 | Q | 10 |
| Hans Rd. | 8 | G | 4 |
| Hantsfield Rd. | 6 | A | 4 |
| Hanwell St. | 10 | M | 3 |
| Hapton St. | 20 | K | 7 |
| Harbord St. | 23 | R | 6 |
| Harcourt St. | 19 | H | 8 |
| Harding St. | 24 | S | 6 |
| Hardman St. | 33 | R | 9 |
| Hardwick St. | 22 | P | 7 |
| Hardy St. | 33 | R | 10 |
| Hare Pl. | 31 | N | 9 |
| Harebell St. | 18 | H | 8 |
| Harewood St. | 21 | M | 5 |
| Harford St. | 32 | Q | 9 |
| Harke St. | 23 | S | 6 |
| Harlech St. | 18 | G | 5 |
| Harley St. | 6 | A | 2 |
| Harlow St. | 35 | V | 10 |
| Harold St. | 24 | T | 6 |
| Harper Rd. | 7 | D | 2 |
| Harper St. | 22 | P | 7 |
| Harrington Dock | 35 | W | 12 |
| Harrington St. | 32 | P | 11 |
| Harrison Drive, Wallasey | 38 | A | 1 |
| Harrison Park, Wallasey | 38 | A | 1 |
| Harrogate St. | 21 | M | 6 |
| Harrow Rd. | 10 | K | 4 |
| Harrowby St. | 24 | T | 8 |
| Hart St. | 22 | P | 9 |
| Hartington Rd. | 24 | U | 5 |
| Hartley St. | 19 | I | 6 |
| Hartnup St. | 20 | K | 5 |
| Harvey St. | 24 | T | 5 |
| Hatfield Rd. | 17 | D | 5 |
| Hatfield St. | 22 | Q | 7 |
| Hatherley St. | 24 | T | 8 |
| Hatton Garden | 31 | O | 10 |
| Havelock St. | 20 | L | 7 |
| Haverstock Rd. | 12 | P | 2 |
| Hawarden Av. | 15 | W | 4 |
| Hawdon St. | 24 | T | 5 |
| Hawke St. | 32 | P | 9 |
| Hawkesworth St. | 10 | L | 4 |
| Hawkins St. | 12 | P | 4 |
| Hawkstone St. | 25 | W | 9 |
| Hawthorne Grove | 23 | R | 5 |
| Hawthorne Rd. | 17 | D | 6 |
| Hayfield St. | 19 | I | 5 |
| Haylock St. | 35 | W | 10 |
| Haymarket, North | 21 | M | 6 |
| Haymarket, Old | 32 | O | 10 |
| Hazeldale Rd. | 7 | D | 2 |
| Hazlemere Rd. | 12 | Q | 1 |
| Head St. | 34 | T | 10 |
| Heathbank, Wallasey | 38 | A | 3 |
| Heath St. | 23 | R | 8 |
| Heathcote Rd. | 8 | F | 4 |
| Heathcote St. | 24 | T | 6 |

| | | | |
|---|---|---|---|
| Heathfield Rd. | 15 | X | 1 |
| Heathfield St. | 32 | Q | 10 |
| Heber St. | 11 | O | 5 |
| Hector St. | 18 | F | 8 |
| Hedley St. | 30 | K | 10 |
| Helena St. | 23 | R | 6 |
| Helena St., Walton | 7 | E | 4 |
| Hemans St. | 24 | T | 9 |
| Hemans Street, Bootle | 26 | A | 9 |
| Henderson Green | 22 | Q | 6 |
| Hendon Rd. | 12 | P | 2 |
| Henry St., Campbell St. | 33 | Q | 11 |
| Henry St., Edge Lane | 13 | R | 1 |
| Henry Edward St. | 31 | N | 10 |
| Herbert St. | 21 | N | 6 |
| Herbert St., Walton | 7 | D | 4 |
| Herculaneum B'ge | 35 | W | 11 |
| Herculaneum Dock | 35 | X | 11 |
| Herculaneum Dock Station | 35 | W | 11 |
| Hereford Rd. | 15 | W | 1 |
| Heriot St. | 19 | I | 8 |
| Hermia St. | 18 | F | 8 |
| Hermitage, The | 8 | G | 3 |
| Hero St. | 18 | E | 6 |
| Herschel St. | 20 | K | 5 |
| Hertford Drive, Liscard | 38 | B | 2 |
| Hertford Rd. | 17 | E | 8 |
| Heyes St. | 10 | L | 4 |
| Hey Green Rd. | 14 | T | 2 |
| Heyworth St. | 20 | L | 7 |
| Hibbert St. | 21 | M | 7 |
| High St., Wavertree | 14 | V | 1 |
| Higham St. | 21 | M | 8 |
| Highfield Road, Rock Ferry | 37 | C | 4 |
| Highfield Road, Walton | 7 | C | 3 |
| Highfield St. | 31 | N | 11 |
| Highgate St. | 23 | R | 6 |
| High Park Mills | 35 | V | 11 |
| High Park St. | 25 | V | 9 |
| Hilberry Av. | 11 | N | 1 |
| Hilbre St. | 32 | P | 9 |
| Hill St. | 34 | T | 11 |
| Hinderton Road, Tranmere | 36 | B | 3 |
| Hinton St. | 12 | P | 3 |
| Hobart St. | 20 | K | 7 |
| Hockenhall Alley | 31 | O | 11 |
| Hodder St. | 20 | K | 6 |
| Hodges Mount | 35 | V | 9 |
| Hodson Pl. | 21 | N | 6 |
| Hodson St. | 31 | N | 10 |
| Hogarth Rd. | 18 | G | 7 |
| Holbeck St. | 10 | L | 3 |
| Holborn St. | 22 | P | 6 |
| Holden St. | 23 | S | 7 |
| Holdsworth St. | 12 | Q | 4 |
| Holford St. | 22 | O | 7 |
| Holland Pl. | 23 | Q | 6 |
| Holland Rd., Liscard | 38 | B | 2 |
| Holland St. | 12 | Q | 2 |
| Holly Rd. | 13 | Q | 3 |
| Holly St. | 31 | N | 9 |
| Holly St., Bootle | 16 | B | 7 |
| Holly Bank Rd. | 15 | X | 3 |
| Hollyfield Rd. | 6 | B | 3 |
| Holm Lane, Oxton | 36 | A | 3 |
| Holme St. | 29 | H | 10 |
| Holmes St. | 24 | U | 5 |
| Holt Road | 12 | Q | 4 |
| Holt St. | 23 | S | 6 |
| Holy Innocents Church | 23 | S | 7 |
| Holy Trinity Ch., St Anne St. | 21 | O | 9 |
| Holy Trinity Ch., Breck Rd. | 11 | M | 4 |
| Holy Trinity Ch., Church Rd. | 15 | W | 1 |
| Holy Trinity Ch., Parliament St. | 33 | S | 11 |
| Holywell St. | 16 | B | 8 |
| Home for Aged Poor | 11 | N | 3 |
| Homer St. | 35 | X | 10 |
| Homerton Rd. | 12 | P | 2 |
| Hood St. | 32 | P | 10 |
| Hook St. | 30 | K | 9 |
| Hooton Pl. | 16 | A | 8 |
| Hope Hall, Hope St. | 23 | R | 8 |
| Hope Pl. | 33 | R | 9 |
| Hope St. | 23 | R | 9 |
| Hopwood St. | 30 | K | 9 |
| Horatio St. | 31 | M | 9 |
| Hornby Dock | 26 | B | 11 |
| Hornby Pl. | 6 | B | 2 |
| Hornby Rd, Bootle | 16 | A | 7 |
| Hornby Rd., Rice Lane | 7 | C | 3 |
| Hornby St. | 30 | L | 10 |
| Horne St. | 21 | O | 5 |
| Hornsey Rd. | 10 | K | 3 |
| Hose Side Road, Liscard | 38 | A | 1 |
| Horsfall St. | 35 | W | 11 |
| Horsley St. | 22 | P | 7 |
| Hospital, Bootle | 27 | D | 9 |
| Hotham St. | 32 | P | 9 |
| Hotspur St. | 18 | F | 8 |
| Houghton St. | 32 | P | 10 |
| Houlding St. | 10 | K | 4 |
| Houlgrave St. | 30 | K | 10 |
| Houlton St. | 12 | P | 4 |
| Howat St. | 21 | M | 5 |
| Howe St., Bootle | 27 | E | 10 |
| Howe St., Great Homer St. | 20 | L | 8 |
| Howley St. | 19 | H | 8 |
| Hoylake Rd., Birkenhead | 38 | A | 4 |
| Hughes St. | 21 | N | 5 |
| Hughson St. | 34 | U | 10 |
| Humber St. | 19 | G | 7 |
| Hume St. | 23 | S | 6 |
| Hunt St. | 20 | M | 5 |
| Hunter St. | 31 | O | 10 |
| Hunter's Lane | 15 | V | 1 |
| Huntly Rd. | 12 | P | 3 |
| Hurlingham Rd. | 8 | G | 1 |
| Hurry St. | 35 | X | 10 |
| Hurst St. | 33 | Q | 12 |
| Huskisson Dock & Branches | 29 | G | 11 |
| Huskisson Dock Station | 29 | H | 10 |
| Huskisson Goods Station | 29 | I | 9 |
| Huskisson's Monument, Canning Pl. | 32 | Q | 11 |
| Huskisson's Monument, St James Cemetery | 33 | S | 9 |
| Huskisson St. | 23, 33 | S | 9 |
| Hutchinson St. | 22 | O | 6 |
| Hyde St. | 22 | P | 7 |
| Hygeia St. | 21 | N | 5 |
| Hyslop St. | 34 | T | 10 |
| Ibstock Rd. | 16 | A | 7 |
| Ida St. | 18 | F | 7 |
| Iden St. | 22 | P | 7 |
| Idris St. | 30 | K | 10 |
| Ilford St. | 22 | P | 8 |
| Iliad St. | 21 | M | 8 |
| Ilchester Road, Birkenhead | 38 | A | 4 |
| Imison St. | 7 | D | 5 |
| Imperial Av., Liscard | 38 | B | 2 |
| Imperial Hotel | 32 | P | 10 |
| Imrie St. | 8 | E | 4 |
| Ince Av. | 9 | I | 3 |
| Index St. | 18 | F | 5 |
| India St. | 21 | M | 7 |
| Industrial School | 18 | G | 7 |
| Infant Orphan Asylums | 23 | R | 7 |
| Infectious Diseases Hosp., Bootle | 16 | A | 5 |
| Infectious Diseases Hospital | 7 | D | 4 |
| Infectious Diseases Hosp., Netherfield Rd. North | 20 | L | 7 |
| Ingrave Rd. | 8 | G | 1 |
| Ingrow Rd. | 22 | P | 5 |
| Institute & Schoo. of Arts | 33 | R | 9 |
| Ireton St. | 8 | F | 4 |
| Iris St. | 18 | F | 7 |
| Irlam Rd. | 16 | B | 9 |
| Irvine St. | 23 | Q | 6 |
| Irwell St. | 32 | P | 12 |
| Isaac St. | 35 | W | 10 |
| Isis St. | 24 | U | 6 |
| Islington | 22 | O | 9 |
| Islington Sq. | 22 | O | 7 |
| Ismay St. | 18 | G | 5 |
| Ivanhoe St. | 17 | C | 8 |
| Ivernia Rd. | 8 | F | 2 |
| Ivor St. | 18 | F | 9 |
| Ivy St. | 23 | S | 7 |
| Ivydale Rd. | 7 | D | 1 |
| Ivyleigh | 11 | N | 1 |
| Jackson St. | 34 | U | 10 |
| Jackson's Lane | 31 | O | 12 |
| Jacob St. | 35 | W | 9 |
| Jamaica St. | 33 | S | 11 |
| James St. | 32 | P | 12 |
| James St. Station | 32 | P | 12 |
| Jamieson Rd. | 15 | V | 3 |
| Janet St. | 23 | R | 5 |
| Jasmine St. | 21 | M | 6 |
| Jefferson St. | 21 | M | 7 |
| Jeffery St. | 20 | K | 6 |
| Jenkinson St. | 21 | N | 8 |
| Jenner St. | 34 | T | 10 |
| Jermyn St. | 24 | U | 7 |
| Jersey St. | 17 | C | 8 |
| Jervis St. | 22 | P | 9 |
| Jesmond St. | 14 | T | 4 |
| Jessica St. | 18 | F | 8 |
| Jevons St. | 35 | X | 10 |
| Jews' Burial Grd. | 7 | D | 2 |
| Jews' Cemetery, Deane Rd. | 12 | Q | 4 |
| Jews' Synagogue, Hope Pl. | 33 | R | 9 |
| Jews' Synagogue, Preston St. | 24 | T | 8 |
| Job St. | 22 | P | 6 |
| Johnson St. | 31 | O | 10 |
| Johnstone St. | 27 | D | 9 |
| Jolliffe St. | 24 | U | 8 |
| Jones St. | 32 | Q | 9 |
| Jordan Pl. | 34 | U | 11 |
| Jordan St. | 33 | S | 11 |
| Jubilee Drive | 22 | Q | 6 |
| Jubilee St. | 22 | P | 7 |
| Judges' Drive, The | 11 | O | 3 |

| | | | |
|---|---|---|---|
| Juliet St. | 18 | F | 8 |
| July Rd. | 11 | M | 2 |
| July St. | 16 | A | 7 |
| June Rd. | 11 | N | 2 |
| June St. | 16 | B | 7 |
| Juniper St. | 29 | G | 9 |
| Juno St. | 23 | R | 6 |
| Jupiter St. | 11 | M | 4 |
| Juvenal St. | 21 | M | 9 |
| Kearney Pl. | 31 | M | 10 |
| Kearsley St. | 19 | I | 7 |
| Keats St. | 16 | A | 8 |
| Keble Rd. | 18 | E | 8 |
| Keble St. | 22 | P | 6 |
| Kedleston St. | 35 | X | 9 |
| Keith Av. | 8 | G | 4 |
| Kellitt Rd. | 14 | V | 3 |
| Kelso Rd. | 12 | P | 3 |
| Kelvin Grove | 25 | V | 8 |
| Kemble St. | 22 | P | 5 |
| Kemlyn Rd. | 10 | K | 4 |
| Kempston St. | 22 | P | 8 |
| Kempton Rd. | 14 | T | 3 |
| Kenilworth St. | 17 | C | 8 |
| Kenmare Rd. | 15 | V | 3 |
| Kensington | 22 | P | 5 |
| Kensington Gdns. | 22 | Q | 5 |
| Kensington St. | 22 | P | 6 |
| Kent Sq. | 33 | R | 11 |
| Kent St. | 33 | R | 10 |
| Kent Street, Bootle | 16 | C | 6 |
| Kepler St. | 21 | M | 7 |
| Kerford St. | 21 | N | 7 |
| Kew St. | 20 | L | 8 |
| Kiddmann St. | 7 | E | 4 |
| Kilshaw St. | 21 | N | 5 |
| Kimberley St. | 24 | T | 8 |
| Kinder St. | 22 | O | 7 |
| King St. | 32 | P | 11 |
| King St., Egremont | 39 | C | 2 |
| King Edward St. | 31 | N | 12 |
| King Edward VII. Statue | 32 | P | 13 |
| Kingfield Rd. | 6 | B | 3 |
| Kinglake St. | 23 | R | 6 |
| King's Docks | 33 | R | 12 |
| King's Rd. | 17 | E | 8 |
| Kingsley Rd. | 24 | T | 7 |
| Kingsway, Liscard | 38 | B | 2 |
| Kinmel St. | 25 | V | 8 |
| Kirby St. | 21 | O | 8 |
| Kirk St., Bootle | 27 | C | 9 |
| Kirk St., Kirkdale Rd. | 20 | I | 7 |
| Kirkdale Home | 18 | G | 7 |
| Kirkdale Recreation Ground | 19 | G | 7 |
| Kirkdale Rd. | 19 | I | 7 |
| Kirkdale Station | 18 | F | 7 |
| Kirkdale Vale | 19 | I | 6 |
| Kirkstall St. | 19 | H | 6 |
| Kitchen St. | 33 | R | 11 |
| Kitchener Drive | 6 | A | 2 |
| Knight St. | 33 | R | 10 |
| Knowsley Rd. | 16 | A | 7 |
| Knowsley View | 21 | N | 5 |
| Laburnum Pl. | 17 | C | 7 |
| Laburnum Rd. | 12 | Q | 2 |
| Lace St. | 31 | O | 10 |
| Laird St., Birkenhead | 36 | A | 1 |
| Lake St. | 20 | K | 5 |
| Lamb St. | 19 | I | 9 |
| Lambert St. | 22 | O | 9 |
| Lambeth Rd. | 19 | I | 8 |
| Lampeter Rd. | 10 | L | 2 |
| Lamport St. | 34 | U | 10 |
| Lancaster Av. | 25 | V | 5 |
| Lancaster Street, Stanley Rd. | 20 | K | 8 |
| Lancaster Street, Walton | 7 | E | 4 |
| Lance St. | 21 | M | 6 |
| Lancefield Rd. | 6 | B | 3 |
| Lancelot's Hey | 31 | O | 12 |
| Landseer Rd. | 21 | M | 6 |
| Langdale Rd. | 15 | W | 3 |
| Langdale St. | 17 | C | 7 |
| Langham St. | 19 | H | 5 |
| Langrove St. | 20 | M | 8 |
| Langsdale St. | 21 | O | 8 |
| Langton Branch Dock | 27 | C | 10 |
| Langton Dock | 27 | D | 11 |
| Langton Rd. | 14 | U | 4 |
| Langton St. | 27 | C | 11 |
| Langtry Rd. | 18 | G | 7 |
| Lansdowne Pl. | 20 | L | 6 |
| Larchdale Rd. | 7 | D | 2 |
| Larch Lea | 11 | M | 4 |
| Larkfield View | 14 | T | 2 |
| Latham St. | 19 | I | 9 |
| Latimer St. | 30 | K | 9 |
| Lauder Rd. | 13 | Q | 3 |
| Laurel Rd. | 12 | Q | 3 |
| Lauriston Rd. | 9 | H | 1 |
| Lavan St. | 21 | O | 6 |
| Lavrock Bank | 35 | W | 11 |
| Lawrence Grove | 14 | V | 3 |
| Lawrence Rd. | 14 | U | 4 |
| Lawrence St. | 31 | M | 9 |
| Lawton St. | 32 | Q | 10 |
| Laxey St. | 34 | U | 10 |
| Layland St. | 23 | S | 6 |
| Leadenhall St. | 20 | K | 6 |
| Leander St. | 22 | Q | 9 |
| Lear Road | 13 | R | 1 |
| Leasowe Rd. | 6 | A | 1 |
| Leasowe Road, Wallasey | 38 | A | 2 |
| Leda St. | 24 | T | 6 |
| Ledward St. | 35 | V | 10 |
| Leece St. | 33 | R | 9 |
| Leeds St. | 31 | N | 11 |
| Leeds & Liverpool Canal | 16 | B | 6 |
| Leeds & Liverpool Canal | 30 | L | 10 |
| Leicester Rd. | 16 | B | 5 |
| Leigh St. | 32 | P | 10 |
| Leighton St. | 18 | F | 6 |
| Leison St. | 19 | I | 8 |
| Lemon St. | 19 | I | 9 |
| Lennox St. | 12 | Q | 5 |
| Lenthall St. | 8 | F | 4 |
| Leonora St. | 35 | W | 9 |
| Leopold Rd. | 22 | Q | 6 |
| Lesseps Rd. | 24 | U | 5 |
| Lester Gdns. | 19 | I | 7 |
| Lestock St. | 34 | T | 10 |
| Leta St. | 8 | G | 4 |
| Letitia St. | 35 | V | 9 |
| Letterstone St. | 21 | M | 6 |
| Leven St. | 18 | G | 6 |
| Lewis's Establishment | 32 | P | 10 |
| Leyden St. | 30 | I | 9 |
| Liberty St. | 14 | U | 3 |
| Library, Rice Lane | 7 | C | 2 |
| Lidderdale Rd. | 15 | W | 3 |
| Liffey St. | 24 | U | 7 |
| Lightbody St. | 30 | K | 11 |
| Lightwood St. | 24 | T | 5 |
| Lilford Av. | 6 | A | 2 |
| Lilley Rd. | 12 | Q | 3 |
| Lillian Rd. | 10 | L | 4 |
| Lily Grove, Dorothy St. | 23 | R | 5 |
| Lily Grove, Walton | 9 | G | 2 |
| Lime Grove | 24 | U | 6 |
| Lime St. | 32 | P | 10 |
| Lime St. Station, L.M.S. | 32 | P | 9 |
| Limekiln Lane | 30 | L | 9 |
| Lime Kiln Lane, Poulton | 38 | B | 3 |
| Linacre Bridge | 16 | A | 6 |
| Linacre Lane | 16 | A | 6 |
| Lincoln Drive, Liscard | 38 | B | 2 |
| Lincoln St. | 27 | E | 9 |
| Lind St. | 18 | F | 5 |
| Linden St. | 23 | S | 7 |
| Lindley St. | 24 | T | 5 |
| Lindsay Rd. | 9 | I | 1 |
| Ling St. | 22 | Q | 5 |
| Linnet Lane | 25 | X | 7 |
| Linton St., Goodison St. | 8 | G | 5 |
| Linton St., West Derby Rd. | 11 | O | 4 |
| Liscard, Wallasey | 38 | B | 2 |
| Liscard Rd. | 14 | U | 4 |
| Liscard Rd., Egremont | 38 | B | 3 |
| Liscard & Poulton Stn., Wallasey | 38 | A | 3 |
| Liscard & Wallasey Rd., Wallasey | 38 | A | 2 |
| Lissant St. | 23 | S | 6 |
| Lister Drive | 12 | O | 1 |
| Lister Rd. | 12 | Q | 3 |
| Liston St. | 8 | E | 4 |
| Litherland Rd. | 16 | B | 7 |
| Little Canning St. | 23 | S | 9 |
| Littledale Road, Seacombe | 39 | C | 3 |
| Little Howard St. | 30 | M | 11 |
| Little Woolton St. | 22 | Q | 7 |
| Liver Buildings | 32 | O | 12 |
| Liver Cres. | 19 | G | 6 |
| Liver St. | 33 | Q | 11 |
| Liverpool College & Police Athletic Ground | 12 | Q | 1 |
| Liverpool Football Ground | 10 | K | 4 |
| Liverpool Industrial School | 18 | G | 6 |
| Liverpool Parish Workhouse, Brownlow Hill | 22 | Q | 8 |
| Livingstone Street, Birkenhead | 36 | B | 2 |
| Llanrwst St. | 34 | U | 10 |
| Lloyd St. | 21 | N | 6 |
| Lochinvar St. | 7 | E | 4 |
| Lockerby Rd. | 12 | Q | 3 |
| Lockhart St. | 35 | W | 11 |
| Lodge Lane | 24 | U | 6 |
| Lodwick St. | 28 | E | 9 |
| Lombard St. | 11 | N | 4 |
| Lomond Rd. | 13 | R | 1 |
| London Rd. | 32 | P | 9 |
| L.M.S. Goods Stn. | 26 | B | 10 |
| L.M.S. Goods Stn. | 27 | C | 9 |
| L.M.S. Goods Stn. | 27 | C | 10 |
| Long Lane | 14 | T | 1 |
| Longfellow St. | 24 | T | 6 |
| Longfellow Street, Bootle | 26 | A | 9 |
| Longville St. | 35 | V | 11 |
| Lonsdale St. | 24 | S | 7 |
| Loraine St. | 20 | L | 6 |
| Lord St. | 32 | P | 11 |
| Lord St., Birkenhead | 36 | B | 2 |
| Lord Nelson St. | 32 | P | 9 |

| | | | |
|---|---|---|---|
| Lorne St. | 12 | Q | 2 |
| Lorton St. | 24 | T | 6 |
| Lostock Rd. | 12 | Q | 3 |
| Lothair Rd. | 10 | K | 5 |
| Lothian St. | 24 | V | 9 |
| Loudon Grove | 24 | U | 8 |
| Louis St. | 20 | K | 8 |
| Louisa St. | 20 | K | 6 |
| Lovat St. | 23 | R | 6 |
| Love Lane | 30 | L | 11 |
| Lovers' La., Oxton | 36 | A | 3 |
| Low Hill | 22 | O | 6 |
| Lowell St. | 18 | F | 5 |
| Lower Bank View | 28 | E | 10 |
| Lower Breck Rd. | 11 | M | 3 |
| Lower Castle St. | 32 | O | 12 |
| Lower Mersey View | 28 | E | 9 |
| Lower Milk St. | 31 | N | 11 |
| Lowndes Rd. | 11 | M | 1 |
| Lowther St. | 24 | T | 7 |
| Low Wood St. | 22 | P | 6 |
| Loxdale St. | 35 | X | 10 |
| Ludlow St. | 18 | G | 5 |
| Ludwig Rd. | 10 | M | 4 |
| Luke St. | 34 | T | 9 |
| Lundie St. | 21 | M | 5 |
| Lune St. | 20 | K | 6 |
| Lurgan Rd. | 12 | Q | 3 |
| Lusitania Rd. | 8 | F | 3 |
| Luther St. | 20 | K | 8 |
| Luton Grove | 19 | H | 6 |
| Luton St. | 29 | I | 10 |
| Luxmore Rd. | 8 | G | 4 |
| Luxor St. | 23 | S | 6 |
| Lyceum News Room | 32 | Q | 10 |
| Lydia Ann St. | 33 | Q | 11 |
| Lydiate St. | 24 | T | 7 |
| Lyell St. | 20 | L | 5 |
| Lynedoch St. | 21 | O | 5 |
| Lynholme Rd. | 10 | K | 3 |
| Lynwood Rd. | 6 | B | 2 |
| Lyon Rd. | 10 | L | 4 |
| Lyons St. | 28 | E | 10 |
| Lyric Theatre | 19 | I | 7 |
| Lyster Rd. | 27 | B | 10 |
| Lytton St. | 21 | O | 7 |
| Macaulay St. | 23 | S | 6 |
| Macbeth St. | 18 | F | 8 |
| Macdonald St. | 14 | U | 3 |
| Mackenzie St. | 21 | M | 6 |
| M'Leod St. | 21 | M | 5 |
| Maddox St. | 31 | M | 9 |
| Maddrell St. | 30 | L | 11 |
| Madelaine St. | 24 | U | 8 |
| Madeley St. | 12 | O | 4 |
| Madryn St. | 25 | V | 8 |
| Magazine La., New Brighton | 38 | B | 1 |
| Magazine Promen., New Brighton | 38 | B | 1 |
| Magdala St. | 24 | T | 6 |
| Magnum St. | 20 | L | 7 |
| Maguire St. | 31 | M | 10 |
| Maitland St. | 24 | T | 6 |
| Major St. | 20 | K | 8 |
| Makin St. | 8 | E | 5 |
| Malcolm St. | 18 | E | 9 |
| Malden Rd. | 12 | P | 4 |
| Mallow Rd. | 12 | P | 4 |
| Malton Rd. | 16 | B | 7 |
| Malta St. | 35 | V | 10 |
| Malvern Rd. | 12 | O | 4 |
| Malwood St. | 35 | W | 10 |
| Manchester Dock | 32 | P | 12 |
| Manchester St. | 32 | O | 10 |
| Mandeville St. | 8 | F | 5 |
| Manestys Lane | 32 | P | 11 |
| Manfred St. | 22 | P | 7 |
| Mann Island | 32 | P | 12 |
| Mann St. | 34 | T | 11 |
| Mann St., Bootle | 28 | E | 9 |
| Mannering Rd. | 25 | X | 7 |
| Manningham Rd. | 10 | L | 3 |
| Manor Hill, Claughton | 36 | A | 2 |
| Manor Rd., Liscard | 38 | B | 2 |
| Mansell Rd. | 12 | O | 4 |
| Mansfield St. | 21 | N | 8 |
| Manton Rd. | 12 | P | 4 |
| Maple Grove | 24 | V | 6 |
| Marble St. | 32 | P | 10 |
| March Rd. | 11 | N | 2 |
| Marchfield Rd. | 6 | B | 3 |
| Marcot Rd. | 12 | P | 2 |
| Margaret Rd. | 18 | F | 5 |
| Margaret St. | 21 | N | 6 |
| Maria Rd. | 7 | E | 4 |
| Marine Parade | 30 | L | 13 |
| Marine Park, New Brighton | 38 | B | 1 |
| Marine Promenade, New Brighton | 38 | B | 1 |
| Mariners' Home, Egremont | 38 | B | 2 |
| Marion St., Birkenhead | 36 | B | 2 |
| Marius St. | 19 | H | 5 |
| Mark St. | 20 | I | 7 |
| Market St. | 32 | P | 10 |
| Market St., Birkenhead | 36 | B | 2 |
| Markfield Rd. | 16 | A | 7 |
| Markhill House | 17 | D | 5 |
| Marlborough Rd. | 11 | M | 1 |
| Marlborough St. | 31 | N | 10 |
| Marlowe Rd., Liscard | 38 | B | 3 |
| Marlsford St. | 12 | O | 4 |
| Marmaduke St. | 23 | R | 6 |
| Marmion Rd. | 25 | X | 7 |
| Marmion Ter. | 35 | W | 11 |
| Marmonde St. | 19 | H | 6 |
| Marquis St. | 22 | P | 8 |
| Marsden St. | 22 | O | 6 |
| Marsh Lane | 16 | A | 8 |
| Marsh Lane and Strand Rd. Stn. | 16 | B | 8 |
| Marsh St. | 18 | F | 7 |
| Marshall St. | 35 | V | 10 |
| Martensen St. | 23 | R | 6 |
| Martin's La., Liscard | 38 | B | 2 |
| Marwood St. | 20 | K | 7 |
| Mary Ann St. | 32 | Q | 9 |
| Marybone | 31 | N | 10 |
| Maryland St. | 33 | R | 9 |
| Mason St. | 23 | R | 6 |
| Maternity Home | 23 | R | 8 |
| Mather St. | 35 | W | 9 |
| Mathew St. | 32 | P | 11 |
| Matlock Av. | 6 | A | 2 |
| Matthew St. | 27 | D | 9 |
| Maud St. | 24 | U | 8 |
| Mauretania Rd. | 8 | F | 3 |
| Mawdsley St. | 29 | H | 9 |
| Maxton Rd. | 12 | P | 4 |
| May St. | 32 | Q | 9 |
| May St., Bootle | 16 | A | 7 |
| Mayfields | 19 | G | 6 |
| Maynard St. | 24 | T | 6 |
| Mazzini St. | 21 | M | 7 |
| Meaburn St. | 22 | O | 7 |
| Meadow St. | 31 | N | 9 |
| Medical Institute, Mt. Pleasant | 23 | R | 8 |
| Medlock St. | 19 | G | 7 |
| Mela St. | 22 | O | 6 |
| Melbourne St. | 20 | K | 7 |
| Meliden Road | 13 | R | 2 |
| Melling Rd. | 16 | A | 7 |
| Melrose Av. | 18 | F | 7 |
| Melrose Rd. | 18 | F | 7 |
| Melville Chambs., Lord St. | 32 | P | 11 |
| Melville Pl. | 23 | R | 7 |
| Melville St. | 35 | V | 9 |
| Memphis St. | 23 | S | 6 |
| Menai St. | 30 | K | 10 |
| Menzies St. | 35 | X | 9 |
| Mercer Court | 32 | P | 12 |
| Mere Hall, Birkenhead | 36 | A | 3 |
| Mere Lane | 20 | L | 6 |
| Merivale St. | 13 | R | 5 |
| Merlin St. | 24 | U | 9 |
| Mersey Pk., Tranmere | 36 | B | 3 |
| Mersey Rd., Tranmere | 37 | C | 3 |
| Mersey St. | 32 | Q | 11 |
| Mersey Tunnel | 32 | P | 13 |
| Merton Grove | 17 | C | 8 |
| Merton Rd. | 17 | C | 8 |
| Methuen St. | 14 | U | 3 |
| Micawber St. | 34 | U | 9 |
| Micklefield Rd. | 15 | W | 2 |
| Middle St. | 30 | K | 10 |
| Middlesex Rd. | 16 | B | 5 |
| Midghall St. | 31 | N | 10 |
| Mildred St. | 23 | R | 7 |
| Mile End | 30 | M | 9 |
| Miles St. | 35 | W | 9 |
| Milford St. | 29 | I | 10 |
| Mill Lane | 32 | O | 9 |
| Mill Lane, Bootle | 17 | C | 6 |
| Mill Lane, Liscard | 38 | B | 3 |
| Mill Lane Fever Hosp., Wallasey | 38 | B | 3 |
| Mill Lane, Stanley Park | 9 | I | 4 |
| Mill Rd. | 21 | N | 6 |
| Mill St. | 34 | T | 10 |
| Miller St. | 35 | W | 9 |
| Miller St., Rose Vale | 20 | L | 8 |
| Millers Bridge | 27 | D | 9 |
| Millvale St. | 12 | O | 4 |
| Milman Rd. | 8 | G | 4 |
| Milner's Safe Wks. | 24 | S | 6 |
| Milner St. | 24 | T | 6 |
| Milroy St. | 23 | R | 5 |
| Milton Rd. | 13 | R | 2 |
| Milton St. | 31 | N | 10 |
| Milton St., Bootle | 16 | A | 9 |
| Milverton St. | 12 | O | 4 |
| Mindale Rd. | 14 | U | 1 |
| Minera St. | 20 | M | 7 |
| Minshull St. | 22 | Q | 7 |
| Minto St. | 12 | Q | 5 |
| Miranda Rd. | 18 | E | 7 |
| Mirfield St. | 12 | O | 4 |
| Miriam Rd. | 10 | K | 4 |
| Miskelly St. | 19 | G | 9 |
| Miston St. | 19 | G | 9 |
| Mitford St. | 20 | L | 7 |
| Mitylene St. | 20 | K | 7 |
| Modred St. | 34 | U | 9 |
| Moira St. | 22 | P | 7 |
| Molyneux Rd. | 22 | P | 4 |
| Molyneux St. | 23 | S | 7 |
| Molyneux Street, Bootle | 27 | D | 9 |
| Mona St. | 23 | S | 7 |
| Monastery Rd. | 10 | L | 2 |
| Monk St. | 20 | L | 6 |
| Monro St. | 35 | W | 10 |
| Montague St. | 22 | P | 7 |
| Montfield Rd. | 6 | B | 3 |

| Street | Map | Square | |
|---|---|---|---|
| Monument Place, London Rd. | 22 | P | 8 |
| Moon St. | 22 | Q | 7 |
| Moor Place | 22 | P | 8 |
| Moor St. | 32 | P | 12 |
| Moore St. | 16 | A | 8 |
| Moorfields | 32 | O | 11 |
| Moorgate St. | 23 | S | 5 |
| Morden St. | 12 | O | 4 |
| Morecambe St. | 11 | N | 2 |
| Morland St. | 21 | M | 6 |
| Morley St. | 19 | I | 7 |
| Morningside Rd. | 17 | D | 7 |
| Mornington St. | 35 | V | 10 |
| Morpeth Dock, Birkenhead | 37 | C | 2 |
| Morpeth St. | 33 | S | 9 |
| Morris St. | 21 | N | 6 |
| Morton St. | 34 | U | 9 |
| Mortuary | 32 | O | 13 |
| Mortuary New Brighton | 38 | B | 1 |
| Moses St. | 35 | W | 10 |
| Moss Grove | 24 | V | 6 |
| Moss Lane | 6 | A | 2 |
| Moss St. | 22 | P | 7 |
| Mossdale Rd. | 6 | B | 2 |
| Mossfield Rd. | 6 | A | 3 |
| Mossley Av. | 15 | X | 3 |
| Mould St. | 20 | K | 8 |
| Mount Pleasant | 22 | Q | 8 |
| Mount Pleasant Rd. Liscard | 38 | B | 2 |
| Mount Rd., New Brighton | 38 | B | 1 |
| Mount Rd., Tranmere | 36 | B | 4 |
| Mount St. | 33 | R | 9 |
| Mount Vernon | 22 | Q | 6 |
| Mt. Vernon Convent | 22 | P | 7 |
| Mt. Vernon Grove | 22 | Q | 6 |
| Mt. Vernon Rd. | 22 | Q | 7 |
| Mt. Vernon St. | 22 | P | 7 |
| Mt Vernon View | 22 | Q | 7 |
| Mount View | 33 | R | 10 |
| Mount Wood, Birkenhead | 36 | B | 4 |
| Mountjoy St. | 20 | L | 7 |
| Moville St. | 35 | W | 9 |
| Mozart St. | 24 | U | 7 |
| Mulberry St. | 23 | R | 8 |
| Mulberry St. Recreation Ground | 23 | R | 8 |
| Mulgrave St. | 24 | T | 8 |
| Mulliner St. | 24 | T | 5 |
| Municipal Offices | 32 | O | 11 |
| Murdoch St. | 14 | S | 4 |
| Muriel St. | 9 | H | 4 |
| Myers St. | 23 | S | 7 |
| Myrtle Grove | 23 | R | 5 |
| Myrtle St. | 23 | R | 8 |
| Nansen Grove | 8 | G | 4 |
| Napier St. | 21 | O | 7 |
| Napier St., Bootle | 27 | D | 10 |
| Naseby St. | 8 | F | 4 |
| Nash Grove | 31 | N | 9 |
| Nash St. | 31 | N | 9 |
| Naylor St. | 31 | N | 10 |
| Navy League Sea Training Home, Liscard | 38 | B | 2 |
| Nebo St. | 14 | U | 3 |
| Necropolis Gdns. | 21 | O | 6 |
| Needham Rd. | 12 | Q | 4 |
| Neil St. | 20 | K | 7 |
| Nelson Dock | 30 | I | 12 |
| Nelson Dock Stn. | 30 | I | 11 |
| Nelson Gate | 30 | I | 12 |
| Nelson Monument | 32 | O | 12 |
| Nelson Rd. | 23 | R | 6 |
| Nelson St. | 33 | R | 10 |
| Nelson St., Bootle | 27 | D | 10 |
| Nelson St., Wavertree | 14 | U | 2 |
| Neptune St. | 31 | M | 12 |
| Nesfield St. | 19 | I | 6 |
| Neston St. | 18 | G | 5 |
| Nestor St. | 35 | X | 10 |
| Netherby St. | 25 | X | 10 |
| Netherfield Road North | 20 | K | 7 |
| Netherfield Road South | 21 | M | 7 |
| Netley St. | 19 | G | 6 |
| Nevada St. | 17 | C | 7 |
| Nevin St. | 22 | O | 6 |
| Nevison St. | 22 | R | 6 |
| New Quay | 31 | O | 12 |
| New Road | 11 | N | 1 |
| Newark St. | 18 | G | 5 |
| New Bird St. | 33 | S | 11 |
| Newborough Av. | 15 | X | 3 |
| New Brighton, Wallasey | 39 | C | 1 |
| New Brighton Stn., Wallasey | 38 | B | 1 |
| Newburn St. | 8 | F | 4 |
| Newby St. | 19 | H | 5 |
| Newcastle Rd. | 15 | X | 1 |
| New Chester Rd., Tranmere | 37 | C | 4 |
| Newcombe St. | 11 | N | 14 |
| New Ferry, Birkenhead | 37 | C | 4 |
| New Ferry Park, Birkenhead | 37 | C | 4 |
| New Ferry Pier, Birkenhead | 37 | D | 4 |
| New Hall St. | 33 | S | 11 |
| New Henderson St. | 34 | T | 11 |
| Newington | 32 | Q | 10 |
| Newlands St. | 21 | M | 6 |
| Newman St. | 19 | H | 8 |
| Newport St. | 29 | I | 10 |
| Newsham Drive | 11 | N | 3 |
| Newsham House | 11 | N | 3 |
| Newsham Park | 11 | O | 2 |
| Newsham St. | 20 | L | 8 |
| Newstead Rd. | 24 | T | 6 |
| Newton St. | 34 | T | 9 |
| Nicander Rd. | 15 | X | 3 |
| Nicholson St. | 20 | L | 7 |
| Nickleby St. | 34 | U | 9 |
| Nile St. | 33 | S | 10 |
| Nimrod St. | 18 | G | 5 |
| Nith St. | 19 | G | 7 |
| Nithsdale Rd. | 15 | W | 3 |
| Nixon St. | 8 | E | 4 |
| Noel St. | 24 | T | 6 |
| Norfolk St., Bootle | 16 | B | 6 |
| Norfolk St., St James St. | 33 | S | 11 |
| Norgate St. | 19 | I | 5 |
| Norman St., Birkenhead | 36 | A | 2 |
| Normanby St. | 24 | T | 7 |
| North Corporation Yard | 29 | H | 9 |
| North Dingle | 19 | G | 7 |
| North Docks Goods Station | 30 | I | 11 |
| North Dock Yard | 27 | E | 9 |
| North Hill St. | 24 | U | 8 |
| North Jetty | 28 | E | 11 |
| North John St. | 32 | P | 11 |
| North Park, Bootle | 16 | A | 7 |
| North Rd., Tranmere | 36 | B | 3 |
| North St | 31 | O | 10 |
| North View | 23 | Q | 6 |
| North Wall Lighthouse | 26 | B | 11 |
| Northampton St. | 31 | N | 11 |
| Northbrook St. | 24 | T | 8 |
| Northcote Rd. | 7 | D | 3 |
| Northcote St. | 21 | M | 6 |
| Northdale Rd. | 14 | U | 1 |
| Northern P. O. | 19 | I | 7 |
| Northfield Rd. | 6 | A | 4 |
| North Mersey and Alexandra Docks Goods Station | 26 | B | 10 |
| North Shore Mills | 29 | I | 9 |
| Northumberland St. | 34 | U | 10 |
| Northumberland Ter. | 20 | K | 7 |
| Norton St., Bootle | 16 | A | 8 |
| Norton St., London Rd. | 22 | O | 9 |
| Norwich Rd. | 15 | X | 1 |
| Norwood Grove | 11 | N | 4 |
| Nottingham St. | 20 | M | 7 |
| Nova Scotia | 32 | P | 12 |
| Nursery St. | 20 | K | 8 |
| Nurses' Home, Mill Rd. | 21 | O | 5 |
| Nuttall St. | 23 | R | 5 |
| Oak St., Bootle | 16 | B | 7 |
| Oak St., Wavertree | 14 | U | 3 |
| Oak Bank Rd. | 15 | X | 3 |
| Oakdale Recreation Grd., Seacombe | 38 | B | 3 |
| Oakdale Rd. | 7 | C | 1 |
| Oakdene Rd. | 10 | K | 3 |
| Oakes St. | 22 | P | 8 |
| Oakfield | 10 | L | 4 |
| Oakfield Rd. | 10 | L | 4 |
| Oakleigh | 11 | N | 1 |
| Oban Rd. | 10 | L | 3 |
| Oberon St. | 18 | F | 8 |
| Observatory, Bidston | 38 | A | 4 |
| Odsey St. | 12 | Q | 4 |
| Ogwen St. | 21 | O | 6 |
| Oil St. | 30 | L | 12 |
| Old Barn Rd. | 10 | M | 4 |
| Old Chester Road, Tranmere | 37 | C | 3 |
| Old Church Yard | 32 | O | 12 |
| Old Hall St. | 31 | N | 12 |
| Oldham Pl. | 33 | Q | 9 |
| Oldham St. | 33 | Q | 9 |
| Old Haymarket | 32 | O | 10 |
| Old Leeds St. | 31 | N | 12 |
| Olive St. | 23 | R | 7 |
| Olive Vale | 14 | U | 1 |
| Oliver St. | 23 | S | 7 |
| Oliver St., Birkenhead | 36 | B | 2 |
| Olivia St. | 18 | F | 7 |
| Olney St. | 8 | E | 5 |
| Olton St. | 14 | T | 2 |
| Olympia | 22 | O | 5 |
| Ono St. | 14 | U | 3 |
| Onslow Rd. | 12 | P | 3 |
| Opie St. | 20 | L | 8 |
| Orby St. | 30 | K | 9 |
| Orchard St. | 13 | S | 1 |
| Oregon St. | 17 | C | 7 |
| Orford St. | 14 | U | 1 |
| Oriel Rd., Bootle | 17 | C | 8 |
| Oriel Rd., King's Rd. | 18 | F | 8 |
| Oriel St. | 31 | N | 10 |
| Orient St. | 10 | L | 6 |
| Orlando St. | 18 | F | 8 |
| Ormond St. | 31 | O | 12 |
| Orphan Drive | 11 | O | 1 |

| | | | |
|---|---|---|---|
| Orphan St. | 23 | **R** | **7** |
| Orphanage, Beacon Lane | 20 | **K** | **6** |
| Orrell Lane | 6 | **A** | **2** |
| Orrell Park Stn. | 6 | **A** | **2** |
| Orry St. | 20 | **K** | **9** |
| Orus St. | 18 | **F** | **7** |
| Orwell Rd. | 19 | **H** | **7** |
| Osborne Grove | 21 | **M** | **6** |
| Osborne Rd., Belmont Rd. | 11 | **M** | **3** |
| Osborne Rd., Tue Brook | 11 | **M** | **1** |
| Osterley Gdns. | 6 | **A** | **2** |
| Oswald St. | 20 | **L** | **8** |
| Othello St. | 18 | **F** | **8** |
| Ottley Rd. | 12 | **P** | **3** |
| Ouse St. | 35 | **V** | **9** |
| Overbury St. | 23 | **S** | **6** |
| Overton St. | 23 | **R** | **6** |
| Owen Rd. | 19 | **G** | **8** |
| Owen St. | 23 | **S** | **6** |
| Oxford Rd. | 17 | **D** | **6** |
| Oxford St. | 23 | **R** | **8** |
| Oxford St. East | 23 | **R** | **7** |
| Oxton, Birkenhead | 36 | **A** | **3** |
| Oxton Rd., Birkenhead | 36 | **B** | **3** |
| Oxton St. | 19 | **G** | **5** |
| Pacific Rd. | 16 | **B** | **9** |
| Paddington | 23 | **Q** | **7** |
| Page St. | 21 | **O** | **8** |
| Pagefield Rd. | 15 | **W** | **1** |
| Paget St. | 30 | **K** | **10** |
| Pagewood St. | 20 | **K** | **6** |
| Paisley St. | 31 | **M** | **12** |
| Pakington St. | 23 | **S** | **6** |
| Palace Rd. | 6 | **A** | **1** |
| Paley St. | 19 | **I** | **6** |
| Pallas St. | 18 | **F** | **7** |
| Pall Mall | 31 | **M** | **11** |
| Palm Grove, Birkenhead | 36 | **A** | **2** |
| Palm St. | 23 | **S** | **7** |
| Palmerston St. | 24 | **T** | **6** |
| Pansy St. | 19 | **H** | **8** |
| Paradise St. | 32 | **P** | **11** |
| Park Drive, Birkenhead | 36 | **A** | **2** |
| Park Hill Rd. | 35 | **W** | **9** |
| Park Lane | 33 | **Q** | **11** |
| Park Palace | 35 | **V** | **10** |
| Park Pl. | 34 | **T** | **10** |
| Park Rd. | 34 | **U** | **10** |
| Park Road East, Birkenhead | 36 | **B** | **2** |
| Park-Road North, Claughton | 36 | **A** | **2** |
| Park Road South, Birkenhead | 36 | **B** | **2** |
| Park Road West, Birkenhead | 36 | **A** | **2** |
| Park St. | 35 | **V** | **11** |
| Park St., Birkenhead | 36 | **B** | **2** |
| Park St., Bootle | 17 | **C** | **7** |
| Park Vale Rd. | 6 | **B** | **1** |
| Park Way | 24 | **T** | **8** |
| Parker St. | 32 | **P** | **10** |
| Parkfield Rd. | 25 | **X** | **7** |
| Parkinson Rd. | 7 | **D** | **2** |
| Parliament Pl. | 33 | **S** | **9** |
| Parliament St. | 33 | **S** | **11** |
| Parr St. | 33 | **Q** | **10** |
| Parron St. | 23 | **Q** | **7** |
| Parton St. | 12 | **P** | **3** |
| Patmos St. | 20 | **K** | **7** |
| Paton St. | 18 | **F** | **8** |
| Patterdale Rd. | 15 | **W** | **3** |
| Patteson St. | 22 | **P** | **5** |
| Paul St. | 31 | **M** | **10** |
| Paulton St. | 35 | **W** | **11** |
| Paxton St. | 20 | **K** | **7** |
| Peach St. | 23 | **Q** | **7** |
| Pearson St. | 14 | **U** | **2** |
| Pecksniff St. | 34 | **U** | **9** |
| Peel Sq. | 31 | **N** | **9** |
| Peel Rd. | 16 | **A** | **9** |
| Peel St. | 25 | **W** | **8** |
| Peel St., Tranmere | 37 | **C** | **3** |
| Peet St. | 23 | **R** | **5** |
| Pellew St. | 32 | **P** | **9** |
| Pelops St. | 18 | **F** | **7** |
| Pembroke Pl. | 22 | **P** | **8** |
| Pembroke Rd. | 17 | **D** | **8** |
| Pembroke St. | 22 | **P** | **8** |
| Pendennis St. | 11 | **M** | **4** |
| Penfield Rd. | 6 | **A** | **3** |
| Pengwern St. | 25 | **V** | **8** |
| Penkett Rd., Liscard | 38 | **B** | **2** |
| Penrhyn St. | 20 | **L** | **8** |
| Penrith St. | 34 | **T** | **9** |
| Penrose St. | 20 | **K** | **6** |
| Pentland Av. | 8 | **G** | **4** |
| Penton St. | 22 | **O** | **5** |
| Penuel Rd. | 8 | **F** | **4** |
| Peover St. | 31 | **N** | **9** |
| Percy St. | 33 | **S** | **9** |
| Percy St., Bootle | 16 | **A** | **8** |
| Perry St. | 34 | **T** | **11** |
| Perth St. | 21 | **O** | **6** |
| Peter Rd. | 18 | **F** | **5** |
| Peter St. | 32 | **P** | **10** |
| Peterborough Rd. | 15 | **X** | **1** |
| Peter's Lane | 32 | **P** | **11** |
| Peveril St. | 7 | **E** | **4** |
| Philharmonic Hall | 23 | **R** | **9** |
| Phillimore Rd. | 12 | **P** | **4** |
| Phillips St. | 31 | **N** | **11** |
| Phoebe Anne St. | 21 | **N** | **6** |
| Phythian St. | 22 | **P** | **6** |
| Pickering St. | 21 | **M** | **5** |
| Pickop St. | 31 | **N** | **10** |
| Pickwick St. | 34 | **U** | **10** |
| Picton Grove | 14 | **T** | **3** |
| Picton Reading Room | 32 | **O** | **10** |
| Picton Rd. | 14 | **T** | **3** |
| Pier Head Station | 32 | **O** | **12** |
| Pighue Lane | 13 | **S** | **1** |
| Pilgrim St. | 33 | **R** | **9** |
| Pilot Grove | 14 | **T** | **3** |
| Pim Hill St. | 24 | **U** | **8** |
| Pindar St. | 21 | **N** | **5** |
| Pine Gro., Bootle | 16 | **B** | **6** |
| Pine Gro., Crown St. | 23 | **S** | **7** |
| Pine St. | 23 | **S** | **7** |
| Pinehurst Rd. | 10 | **K** | **3** |
| Pinner St. | 13 | **R** | **2** |
| Pitt St. | 33 | **Q** | **11** |
| Plan St. | 22 | **O** | **7** |
| Playhouse | 32 | **P** | **10** |
| Pleasant Hill St. | 34 | **T** | **11** |
| Pleasant Street, Bootle | 27 | **C** | **9** |
| Pleasant Street, Harford St. | 32 | **Q** | **9** |
| Pleasant View | 13 | **R** | **1** |
| Pleasant View, Sellar St. | 19 | **H** | **7** |
| Plimsoll St. | 23 | **R** | **5** |
| Plumer St. | 14 | **U** | **3** |
| Plumpton St. | 21 | **N** | **7** |
| Pluto St. | 19 | **I** | **8** |
| Pollock St. | 22 | **P** | **5** |
| Pomfret St. | 24 | **T** | **8** |
| Pomona St. | 22 | **Q** | **9** |
| Ponsonby St. | 24 | **U** | **7** |
| Poplar St. | 21 | **M** | **6** |
| Porter St. | 30 | **L** | **12** |
| Portia St. | 18 | **F** | **8** |
| Portland Pl. | 20 | **M** | **8** |
| Portland St. | 30 | **L** | **10** |
| Portland St., New Brighton | 38 | **B** | **1** |
| Portman Rd. | 14 | **U** | **4** |
| Port Sanitary Offices | 32 | **O** | **13** |
| Portwood St. | 24 | **T** | **6** |
| Potter St. | 20 | **K** | **8** |
| Poulton, Wallasey | 38 | **B** | **3** |
| Poulton Rd., Seacombe | 38 | **B** | **3** |
| Powis St. | 25 | **V** | **8** |
| Pownall Sq. | 31 | **N** | **11** |
| Pownall St. | 33 | **Q** | **11** |
| Premier St. | 20 | **L** | **6** |
| Prenton, Birkenhead | 36 | **A** | **4** |
| Prenton Rd. East, Tranmere | 36 | **B** | **3** |
| Prenton Rd. West, Tranmere | 36 | **B** | **4** |
| Prenton Reservoir, Birkenhead | 36 | **B** | **4** |
| Prescot Drive | 12 | **P** | **2** |
| Prescot Rd. | 12 | **Q** | **3** |
| Prescot St. | 22 | **P** | **7** |
| Preston Grove | 11 | **N** | **3** |
| Preston Road Station | 7 | **C** | **2** |
| Preston St. | 32 | **O** | **10** |
| Priam St. | 18 | **F** | **8** |
| Price St. | 32 | **Q** | **11** |
| Price St., Birkenhead | 36 | **B** | **1** |
| Priest St. | 24 | **T** | **6** |
| Primrose Hill | 31 | **O** | **10** |
| Primrose St. | 19 | **H** | **8** |
| Prince Albert Statue | 32 | **P** | **10** |
| Prince Alfred Rd. | 15 | **W** | **1** |
| Prince Edwin Lane | 21 | **M** | **8** |
| Prince Edwin St. | 21 | **M** | **8** |
| Princefield Rd. | 6 | **A** | **3** |
| Prince Rupert St. | 21 | **N** | **7** |
| Prince William St. | 34 | **T** | **10** |
| Prince's Av. | 24 | **U** | **8** |
| Prince's Dock | 31 | **N** | **13** |
| Prince's Dock Stn. | 31 | **N** | **12** |
| Prince's Gate | 25 | **V** | **7** |
| Prince's Half Tide Dock | 31 | **M** | **12** |
| Prince's Landing Stage | 31 | **N** | **13** |
| Prince's Parade | 31 | **N** | **13** |
| Prince's Park | 25 | **V** | **7** |
| Prince's Park Ter. | 25 | **V** | **7** |
| Prince's Rd. | 24 | **T** | **8** |
| Prince's St. | 32 | **O** | **11** |
| Prince's St., Bootle | 27 | **E** | **9** |
| Pringle St. | 11 | **O** | **1** |
| Priory Grove | 20 | **L** | **6** |
| Priory Hill | 20 | **L** | **7** |
| Priory Mount | 20 | **L** | **7** |
| Priory Rd., Heyworth St. | 20 | **L** | **7** |
| Priory Rd., Townsend Lane | 10 | **L** | **3** |
| Priory St. | 20 | **L** | **6** |
| Proctor St. | 11 | **O** | **4** |
| Promenade Pier, New Brighton | 38 | **B** | **1** |
| Prophet St. | 34 | **U** | **10** |
| Prospect St. | 22 | **P** | **7** |
| Prospect Vale | 12 | **P** | **2** |
| Prospect Vale, Wallasey | 38 | **A** | **2** |

Prudential Insurance Buildings, Dale St. . 32 O 11
Prudhoe St. . 22 P 8
Prussia St. . 31 N 12
Pudsey St. . 32 P 9
Pugin St. . 19 H 6
Pulford St. . 20 I 5
Pumpfields . 31 M 11
Purcell Pl. . 31 M 10
Pym St. . 8 F 5
Pyramid St. 20 L 7
Quarantine Gr'nd, Rock Ferry . 37 D 3
Quarry Rd. . 18 E 6
Queen Sq. . 32 P 10
Queen St. . 31 N 12
Queen Anne St. . 21 O 8
Queen's Docks . 33 S 12
Queen's Drive . 8 F 3
Queen's Graving Dock . 33 S 12
Queen's Road, Bootle . 17 E 8
Queen's Rd., Breck Rd. . 21 M 5
Queen's Statue . 32 P 9
Queensland St. . 23 R 6
Queen Victoria Statue . 32 P 12
Quorn St. . 22 Q 5
Rachel St. . 21 M 9
Radcliffe St. . 21 O 7
Radnor Drive, Liscard . 38 B 2
Radnor Pl. . 11 N 2
Radstock Rd. . 12 P 3
Raffles St. . 33 S 10
Ragged School . 20 K 8
Rake Farm . 9 H 2
Rake House . 9 G 3
Raleigh St. . 28 E 10
Ramilies Rd. . 15 X 2
Randolph St. . 19 I 5
Ranelagh Pl. . 32 P 10
Ranelagh St. . 32 P 10
Rankin St. . 35 W 10
Rappart Rd., Seacombe . 39 C 3
Rathbone Pl. . 33 R 10
Rathbone Rd. and Depot . 14 T 1
Rathbone St. . 33 S 10
Rawcliffe Rd. . 7 C 3
Rawlins St. . 12 Q 2
Raymond St. . 30 L 10
Reading St. . 19 H 8
Recreation St. . 17 C 6
Rector Rd. . 10 L 2
Rectory St. . 35 W 10
Red Noses, Wallasey . 38 A 1
Redbourne St. . 11 M 3
Redbrook St. . 11 M 3
Redcar St. . 11 M 3
Red Cross St. . 32 P 12
Redfern St. . 18 G 8
Redgrave St. . 12 Q 4
Red Rock St. . 11 N 5
Redvers Drive . 6 A 2
Reform St. . 13 S 1
Regent Rd. . 27 B 10
Regent St. . 30 L 12
Rembrandt St. . 19 I 6
Rendal St. . 21 M 6
Renfrew St. . 22 P 6
Rennie St. . 19 I 6
Renshaw St. . 32 Q 10
Reservoir St. . 21 N 6
Revenue Buildings 32 Q 12
Reynolds St. . 21 N 5
Rhiwlas St. . 25 V 8
Rhyl St., Bootle . 16 A 8
Rhyl St., Toxteth St. . 35 V 10
Ribble St. . 20 K 6
Rice Lane . 6 C 2
Rice Lane, Egremont . 39 C 2
Rice St. . 33 R 9
Richardson St. . 24 U 5
Richmond Grove . 21 M 6
Richmond Park . 11 M 3
Richmond Row 21, 31 N 9
Richmond St. . 32 P 10
Richmond Ter. . 11 M 5
Rickman St. . 19 H 7
Ridgeway St. . 13 R 4
Ridley Rd. . 12 P 4
Rigby St. . 31 N 12
Rimrose Rd. . 26 A 9
Ripon St. . 8 G 4
Rishton St. . 21 M 6
Rita Grove . 13 Q 2
Ritson St. . 24 U 7
River Avon St. . 24 T 6
River View, Seacombe . 39 C 3
Riverside Station 31 O 13
Rivington St. . 20 K 6
Roache St. . 35 V 10
Robarts Rd. . 10 L 4
Roberts St. . 31 N 12
Robertson St. . 34 U 11
Robsart St. . 20 L 8
Robson St. . 20 K 6
Roby St. . 16 A 7
Rochester Rd. . 10 L 3
Rock Ferry, Birkenhead . 37 C 4
Rock Ferry Pier, Birkenhead . 37 C 4
Rock Ferry Stn., Birkenhead . 37 C 4
Rock Lane East, Rock Ferry . 37 C 4
Rock Lane West, Rock Ferry . 37 C 4
Rock Park, Birkenhead . 37 C 4
Rock St. . 32 Q 9
Rockbrook St. . 34 T 10
Rockfield Rd. . 19 I 5
Rockhouse St. . 11 N 3
Rockingham St. . 19 I 9
Rockley St. . 19 H 6
Rockwood St. . 22 O 6
Rocky Lane . 11 N 3
Roden St. . 21 N 7
Roderick Rd. . 8 F 3
Rodney St. . 33 R 9
Rodney Street, Brunswick Pl. . 28 F 9
Rodney St., Bootle 27 D 10
Roe St. . 32 P 10
Rokeby St. . 21 N 8
Rokesmith St. . 24 T 5
Rolfe St. . 22 P 5
Rollo St. . 19 I 7
Roman Catholic Orphanage . 23 S 8
Romeo St. . 18 F 8
Romer Rd. . 12 P 4
Romilly St. . 22 P 5
Romley St. . 18 F 5
Romulus St. . 13 R 2
Rooney St. . 28 F 9
Roper St. . 35 V 10
Rosalind St. . 18 F 8
Roscoe Gdns. . 32 Q 9
Roscoe Lane . 33 R 10
Roscoe St. . 33 Q 9
Roscommon St. . 21 M 8
Rose Brewery . 14 U 2
Rose Cottage . 10 K 1
Rose Hill . 31 N 9
Rose Pl. . 31 N 9
Rose St. . 32 P 10
Rose Vale . 20 M 8
Rosebery St. . 24 T 8
Rossett Av. 15 W 4
Rossett St. . 11 N 2
Rossmore Gdns. . 9 I 2
Rothesay St. . 21 N 8
Rothwell St. . 21 M 5
Rotunda Theatre 20 K 8
Rowson St., New Brighton . 38 B 1
Roxburgh St. . 18 F 6
Royal Assembly Rooms . 33 R 10
Royal Court Theatre . 32 P 10
Royal Hippodrome 22 O 6
Royal Infirmary . 22 P 8
Royal Institute . 33 Q 10
Royal Insurance Buildings . 32 O 11
Royal Southern Hospital . 34 T 11
Royal St. . 19 I 6
Royden St. . 35 W 10
Royston St. . 23 R 5
Rubens St. . 19 I 6
Ruby St. . 35 X 10
Rufford Rd. 12 P 3
Rullerton Road, Liscard . 38 B 3
Rumford Pl. . 31 O 12
Rumford St. . 32 O 12
Rumney Rd. . 18 G 6
Rumney Rd. West 18 G 7
Rupert Grove . 21 M 7
Rupert Hill . 21 N 7
Rupert Lane . 21 N 7
Rupert Lane Recreation Ground 21 M 7
Rupert St. . 21 N 6
Ruskin St. . 18 F 6
Russell Pl. . 22 Q 9
Russell Rd. . 15 X 2
Russell St. . 22 P 9
Ruth St. . 21 N 8
Ruthin St. . 22 P 6
Rutland Av. . 15 W 4
Rutland Street, Bootle . 16 B 6
Rutland Street, Hamilton Rd. . 20 L 6
Rutter St. . 34 U 11
Rydal St. . 20 L 5
Ryder St. . 13 S 5
Rymer Grove . 8 G 4
Sackville St. . 21 M 8
Sadler St. . 22 O 7
Sailors' Home . 32 Q 11
St Agnes Rd. . 19 G 8
St Agnes's Church, Ullet Rd. . 25 W 5
St Aidan's Church 19 I 8
St Aidan's Theological College, Claughton . 36 A 2
St Albans, Whitfield Rd. . 21 N 5
St Albans Church, Lime Kiln Lane 31 M 9
St Albans Rd. . 17 D 8
St Ambrose Church 21 M 7
St Ambrose Grove 10 L 4

St Andrew Rd. . 10 L 4
St Andrew St. . 22 P 8
St Andrew's Ch'ch 13 R 2
St Anne St. . 21 N 9
St Anne Street, Birkenhead . 36 B 1
St Anne's Church 21 N 9
St Anthony's R.C. Church . . 20 L 8
St Arnaud St. . 23 S 6
St Athanasius' Church . . 19 H 7
St Augustine's Ch., Shaw St. . . 21 O 7
St Bartholomew's Ch., Naylor St. 31 N 10
St Bede's Church, Hartington Rd. 25 V 6
St Benedict's Ch. 21 M 7
St Bride St. . 23 S 8
St Bride's Church 33 S 9
St Bridget's Ch'ch 14 U 3
St Catherine's Ch., Chatham St. . 23 R 8
St Catherine's Ch., Tunnel Rd. . 23 S 5
St Catherine's Rd. 17 D 8
St Chad's Church 19 I 6
St Chrysostom St. 21 N 6
St Chrysostom's Church . . 21 N 6
St Clare Rd. 15 V 3
St Clare's R.C. Ch. 15 V 5
St Clement's Ch. . 24 T 6
St Cleopas Church 35 W 10
St Clement's Ch. . 24 T 6
St Columba's Ch., Pleasant St. . 22 Q 9
St Columba's Ch., Smithdown Rd. 15 W 3
St Cuthbert's Ch. 20 K 6
St Cyprian's Ch. . 13 R 5
St David's Rd. . 10 L 4
St Domingo Grove 20 L 5
St Domingo Rd. . 20 K 7
St Domingo Vale 20 L 5
St Dunstan's Ch. 14 T 5
St Edmond's Rd. 17 D 8
St Edward's R.C. College . . 20 K 6
St Gabriel's Ch. . 35 V 11
St George's Church 20 L 7
St George's Cres. . 32 P 11
St George's Hall, Lime St. . . 32 O 10
St George's Hill . 20 M 7
St George's Rd., Wallasey . . 38 A 2
St George's R.C. Industrial School Athletic Ground 21 N 3
St George's St. . 20 M 7
St Hilda St. . 19 H 6
St James' Cemet'y 33 S 9
St James' Church 34 T 10
St James' Mount . 33 S 10
St James' Pl. . 34 T 10
St James' Rd. . 33 S 10
St James' Road, New Brighton . 38 B 1
St James' St. . 33 R 11
St James the Less Church . . 20 K 8
St John Baptist Church . . 35 V 10
St John's Av. . 6 B 2
St John's Church, Bootle . . 18 E 9
St John's Church, Holly Rd. . 13 Q 3
St John's Church, Rice Lane . 6 B 2
St John the Evangelist Church . 21 M 5
St John's Gdns. . 32 O 10
St John's Lane . 32 P 10
St John's Market 32 P 10
St John's Rd. . 18 E 9
St Joseph R.C. Ch. 31 N 9
St Jude's Church 22 P 7
St Lawrence Ch. . 18 G 6
St Luke's Church, Berry St. . 33 R 9
St Luke's Church, Walton . . 9 G 5
St Margaret's Ch., Belmont Rd. . 11 N 3
St Margaret's Ch., Princes Rd. . 24 T 9
St Margaret's Gro. 11 N 3
St Martin St. . 30 L 9
St Martin's Church 30 L 9
St Martin's Market 31 M 9
St Mary Magdalene Church . . 22 P 8
St Mary's Av. . 8 F 3
St Mary's Church, Bootle . . 27 C 9
St Mary's Church, Sandown Park . 14 T 1
St Mary's Church, Towerlands St. 23 Q 6
St Mary's Church, Walton . . 8 E 4
St Mary's Grove . 8 F 3
St Mary's Lane . 8 F 3
St Mary's Pl. . 8 F 3
St Matthew's Ch., Hill St. . . 34 T 10
St Matthew's Ch., Scotland Rd. . 20 L 9
St Matthias Ch., Gt. Howard St. 30 L 11
St Michael's Ch. . 33 R 11
St Nathaniel's Ch. 24 S 7
St Nicholas Ch., Chapel St. . 32 O 12
St Nicholas Pl. . 32 O 12
St Patrick's Chapel 34 T 10
St Paul Rd., Tranmere . . 37 C 3
St Paul's Church, Belvidere Rd. . 25 W 8
St Paul's Church, Brasenose Rd. . 18 F 9
St Paul's Church, St Paul's Sq. . 31 N 12
St Paul's Eye Hospital . . 31 N 12
St Paul's Rd., Seacombe . . 39 C 3
St Paul's School . 35 W 9
St Paul's Sq. . 31 N 12
St Peter's Church, Sackville St. . 21 M 8
St Peter's Road, Rock Ferry . 37 C 4
St Philemon's Ch., Windsor St. . 34 U 9
St Philip's Church, Sheil Rd. . 12 P 4
St Polycarp's Ch. 20 L 7
St Saviour's Ch., Breckfield Rd. North . . 20 L 6
St Saviour's Ch., Up. Huskisson Street . . 24 S 8
St Silas Church, High Park St. . 25 V 9
St Silas Church, Pembroke Pl. . 22 P 8
St Silas St. . . 25 V 9
St Simon and St Jude's Church . 10 K 4
St Simon's Church 32 P 9
St Stephen St. . 32 O 10
St Stephen's Ch., Byrom St. . 32 O 10
St Stephen's Ch., Grove St. . 23 R 7
St Thomas Ch., Warwick St. . 34 U 11
St Timothy's Ch. 21 N 8
St Titus's Church 31 M 9
St Vincent of Paul R.C. Church . 33 S 10
St Vincent St. East 32 P 9
St Xavier's R.C. Church . . 21 O 8
Saker St. . 19 I 5
Salisbury Dock . 30 K 12
Salisbury Gates, N. and S. . 30 K 12
Salisbury Rd. . 14 T 4
Salisbury Road, Bootle . . 16 A 8
Salisbury Road, Breckfield Rd. . 20 L 5
Salisbury Road, Walton . . 7 D 3
Salisbury St. . 21 N 8
Salisbury Ter. . 14 U 1
Salop St. . 19 H 6
Salthouse Dock . 32 Q 12
Saltney St. . . 30 K 12
Sampson St. . 21 M 7
Samuel St. . . 20 L 7
Sand St., Cotton St. . . . 30 L 11
Sand St. South . 33 S 10
Sandbeck St. . 35 X 10
Sandcliffe Road, Wallasey . . 38 A 1
Sandeman Rd. . 9 I 1
Sandfield Farm . 17 E 6
Sandhead St. . 14 T 4
Sandheys St. . 19 I 7
Sandhills Bridge . 29 H 9
Sandhills Lane . 29 H 10
Sandhills Station . 29 H 9
Sandon Dock . 29 H 11
Sandon Rd. . 7 D 3
Sandon St. . . 23 S 8
Sandon Ter. . 33 S 9
Sandon & Canada Goods Station . 29 H 10
Sandon Half Tide Dock . . 29 H 12
Sandown Fields . 14 U 1
Sandown Lane . 14 U 1
Sandown Park . 14 T 1
Sandringham Rd. 11 M 1
Sandy Lane . 27 D 9
Sandy Lane, Wallasey . . 38 A 2
Sarah St. . 21 N 6
Saxon St. . 11 N 4
Saxonia Rd. . 8 F 3
Saxony Rd. . 22 P 6
Scholar St. . . 24 T 5
Schomberg St. . 22 O 5
School Lane . 32 P 11
Scorton St. . . 11 N 2
Scotch Church, Oldham St. . 33 Q 9
Scotland Pl. . 31 N 10
Scotland Rd. . 20 M 9
Scott St. . 16 A 8
Scourfield St. . 13 R 5

| | | | |
|---|---|---|---|
| Sea Brow | 32 | P | 12 |
| Sea Rd., Wallasey | 38 | A | 1 |
| Seabank Rd., Liscard | 38 | B | 2 |
| Seacombe & Stn., Wallasey | 39 | C | 3 |
| Seacombe Prom., Wallasey | 39 | C | 3 |
| Seacome St. | 20 | K | 8 |
| Seafield Rd. | 6 | B | 3 |
| Seaforth St. | 27 | C | 9 |
| Seaforth Sands Station | 26 | A | 10 |
| Seaman Rd. | 15 | V | 3 |
| Seamen's Orphanage | 11 | O | 1 |
| Seaton St. | 12 | Q | 5 |
| Sea View Rd. | 26 | A | 9 |
| Seaview Rd., Liscard | 38 | B | 2 |
| Sedley St., Breck Rd. | 11 | M | 4 |
| Sedley St., Brompton Rd. | 13 | R | 2 |
| Seel St. | 32 | Q | 10 |
| Sefton Drive | 25 | W | 6 |
| Sefton Park | 25 | W | 5 |
| Sefton Park Stn. | 15 | X | 3 |
| Sefton Rd. | 7 | C | 2 |
| Sefton St. | 34 | U | 12 |
| Sefton St., High Park St. | 35 | V | 9 |
| Segrave St. | 32 | P | 9 |
| Seiont Ter. | 34 | V | 10 |
| Selborne St. | 24 | T | 8 |
| Selby Rd. | 6 | A | 2 |
| Seldon St. | 22 | P | 6 |
| Sellar St. | 19 | H | 7 |
| Selwyn St. | 18 | F | 6 |
| September Rd. | 11 | M | 2 |
| Serpentine Road, Egremont | 38 | B | 2 |
| Sessions Court, Birkenhead | 37 | C | 2 |
| Sessions Rd. | 19 | H | 7 |
| Severn St. | 20 | K | 7 |
| Severs St. | 21 | N | 5 |
| Seville St. | 20 | K | 7 |
| Seymour St. | 22 | P | 9 |
| Seymour Street, Bootle | 27 | D | 10 |
| Shadwell St. | 30 | I | 10 |
| Shaftesbury St. | 34 | U | 10 |
| Shakespeare St. | 26 | A | 9 |
| Shakespeare Theat. | 32 | O | 9 |
| Shakespeare St. | 21 | N | 5 |
| Shallcross St. | 21 | N | 5 |
| Shallot St. | 24 | U | 8 |
| Shannon St. | 22 | Q | 9 |
| Sharp St. | 19 | I | 7 |
| Shaw St. | 21 | N | 7 |
| Shaw's Alley | 33 | Q | 11 |
| Sheil Park | 11 | N | 4 |
| Sheil Rd. | 11 | O | 3 |
| Shelley St. | 34 | U | 11 |
| Shelley Street, Bootle | 16 | A | 8 |
| Shenstone St. | 23 | R | 6 |
| Shenstone Street, Bootle | 26 | A | 9 |
| Shepston Av. | 8 | G | 4 |
| Sherdley St. | 22 | Q | 7 |
| Sheridan Pl. | 27 | E | 9 |
| Sheridan St. | 21 | M | 8 |
| Sheriff St. | 21 | M | 8 |
| Sherlock St. | 19 | I | 6 |
| Sherwood St. | 30 | L | 11 |
| Shimmin St. | 23 | R | 6 |
| Shore Rd., Birkenhead | 37 | C | 2 |
| Shore Rd. | 26 | A | 10 |
| Shotwick St. | 13 | R | 2 |
| Shrewsbury Rd., Oxton | 36 | A | 3 |
| Shrewsbury Road N., Claughton | 36 | A | 2 |
| Sidney Pl. | 23 | R | 6 |
| Sidney Rd. | 17 | E | 6 |
| Silverdale Av. | 11 | N | 1 |
| Silvester St. | 30 | L | 10 |
| Sim St. | 21 | O | 8 |
| Simms Rd. | 11 | M | 1 |
| Singleton Avenue, Birkenhead | 36 | B | 3 |
| Simpson St. | 33 | R | 11 |
| Sinclair St. | 12 | Q | 4 |
| Sirdar St. | 23 | S | 6 |
| Sir Howard St. | 23 | S | 8 |
| Sir Thomas St. | 32 | O | 11 |
| Skating Rink | 32 | P | 9 |
| Skelhorne St. | 32 | P | 9 |
| Skerries Rd. | 10 | K | 4 |
| Skipton Rd. | 10 | K | 3 |
| Skirving St. | 20 | K | 8 |
| Slade St. | 30 | K | 9 |
| Slater St. | 32 | Q | 10 |
| Slatey Rd., Birkenhead | 36 | A | 2 |
| Sleepers Hill | 19 | I | 5 |
| Smallpox Hosp., Birkenhead | 38 | A | 4 |
| Smeaton St. | 18 | F | 6 |
| Smith St. | 19 | I | 8 |
| Smithdown Lane | 23 | R | 7 |
| Smithdown Rd. | 15 | W | 4 |
| Smithfield St. | 31 | N | 11 |
| Smithy Lane | 8 | E | 4 |
| Smollett St. | 22 | P | 5 |
| Smyrna Road, Bootle | 16 | B | 7 |
| Snaefell Av. | 11 | N | 1 |
| Snowden St. | 30 | K | 10 |
| Snowdrop St. | 19 | H | 8 |
| Soho Sq. | 21 | O | 8 |
| Soho St. | 21 | N | 8 |
| Solomon St. | 22 | P | 5 |
| Solon St. | 13 | R | 5 |
| Solva St. | 21 | N | 6 |
| Solway St. | 24 | U | 7 |
| Somerset Pl. | 11 | N | 2 |
| Somerset Rd. | 16 | B | 5 |
| Somerton St. | 14 | T | 2 |
| Somerville, Wallasey | 38 | B | 3 |
| Sophia St. | 23 | S | 6 |
| South Grove | 35 | X | 9 |
| South St. | 25 | V | 8 |
| South Albert Rd. | 25 | X | 7 |
| Southampton St. | 34 | U | 9 |
| South Bank Rd. | 13 | R | 2 |
| South Castle St. | 32 | P | 11 |
| South Chester St. | 34 | T | 10 |
| South Corporation Yard | 35 | W | 11 |
| Southdale Rd. | 14 | U | 2 |
| South Dock Yard | 34 | T | 12 |
| Southey St. | 16 | A | 8 |
| South Ferry Basin | 34 | T | 12 |
| Southfield Rd. | 6 | A | 3 |
| South Hill Grove | 35 | X | 9 |
| South Hill Rd. | 35 | X | 9 |
| South Hunter St. | 33 | R | 9 |
| South Jetty | 28 | E | 11 |
| South John St. | 32 | P | 11 |
| South Recreation Ground | 7 | E | 7 |
| Southwell St. | 34 | U | 10 |
| Sparling St. | 33 | R | 11 |
| Speke St. | 13 | S | 5 |
| Spekeland Rd. | 14 | T | 5 |
| Spekeland St. | 23 | S | 6 |
| Spekeland Vale | 14 | T | 5 |
| Spellow Lane | 18 | G | 5 |
| Spellow Station | 18 | F | 5 |
| Spencer St., Bootle | 16 | A | 8 |
| Spencer St., Everton Rd. | 21 | N | 6 |
| Spofforth Rd. | 14 | T | 4 |
| Sprainger St. | 30 | L | 11 |
| Spring Grove | 17 | C | 6 |
| Spring St. | 34 | T | 10 |
| Springbank Rd. | 11 | M | 4 |
| Springfield, Prince Alfred Rd. | 15 | W | 1 |
| Springfield Sq. | 19 | H | 6 |
| Springfield St. | 21 | O | 9 |
| Spurgeon St. | 20 | M | 6 |
| Squires St. | 23 | S | 6 |
| Stafford Street, Bootle | 16 | B | 8 |
| Stafford Street, London Rd. | 22 | O | 8 |
| Stalbridge Av. | 15 | X | 2 |
| Stalmine Rd. | 7 | D | 3 |
| Stamford St. | 13 | Q | 4 |
| Stananought St. | 34 | U | 9 |
| Stancliffe St. | 22 | P | 7 |
| Standale Rd. | 14 | U | 1 |
| Standish St. | 31 | N | 10 |
| Stand St. | 22 | P | 7 |
| Stanfield Rd. | 21 | M | 6 |
| Stanhope St. | 34 | T | 11 |
| Stanley | 12 | R | 1 |
| Stanley Athletic Ground | 12 | P | 1 |
| Stanley Dock | 30 | K | 11 |
| Stanley Gdns. | 17 | E | 7 |
| Stanley Hall | 17 | D | 7 |
| Stanley Hospital | 19 | H | 8 |
| Stanley Park | 9 | H | 5 |
| Stanley Park Av., North | 8 | G | 2 |
| Stanley Park Av., South | 9 | H | 2 |
| Stanley Rd. | 20 | I | 8 |
| Stanley Rd., Bidston | 38 | A | 4 |
| Stanley Rd., Bootle | 17 | C | 7 |
| Stanley Station | 12 | Q | 1 |
| Stanley St., Dale St. | 32 | O | 11 |
| Stanley St., Prescot Rd. | 12 | Q | 2 |
| Star St. | 34 | U | 11 |
| Starfield St. | 11 | O | 4 |
| Starkie St. | 22 | O | 7 |
| Steble Grove | 35 | V | 10 |
| Steble St. | 35 | V | 10 |
| Steel St. | 30 | K | 10 |
| Steers St. | 21 | N | 6 |
| Stepney Grove | 8 | G | 4 |
| Sterling St. | 19 | I | 8 |
| Sterne St. | 22 | O | 5 |
| Stevenson St. | 14 | U | 2 |
| Stitt St. | 21 | N | 7 |
| Stockbridge St. | 20 | L | 5 |
| Stockdale St. | 31 | N | 10 |
| Stock Exchange | 32 | O | 11 |
| Stoddart Rd | 8 | F | 3 |
| Stone St. | 30 | L | 11 |
| Stonehill St. | 10 | L | 4 |
| Stonewall St. | 21 | M | 7 |
| Stopford St. | 35 | W | 10 |
| Storeton Road, Birkenhead | 36 | B | 4 |
| Stour St. | 19 | H | 7 |
| Strand Rd. | 27 | B | 9 |
| Strand St. | 32 | P | 12 |
| Strathcona Rd. | 14 | U | 3 |
| Strathmore Rd. | 11 | N | 3 |

| | | | |
|---|---|---|---|
| Strickland St. | 21 | N | 8 |
| Stuart Rd. | 18 | E | 5 |
| Studholme St. | 29 | G | 9 |
| Suburban Rd. | 10 | L | 3 |
| Sudworth House, New Brighton | 38 | B | 1 |
| Sudworth Road, New Brighton | 38 | B | 1 |
| Suffield Rd. | 18 | G | 7 |
| Suffolk St., Bootle | 16 | B | 6 |
| Suffolk St., Duke St. | 32 | Q | 10 |
| Sugnall St. | 23 | R | 9 |
| Summer Gdns. | 19 | H | 7 |
| Summer Seat | 31 | M | 10 |
| Summer Seat, Bootle | 27 | C | 9 |
| Sumner St. | 30 | K | 9 |
| Sun St. | 22 | Q | 7 |
| Sunbury Rd. | 10 | K | 3 |
| Sunlight St. | 11 | N | 3 |
| Sunningdale Rd. | 14 | T | 1 |
| Sunnyside | 25 | V | 8 |
| Surrey St. | 16 | B | 6 |
| Sussex St. | 34 | T | 9 |
| Sussex St., Bootle | 16 | B | 6 |
| Sutcliffe St. | 12 | O | 4 |
| Sutherland St. | 13 | R | 4 |
| Sutton St. | 11 | O | 1 |
| Swanston Av. | 8 | G | 4 |
| Sweeting St. | 32 | O | 11 |
| Swinburne St. | 26 | A | 9 |
| Swiss Rd. | 12 | P | 3 |
| Sybil Rd. | 19 | I | 5 |
| Sycamore St. | 23 | S | 7 |
| Sydenham Av. | 25 | V | 5 |
| Sydney St. | 6 | A | 1 |
| Sykes St. | 21 | N | 6 |
| Sylvania Rd. | 8 | F | 3 |
| Sylvia St. | 18 | F | 8 |
| Syren St. | 18 | F | 9 |
| Tabley Rd. | 14 | U | 4 |
| Tabley St. | 33 | R | 11 |
| Tagus St. | 24 | U | 7 |
| Talbot Rd., Oxton | 36 | A | 3 |
| Talbot Street | 22 | O | 7 |
| Talbot St., Bootle | 16 | B | 8 |
| Taliesin St. | 20 | K | 8 |
| Talton Rd. | 14 | U | 3 |
| Tamworth St. | 35 | V | 11 |
| Tancred Rd. | 19 | I | 5 |
| Taplow St. | 10 | L | 3 |
| Tarbet St. | 34 | T | 9 |
| Tariff St. | 30 | K | 9 |
| Tarleton St. | 32 | P | 10 |
| Tate St. | 19 | H | 5 |
| Tatlock St. | 30 | L | 10 |
| Tatton Rd. | 6 | A | 2 |
| Taunton St. | 14 | T | 2 |
| Tavistock St. | 35 | W | 10 |
| Tawd St. | 19 | H | 6 |
| Tay St. | 25 | V | 9 |
| Taylor St. | 20 | K | 8 |
| Technical School, Bootle | 17 | D | 8 |
| Technical School, Orwell Rd. | 19 | H | 7 |
| Teck St. | 22 | P | 6 |
| Tees St. | 18 | F | 7 |
| Tegid St. | 21 | N | 6 |
| Teilo St. | 25 | V | 9 |
| Telary St. | 30 | L | 10 |
| Tempest Hey | 32 | O | 11 |
| Temple Court | 32 | P | 11 |
| Temple Lane | 32 | O | 11 |
| Temple St. | 32 | O | 11 |
| Tennyson St. | 34 | T | 9 |
| Tennyson Street, Bootle | 16 | A | 9 |
| Tenterden St. | 30 | L | 9 |
| Tetlow St. | 19 | H | 6 |
| Teulon St. | 19 | H | 6 |
| Thackeray St. | 24 | T | 9 |
| Thames St. | 24 | T | 7 |
| The Elms | 25 | X | 8 |
| The Strand | 32 | P | 12 |
| Thirlmere Rd. | 10 | L | 5 |
| Thistlewood Rd. | 13 | R | 2 |
| Thomas St. | 32 | P | 11 |
| Thomaston St. | 20 | K | 8 |
| Thomson St. | 21 | N | 5 |
| Thorburn Road, New Ferry | 37 | C | 4 |
| Thorburn St. | 23 | R | 5 |
| Thorncliff St. | 21 | M | 8 |
| Thorndale St. | 19 | I | 6 |
| Thornes Rd. | 22 | P | 5 |
| Thornfield Rd. | 6 | B | 2 |
| Thornton Pl. | 35 | W | 11 |
| Thornton Rd. | 16 | A | 7 |
| Thornycroft Rd. | 14 | V | 4 |
| Threlfall St. | 25 | W | 9 |
| Throstle Nest | 7 | D | 3 |
| Thurlow St. | 31 | N | 9 |
| Thurnham St. | 11 | N | 3 |
| Thurston Rd. | 10 | L | 3 |
| Tiber St. | 24 | U | 7 |
| Tide Gauge House | 27 | D | 11 |
| Tillard St. | 19 | H | 8 |
| Tillotson St. | 22 | Q | 7 |
| Tilney St. | 6 | A | 2 |
| Timber Slipway | 27 | D | 10 |
| Time Gun, Birkenhead | 37 | C | 2 |
| Timpron St. | 24 | T | 5 |
| Tindall St. | 30 | K | 9 |
| Tinsley St. | 20 | K | 5 |
| Tintern St. | 19 | H | 6 |
| Titchfield St. | 30 | L | 10 |
| Tithe Barn St. | 31 | O | 11 |
| Tiverton St. | 14 | T | 2 |
| Tobacco Wareh'se | 30 | K | 11 |
| Toft St. | 13 | Q | 4 |
| Tollemache Rd., Claughton | 36 | A | 2 |
| Tooke St. | 21 | O | 5 |
| Torbock St. | 21 | O | 8 |
| Toronto St. | 28 | F | 9 |
| Torr St. | 20 | K | 7 |
| Tower Buildings | 32 | O | 12 |
| Tower Gardens | 32 | O | 12 |
| Tower Promenade, New Brighton | 38 | B | 1 |
| Towerlands St. | 23 | Q | 6 |
| Town Hall, Dale St. | 32 | O | 12 |
| Town Hall, Walton | 8 | E | 4 |
| Town Hall, Wavertree | 14 | V | 1 |
| Town Station, Birkenhead | 37 | C | 2 |
| Townsend House | 10 | K | 1 |
| Townsend Lane | 10 | L | 2 |
| Townsend St. | 29 | I | 10 |
| Towson St. | 20 | K | 5 |
| Toxteth Chapel | 35 | X | 9 |
| Toxteth Dock | 35 | V | 12 |
| Toxteth Dock Stn. | 35 | V | 12 |
| Toxteth Grove | 35 | X | 9 |
| Toxteth Park Cem. | 24 | U | 5 |
| Toxteth Pk. Workhouse | 15 | V | 4 |
| Toxteth St. | 35 | V | 10 |
| Trafalgar Dock | 30 | L | 12 |
| Trafalgar Road, Egremont | 38 | B | 2 |
| Trafalgar St. | 22 | Q | 9 |
| Tramway Depot | 18 | G | 6 |
| Tramway Depot, Edge Lane | 13 | R | 3 |
| Tramway Depot, Lambeth Rd. | 19 | I | 8 |
| Tramway Depot, Wavertree | 15 | V | 1 |
| Tramway Offices, Hatton Garden | 31 | O | 10 |
| Tranmere Higher, Birkenhead | 36 | B | 3 |
| Tranmere, Lower, Birkenhead | 37 | C | 3 |
| Tranmere Park, Birkenhead | 36 | B | 3 |
| Travers St. | 21 | O | 8 |
| Treborth St. | 25 | V | 8 |
| Trent St. | 29 | I | 10 |
| Trent St., Bootle | 26 | A | 10 |
| Trevelyan St. | 7 | E | 4 |
| Trevor Rd. | 6 | A | 2 |
| Trinity Church, Belvidere Rd. | 25 | W | 8 |
| Trinity Rd. | 17 | D | 8 |
| Troughton St. | 23 | R | 6 |
| Trowbridge St. | 22 | P | 9 |
| Trueman St. | 31 | O | 10 |
| Truro Rd. | 15 | X | 1 |
| Tryon St. | 32 | P | 10 |
| Tuckerman Institute | 34 | S | 10 |
| Tudor St. | 12 | O | 5 |
| Tue Brook | 11 | M | 1 |
| Tue Brook Station | 11 | N | 1 |
| Tulloch St. | 22 | O | 5 |
| Tunnel Rd. | 23 | S | 5 |
| Tunstall St. | 24 | T | 5 |
| Tweed St. | 11 | O | 4 |
| Twickenham St. | 10 | L | 3 |
| Twiss St. | 35 | V | 9 |
| Twyford St. | 10 | L | 3 |
| Tyne St. | 19 | G | 7 |
| Tynemouth St. | 21 | M | 6 |
| Tyrer St. | 32 | P | 10 |
| Ullet Rd. | 25 | W | 5 |
| Ullswater St. | 10 | L | 5 |
| Underhill St. | 11 | M | 4 |
| Underley St. | 24 | T | 5 |
| Union Court | 32 | P | 11 |
| Union St. | 31 | O | 12 |
| Union St., Egremont | 39 | C | 3 |
| University, Brownlow Hill | 22 | Q | 8 |
| University Hall | 13 | Q | 3 |
| University Rd. | 17 | D | 7 |
| Upper Baker St. | 22 | O | 6 |
| Upper Beau St. | 21 | N | 8 |
| Upper Brighton, New Brighton | 38 | B | 1 |
| Upper Canning St. | 23 | S | 7 |
| Upper Duke St. | 33 | R | 10 |
| Upper Essex St. | 35 | V | 10 |
| Up. Frederick St. | 33 | R | 11 |
| Up. Hampton St. | 24 | T | 8 |
| Up. Harrington St. | 34 | T | 10 |
| Upper High St. | 20 | L | 7 |
| Upper Hill St. | 34 | T | 9 |
| Upper Hope Pl. | 23 | R | 9 |
| Up. Huskisson St. | 23 | S | 7 |
| Upper Mann St. | 34 | U | 11 |
| Upper Mason St. | 23 | Q | 6 |
| Upper Milk St. | 31 | N | 11 |
| Upper Newington | 32 | Q | 9 |
| Upper Park St. | 35 | V | 10 |
| Up. Parliament St. | 24 | T | 8 |
| Upper Pitt St. | 33 | R | 10 |
| Upper Pownall St. | 33 | R | 11 |
| Up. Stanhope St. | 34 | T | 10 |
| Up. Warwick St. | 34 | U | 10 |
| Up. William St. | 30 | L | 11 |
| Urmson Rd., Liscard | 38 | B | 2 |

| | | | |
|---|---|---|---|
| Ursula St. | 18 | F | 6 |
| Utting Av. | 9 | I | 1 |
| Uxbridge St. | 23 | S | 5 |
| Vale Park, New Brighton | 38 | B | 1 |
| Valley Rd. | 10 | L | 4 |
| Vandries St. | 30 | L | 12 |
| Vandyke St. | 24 | U | 6 |
| Vane St. | 22 | O | 6 |
| Varthen St. | 20 | K | 5 |
| Vaughan Rd., New Brighton | 38 | B | 1 |
| Vaughan St. | 35 | V | 11 |
| Vauxhall Rd. | 30 | K | 9 |
| Venice St. | 20 | K | 5 |
| Venmore St. | 20 | K | 5 |
| Venus St. | 11 | M | 4 |
| Vere St. | 35 | V | 11 |
| Vermont St. | 16 | B | 7 |
| Vernon St. | 32 | O | 11 |
| Verona St. | 20 | K | 6 |
| Verulam St. | 24 | T | 7 |
| Vescock St. | 30 | L | 9 |
| Vesuvius St. | 19 | I | 8 |
| Vicar Road | 10 | L | 2 |
| Vickers St. | 34 | T | 9 |
| Victor St. | 14 | T | 4 |
| Victoria Dock | 30 | M | 12 |
| Victoria Drive | 6 | A | 2 |
| Victoria Park | 14 | U | 1 |
| Victoria Pk., Tranmere | 36 | B | 4 |
| Victoria Rd. | 11 | M | 1 |
| Victoria Rd., New Brighton | 38 | B | 1 |
| Victoria Rd., Seacombe | 39 | C | 3 |
| Victoria Rd., Tranmere | 36 | B | 3 |
| Victoria Sq. | 31 | M | 9 |
| Victoria St. | 32 | O | 10 |
| Victoria Tunnel | 23 | S | 5 |
| Victoria Yard | 29 | H | 10 |
| Vienna St. | 20 | K | 5 |
| Village Grove | 21 | N | 7 |
| Village Rd., Oxton | 36 | A | 3 |
| Village St. | 21 | N | 7 |
| Villars St. | 32 | P | 9 |
| Vine Pl. | 23 | R | 7 |
| Vine St. | 23 | R | 7 |
| Vining St. | 24 | U | 9 |
| Viola St. | 18 | E | 8 |
| Violet St. | 34 | T | 9 |
| Vipond St. | 21 | N | 5 |
| Virgil St. | 21 | M | 9 |
| Virginia Rd., New Brighton | 38 | B | 1 |
| Virginia Street, Bootle | 16 | B | 7 |
| Virginia St., Oldhall St. | 31 | N | 12 |
| Vittoria St., Birkenhead | 38 | B | 4 |
| Vittoria Wharf, Birkenhead | 36 | B | 1 |
| Vivian St. | 22 | O | 6 |
| Voelas St. | 25 | V | 8 |
| Vron Hill St. | 24 | U | 8 |
| Vulcan St., Bootle | 26 | B | 9 |
| Vulcan St., Great Howard St. | 30 | L | 12 |
| Vyrnwy St. | 20 | K | 5 |
| Wadham Rd. | 18 | E | 8 |
| Wagstaff St. | 34 | T | 9 |
| Wainwright St. | 24 | T | 6 |
| Wakefield St. | 21 | N | 9 |
| Walker St. | 22 | O | 6 |
| Walker Art Gallery, Wm. Brown St. | 32 | O | 9 |
| Wallace St. | 6 | A | 1 |
| Wallasey, Wirral Peninsula | 38 | A | 2 |
| Wallasey Dock | 39 | C | 4 |
| Wallasey Gas Wks, | 38 | B | 3 |
| Wallasey Station | 38 | A | 2 |
| Wallasey (Cattle) Landing Stage | 39 | C | 4 |
| Wallasey Pool | 38 | A | 3 |
| Wallasey Village and Station | 38 | A | 2 |
| Walmsley St. | 30 | I | 10 |
| Walnut St. | 23 | Q | 8 |
| Walpole St. | 23 | S | 6 |
| Walter St. | 30 | K | 11 |
| Waltham Rd. | 10 | L | 3 |
| Walton & Anfield Station | 8 | G | 3 |
| Walton Breck Rd. | 10 | L | 4 |
| Walton Cemetery | 7 | C | 3 |
| Walton Gaol | 6 | B | 3 |
| Walton Hall Av. | 8 | F | 1 |
| Walton Hall Estate | 8 | E | 1 |
| Walton Junct. Stn. | 7 | C | 3 |
| Walton Lane | 9 | G | 4 |
| Walton on the Hill and Station | 8 | E | 4 |
| Walton Park | 7 | C | 3 |
| Walton Rd. | 19 | H | 6 |
| Walton Town Hall | 8 | E | 4 |
| Walton Vale | 6 | A | 1 |
| Walton Villas | 8 | F | 4 |
| Wapping | 32 | Q | 12 |
| Wapping Basin | 33 | R | 12 |
| Wapping Dock | 33 | R | 12 |
| Wapping Goods Station, L.M.S. | 33 | R | 11 |
| Wapping Station | 33 | S | 12 |
| Warbreck Av. | 6 | A | 1 |
| Warbreck Rd. | 6 | A | 1 |
| Warburton St. | 22 | Q | 7 |
| Warden St. | 19 | H | 6 |
| Warham Rd. | 10 | K | 2 |
| Warren Drive, Wallasey | 38 | A | 1 |
| Warren Park, Wallasey | 38 | A | 1 |
| Warren Station, Wallasey | 38 | A | 1 |
| Warren St. | 32 | P | 9 |
| Warwick Rd. | 16 | C | 5 |
| Warwick St. | 34 | U | 11 |
| Wasdale Rd. | 6 | B | 2 |
| Washington St. | 33 | S | 10 |
| Washington St., Bootle | 16 | B | 8 |
| Water St. | 32 | O | 12 |
| Waterhouse St. | 21 | M | 7 |
| Waterloo Rd. | 31 | M | 12 |
| Waterloo Goods Station | 31 | M | 12 |
| Waterloo St. | 15 | V | 1 |
| Waterpark Road, Birkenhead | 36 | A | 4 |
| Water Works St. | 17 | C | 6 |
| Watford Rd. | 10 | K | 4 |
| Watkinson St. | 33 | S | 11 |
| Watmough St. | 21 | N | 8 |
| Watson St., Birkenhead | 36 | B | 2 |
| Wauchope St. | 14 | U | 3 |
| Waverley Rd. | 25 | X | 7 |
| Waverley St. | 17 | C | 9 |
| Wavertree | 14 | U | 1 |
| Wavertree Park | 13 | R | 4 |
| Wavertree Playground | 15 | V | 2 |
| Wavertree Rd. | 23 | S | 5 |
| Wavertree Station | 14 | V | 3 |
| Wavertree Vale | 14 | T | 3 |
| Weardale Rd. | 15 | W | 3 |
| Weaver St. | 7 | E | 5 |
| Webb St. | 24 | T | 5 |
| Webster Rd. | 14 | T | 4 |
| Wedgwood St. | 22 | Q | 5 |
| Weightman Grove | 6 | A | 1 |
| Welbeck Av. | 15 | X | 2 |
| Weldon St. | 8 | E | 5 |
| Welfield Pl. | 25 | W | 9 |
| Well Lane | 17 | C | 6 |
| Well Lane, Tranmere | 36 | B | 3 |
| Well St. | 15 | U | 2 |
| Wellbrow Rd. | 8 | F | 3 |
| Weller St. | 34 | V | 9 |
| Wellesley Rd. | 25 | W | 8 |
| Wellesley Ter. | 25 | W | 8 |
| Wellfield Rd. | 7 | D | 3 |
| Wellington Av. | 15 | V | 4 |
| Wellington Dock | 29 | I | 11 |
| Wellington Fields | 15 | V | 4 |
| Wellington Grove | 14 | U | 2 |
| Wellington Monument | 32 | O | 9 |
| Wellington Road, New Brighton | 38 | B | 1 |
| Wellington Road, Park Rd. | 35 | W | 10 |
| Wellington Road, Picton Rd. | 14 | U | 2 |
| Wellington St. | 31 | M | 9 |
| Wellington Ter. | 25 | V | 9 |
| Wembley Gdns. | 6 | A | 2 |
| Wendell St. | 24 | U | 5 |
| Wenham Rd. | 13 | R | 2 |
| Wenlock Rd. | 10 | K | 3 |
| Wentworth St. | 21 | M | 6 |
| Wernbrook Rd. | 10 | K | 2 |
| Wesleyan Central Halls | 32 | Q | 9 |
| Wesley St. | 34 | T | 10 |
| West St. | 32 | P | 7 |
| West Albert Rd. | 25 | X | 7 |
| Westbank Rd. | 13 | R | 2 |
| Westbank Road, Tranmere | 36 | B | 3 |
| Westbourne Rd., Birkenhead | 36 | B | 2 |
| Westbourne St. | 21 | O | 7 |
| Westcombe Rd. | 10 | K | 2 |
| Westcott Rd. | 10 | L | 4 |
| Westdale Rd. | 14 | U | 2 |
| West Derby Rd. | 21 | O | 5 |
| West Derby Rd., Tue Brook | 11 | N | 1 |
| West Derby St. | 22 | Q | 7 |
| West Derby Union Offices | 22 | O | 6 |
| West Derby Union Test House | 11 | M | 3 |
| West Derby Union Workhouse | 7 | D | 3 |
| West Derby Union Workho. Hosp., Queen's Rd. | 21 | N | 6 |
| Westfield Rd. | 6 | A | 3 |
| Westminster Rd. | 18 | F | 6 |
| Westmoreland Pl. | 30 | L | 9 |
| Westmoreland St. | 31 | N | 11 |
| Westridge House, Birkenhead | 36 | A | 3 |
| West Waterloo Dock | 31 | M | 13 |
| Whalley St. | 35 | W | 10 |
| Wheatland Lane, Seacombe | 39 | C | 3 |
| Whetstone Lane, Birkenhead | 36 | B | 2 |
| Whitaker St. | 34 | T | 9 |
| Whitby St. | 11 | M | 1 |
| Whitcroft Rd. | 12 | P | 3 |

White St. . 33 R 10
Whitechapel . 32 P 10
Whitefield Lane . 18 G 6
Whitefield Rd. . 11 N 4
Whitefield Ter. . 21 N 5
Whiteford St. . 11 N 4
White Rock St. . 11 N 4
Whithorn St. . 14 T 4
Whitland Rd. . 12 P 3
Whitley Gdns. . 21 O 7
Whitley St. . 30 L 11
Whitman St. . 14 U 3
Whittier St. . 24 U 5
Whittle St. . 19 I 7
Wide St. . 22 Q 7
Wightman St. . 22 P 5
Wilberforce Rd. . 8 G 2
Wilbraham St. . 20 L 9
Wilburn St. . 18 G 5
Wilde St. . 32 O 9
Wilfer St. . 24 T 5
Wilkin St. . 19 I 7
William Brown St. 32 O 10
William Henry St. 21 N 8
William Henry St., Bootle . 27 D 9
William Moult St. 20 L 8
Williamson Sq. . 32 P 10
Williamson St. . 32 P 11
Willmer Rd. . 10 K 3
Willoughby St. . 23 S 6
Willowbank Rd., Tranmere . 36 B 3
Willowdale Rd. . 7 C 2
Willows, The, Breck Rd. . 11 M 4
Willows, The, Prescot Rd. . 12 Q 1
Wilmott St. . 21 O 7
Wilson St. . 35 W 9
Wilton St. . 21 O 8
Wimpole St. . 22 Q 5
Winchester Rd. . 40 L 3
Winchfield Rd. . 15 X 2
Windermere St. . 10 M 4
Windermere Ter. . 25 W 7
Windsor Barracks 23 S 6
Windsor Grove . 21 M 6
Windsor Pl., Bootle 17 C 9
WindsorRd., Bootle 16 A 5
Windsor Rd., Tue Brook . 11 N 1
Windsor Rd., Walton Vale . 6 A 1
Windsor St. . 34 T 9
Windsor View . 24 U 6
Winfield Rd. . 6 A 3
Winifred St. . 23 R 6
Winslade Rd. . 8 G 2
Winslow St. . 19 G 5
Winter Gardens, New Brighton . 38 B 1
Winter St. . 22 O 6
Wirral Water Wks, Birkenhead . 36 A 4
Withens Lane, Liscard . 38 B 2
Withers St. . 13 R 1
Wolfe St. . 34 T 11
Wolseley St. . 12 O 4
Wolsey St. . 18 F 8
Wolstenholme Sq. 32 Q 10
Wood Grove . 13 R 1
Wood St. . 32 Q 10
Woodbine St. . 19 H 8
Woodchurch Rd., Oxton . 36 B 3
Woodcroft Rd. . 14 U 4
Woodfield Rd. . 6 B 2
Woodhouse St. . 19 I 6
Woodland Rd. . 9 I 1
Woodruff St. . 35 V 10
Woodside, Birkenhead . 37 C 2
Woodside Graving Docks, Bir'head 37 C 2
Woodside Station, Birkenhead . 37 C 2
Woodside St. . 23 R 6
Woodstock St. . 30 L 9
Woodville Ter. . 11 M 4
Woolhope Rd. . 8 F 2
Wool Warehouse . 30 K 11
Worcester Drive . 10 L 1
Worcester Rd. . 16 B 6
Wordsworth St., Bootle . 16 A 9
Wordsworth St., Lodge Lane . 24 U 6
Worfield St. . 31 N 11
Worthington St. . 34 S 11
Wrayburn St. . 24 T 5
Wren St. . 21 O 6
Wrenbury St. . 13 Q 4
Wrexham St. . 20 K 8
Wright St. . 30 L 9
Wright St., Egremont . 39 C 2
Wulstan St. . 19 H 8
Wyatt St. . 19 I 6
Wye St. . 20 K 6
Wykeham St. . 19 H 8
Wylva Rd. . 10 K 4
Wyncroft St. . 35 X 9
Wynne St. . 22 R 5
Wynnstay St. . 25 V 8
Yanwath St. . 24 T 6
Yates St. . 35 V 10
Yellow Noses, Wallasey . 38 B 1
Yelverton Rd. . 10 K 2
Yew Tree Rd. . 7 C 3
York Avenue . 15 W 5
York St., Duke St. 33 Q 11
York St., Walton 7 E 4
York St., West Derby Rd. . 11 O 4
York Terrace . 20 K 7
Zante St. . 20 I 7

## KEY MAP TO SECTIONS

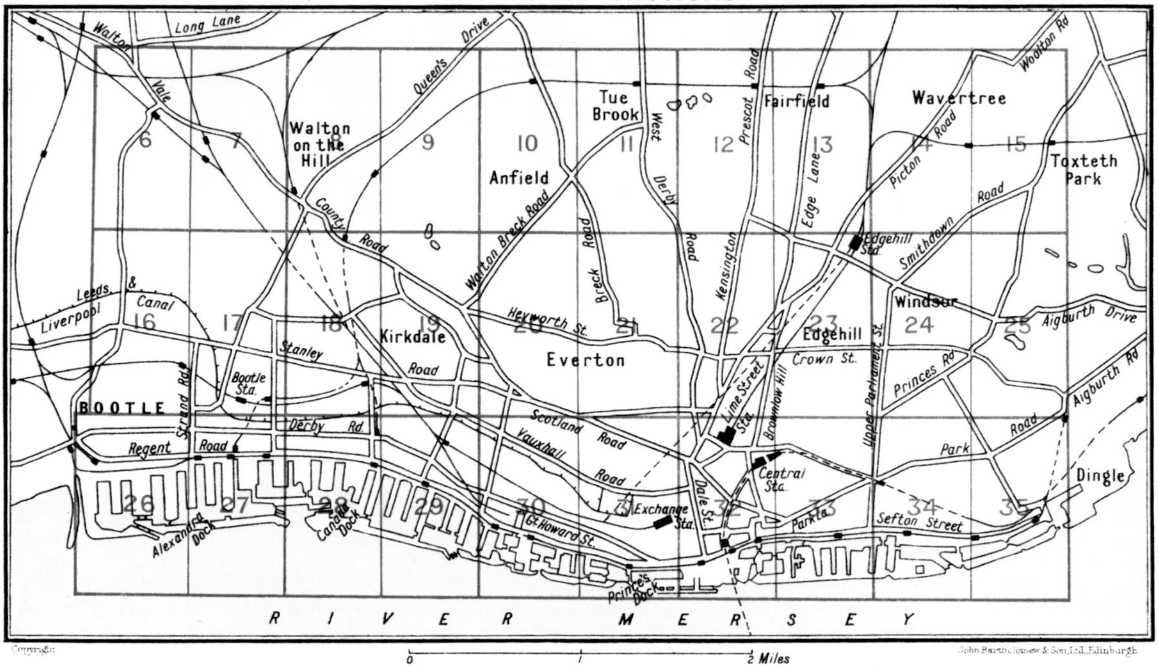
Walton Vale
Long Lane
Queen's Drive
Walton on the Hill
Tue Brook
Fairfield
Wavertree
Wooton Rd
Anfield
West Derby Road
Prescot Road
Picton Road
Toxteth Park
County Road
Walton Breck Road
Breck Road
Kensington
Edge Lane
Edgehill Sta.
Smithdown Road
Leeds & Liverpool Canal
Kirkdale
Heyworth St.
Windsor
Aigburth Drive
Stanley Road
Everton
Edgehill
Crown St.
Princes Rd
Aigburth Rd
Bootle Sta.
BOOTLE
Strand Rd.
Lime Street Sta.
Brownlow Hill
Upper Parliament St.
Derby Rd
Scotland Road
Vauxhall Road
Regent Road
Central Sta.
Park Road
Dingle
Exchange Sta.
Dale St.
Alexandra Dock
Canada Dock
Gt. Howard St.
Park La.
Sefton Street
Princes Dock
R I V E R M E R S E Y
0 1 2 Miles

 John Bartholomew & Son, Ltd., Edinburgh

For Birkenhead and Wallasey see pages 36-37 and 38-39.

2

## MUNICIPAL WARDS

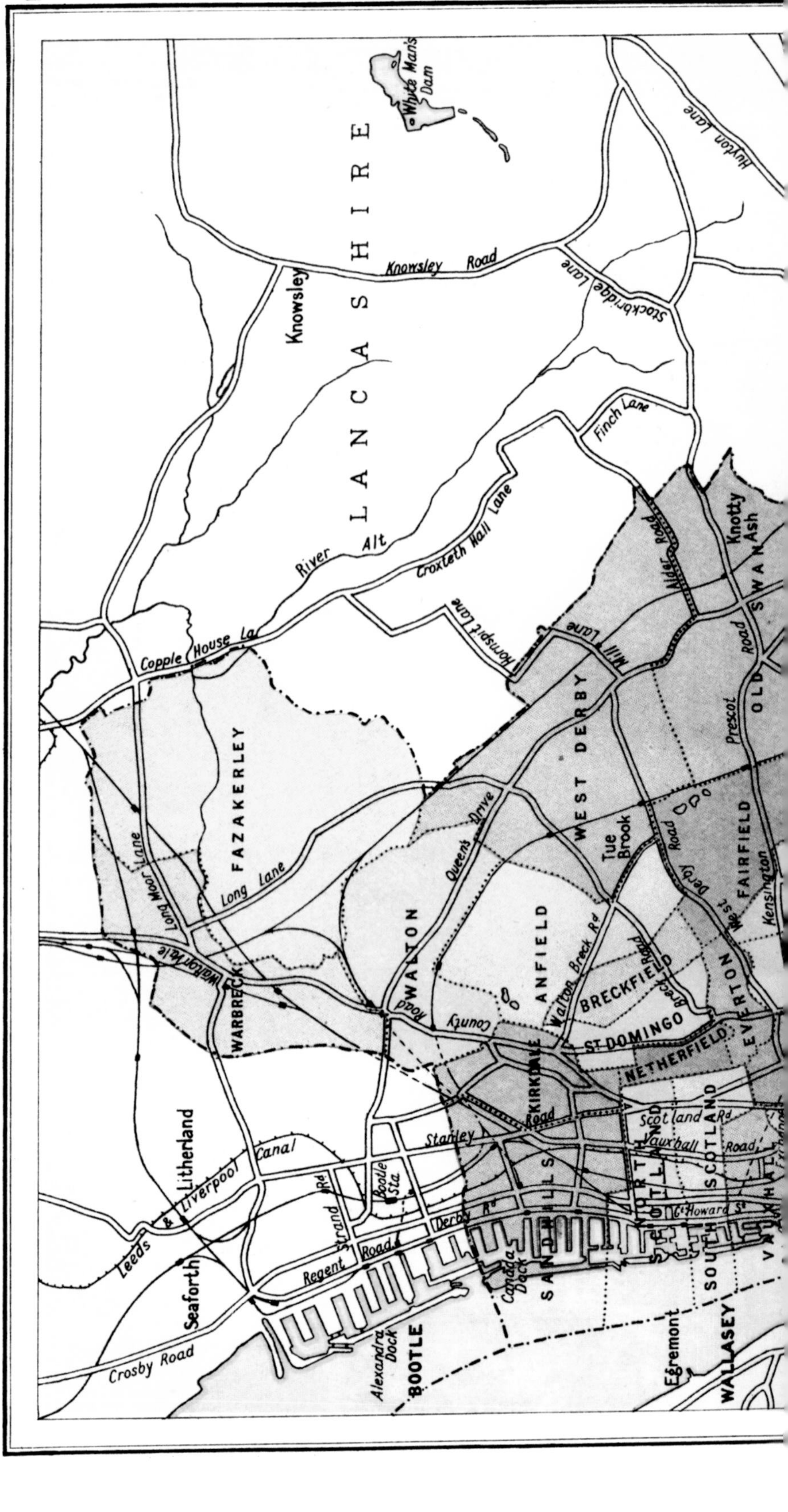

LANCASHIRE
White Man's Dam
Huyton Lane
Knowsley Road
Stockbridge Lane
Knowsley
Finch Lane
River Alt
Croxteth Hall Lane
Hornspit Lane
Copple House La
Alder Road
Knotty Ash
Mill Lane
SWAN
OLD
Road
Prescot
WEST DERBY
FAZAKERLEY
Long Moor Lane
Long Lane
Queens Drive
Tue Brook
Derby Road
West Derby Road
FAIRFIELD
Kensington
WALTON
ANFIELD
Walton Breck Rd
BRECKFIELD
Breck Road
Walton Vale
WARBRECK
Walton Road
County Road
ST DOMINGO
EVERTON
NETHERFIELD
KIRKDALE
Road
Litherland
Leeds & Liverpool Canal
Stanley
Bootle Sta.
Strand Rd
Derby Rd
SANDHILLS
NORTH SCOTLAND
Scotland Rd
Vauxhall Road
SOUTH SCOTLAND
Gt Howard St
VAUXHALL
Seaforth
Regent Road
Canada Dock
SOUTH
Egremont
WALLASEY
Crosby Road
Alexandra Dock
BOOTLE

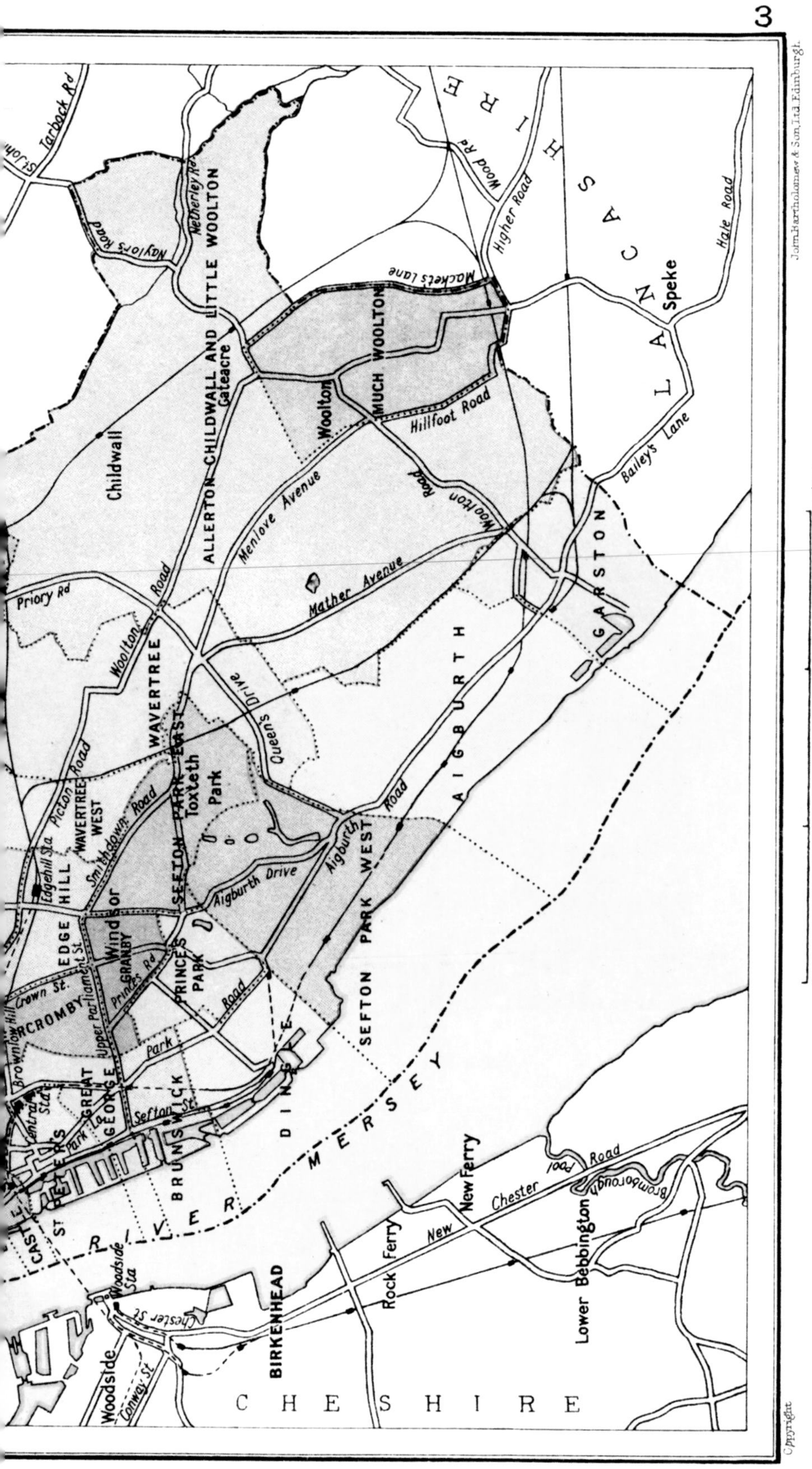
3
LANCASHIRE
CHESHIRE
RIVER MERSEY
Speke
Hale Road
Higher Road
Wood Rd
Mackets Lane
Naylors Road
Netherley Rd
Tarbock Rd
ALLERTON CHILDWALL AND LITTLE WOOLTON
MUCH WOOLTON
Childwall
Gateacre
Woolton
Hillfoot Road
Bailey's Lane
Menlove Avenue
Woolton Road
Mather Avenue
Priory Rd
Woolton Road
GARSTON
AIGBURTH
WAVERTREE
Queens Drive
SEFTON PARK EAST
Toxteth Park
Picton Road
WAVERTREE WEST
Smithdown Road
Edgehill Sta
EDGE HILL
Windsor
GRANBY
Princes Rd
PRINCES PARK
Aigburth Drive
Aigburth Road
SEFTON PARK WEST
SEFTON PARK
DINGLE
Crown St.
Brownlow Hill
ABERCROMBY
Upper Parliament St.
Park Road
GREAT GEORGE
Central Sta
Park La
Sefton St.
BRUNSWICK
ST PETERS
CASTLE ST
Woodside Sta
Woodside
Chester St
Conway St.
BIRKENHEAD
Rock Ferry
New Ferry
New Chester Road
Lower Bebbington
Bromborough Pool
0
1
2
3 Miles
John Bartholomew & Son, Ltd Edinburgh.
Copyright

# PARLIAMENTARY DIVISIONS

4

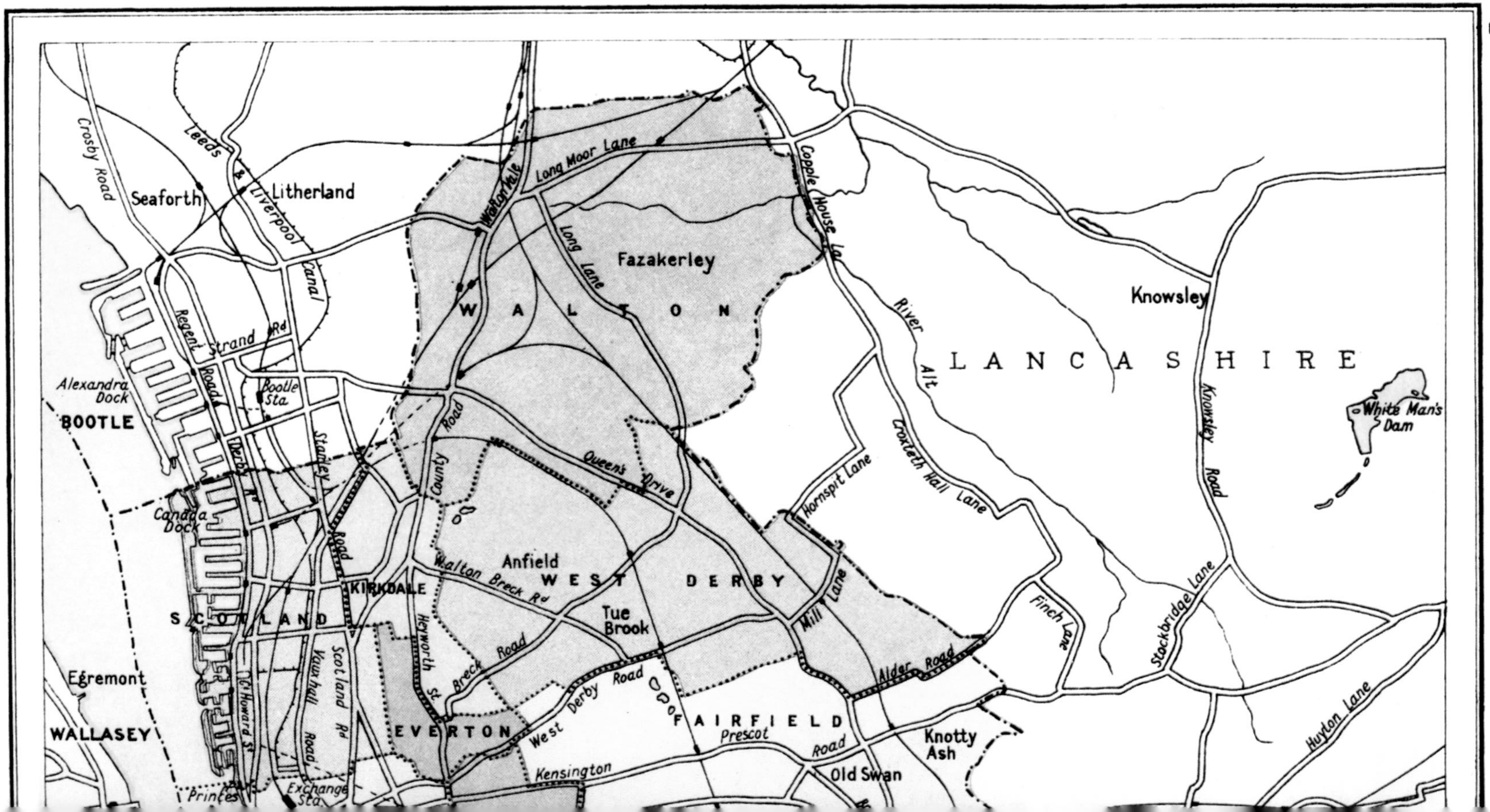

LANCASHIRE
White Man's Dam
Knowsley
Knowsley Road
Huyton Lane
Stockbridge Lane
Finch Lane
Knotty Ash
Old Swan
Croxteth Hall Lane
Hornspit Lane
River Alt
Copple House La
Fazakerley
WALTON
Long Lane
Long Moor Lane
Walton Vale
Litherland
Seaforth
Leeds & Liverpool Canal
Crosby Road
Alexandra Dock
BOOTLE
Regent Road
Strand Rd
Bootle Sta
Derby Rd
Stanley Road
County Road
Queens Drive
Mill Lane
Alder Road
WEST DERBY
Anfield
Walton Breck Rd
Tue Brook
Breck Road
West Derby Road
FAIRFIELD
Prescot Road
Kensington
EVERTON
Heyworth St
KIRKDALE
SCOTLAND
Scotland Rd
Vauxhall Road
Gt Howard St
Canada Dock
Exchange Sta
Princes
Egremont
WALLASEY

5

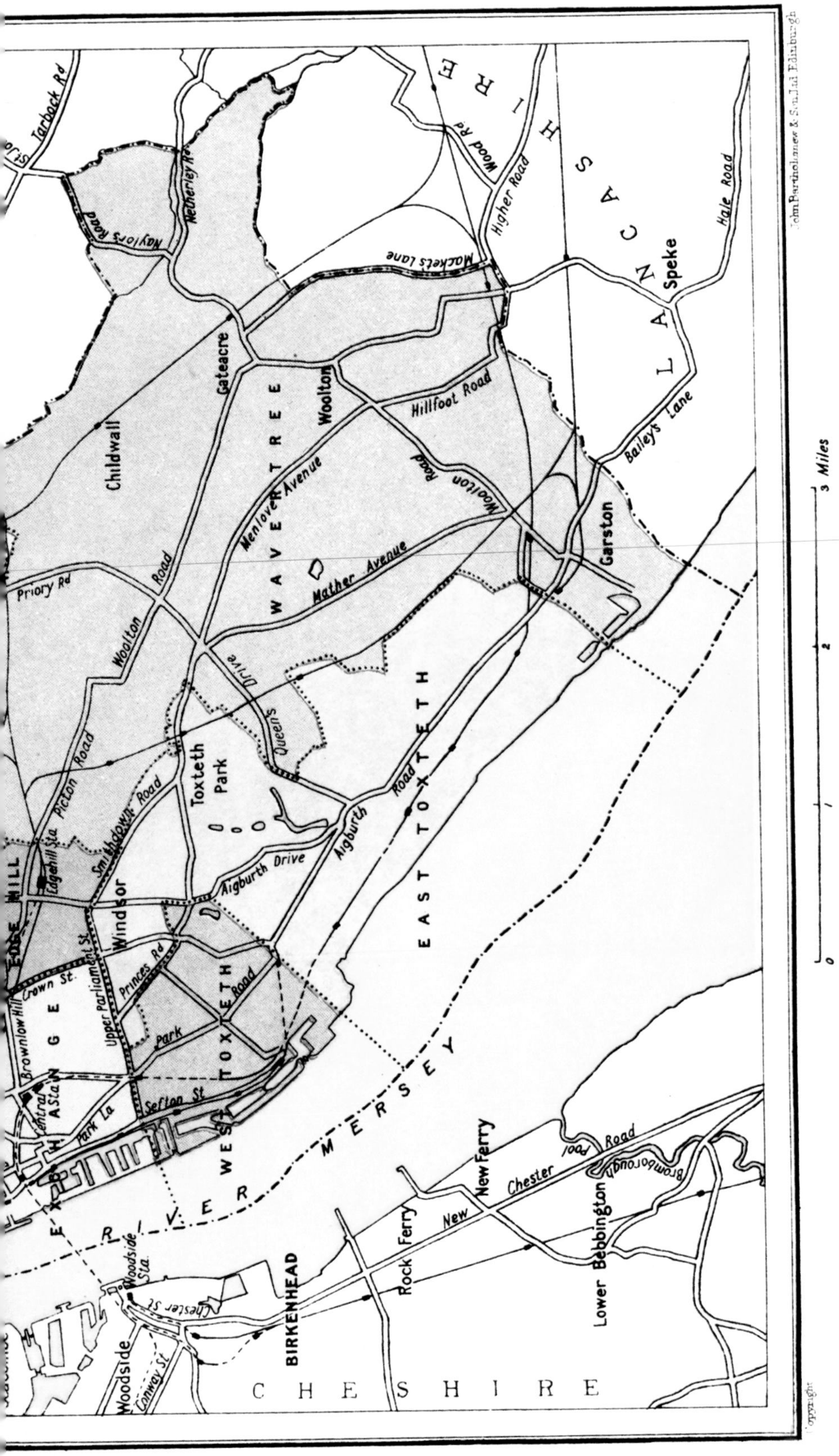

LANCASHIRE
CHESHIRE
RIVER MERSEY
Childwall
Gateacre
Woolton
WAVERTREE
Speke
Garston
Toxteth Park
EAST TOXTETH
WEST TOXTETH
EDGE HILL
Windsor
BIRKENHEAD
Woodside
Woodside Sta.
Rock Ferry
New Ferry
Lower Bebbington
Tarbock Rd
Netherley Rd
Naylors Road
Wood Rd
Higher Road
Hale Road
Mackets Lane
Hillfoot Road
Bailey's Lane
Woolton Road
Menlove Avenue
Mather Avenue
Priory Rd
Queen's Drive
Picton Road
Smithdown Road
Edgehill Sta.
Aigburth Drive
Aigburth Road
Princes Rd
Upper Parliament St.
Crown St.
Brownlow Hill
Central Sta.
Park La
Sefton St
Park
Toxteth Road
Chester St
Conway St
New Chester Road
Bromborough Pool
0
1
2
3 Miles
John Bartholomew & Son, Ltd Edinburgh
Copyright

6

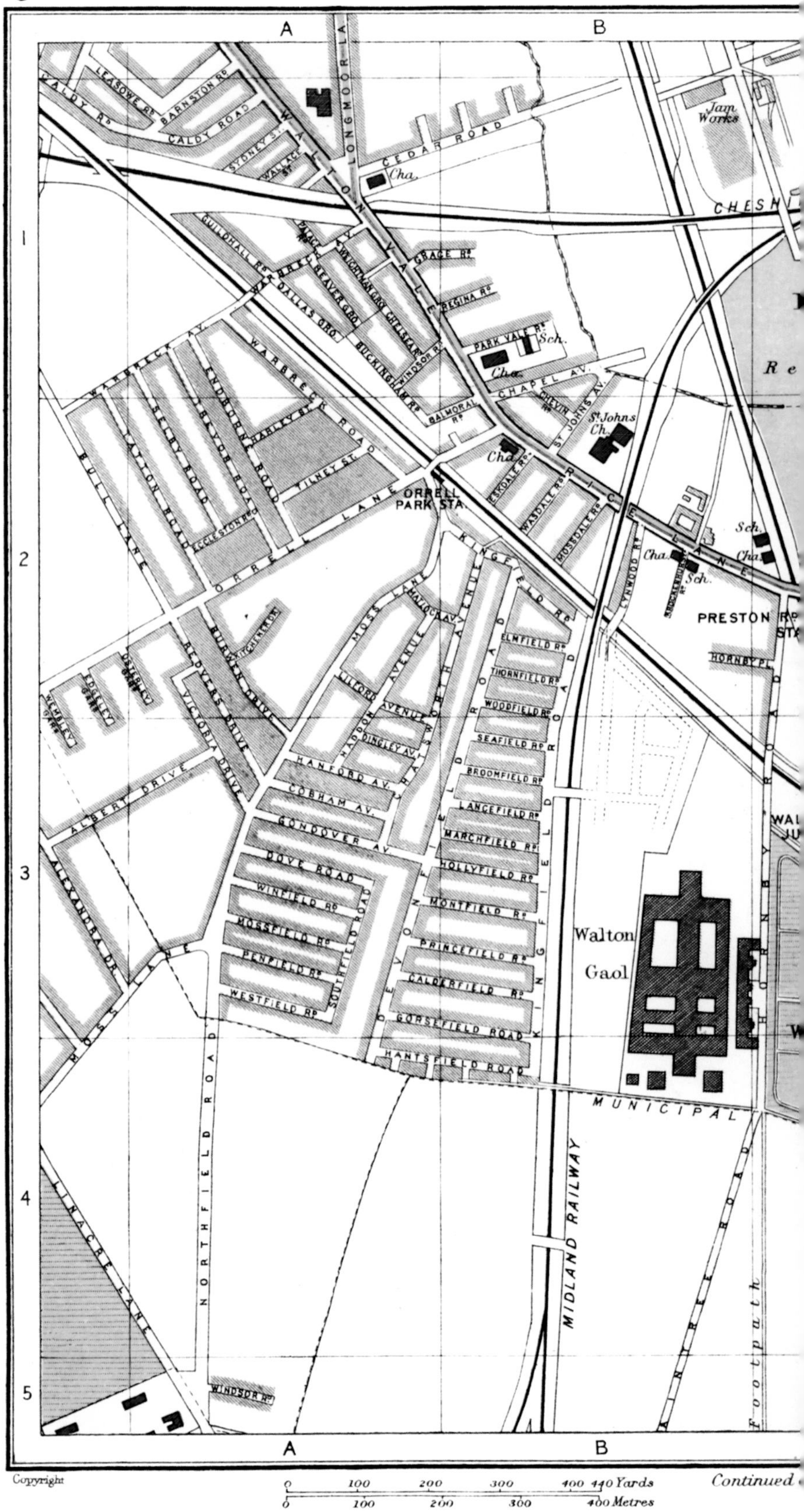
A
B
1
2
3
4
5
CALDY ROAD
LEASOWE RD
BARNSTON RD
CEDAR ROAD
LONGMOOR LA
Jam Works
CHESHI
Cha.
WALTON VALE
GRACE RD
REGINA RD
PARK VALE RD
Sch.
Cha.
CHAPEL AV.
ST JOHNS AV.
St Johns Ch.
BALMORAL RD
WARBRECK ROAD
TILNEY ST.
ORRELL PARK STA.
ORRELL LANE
ESKDALE RD
WASDALL RD
MOSSDALE RD
RICE LANE
Sch.
Cha.
PRESTON RD STA
HORNBY PL.
BULL LANE
ECCLESTON RD
KINGFIELD RD
ELMFIELD RD
THORNFIELD RD
WOODFIELD RD
SEAFIELD RD
BROOMFIELD RD
LANGEFIELD RD
MARCHFIELD RD
HOLLYFIELD RD
MONTFIELD RD
PRINCEFIELD RD
CALDERFIELD RD
GORSEFIELD ROAD
HANTSFIELD ROAD
DEVONFIELD ROAD
KINGFIELD ROAD
HADDON AVENUE
DINGLEY AV.
HANFORD AV.
COBHAM AV.
GONDOVER AV.
DOVE ROAD
WINFIELD RD
MOSSFIELD RD
PENFIELD RD
WESTFIELD RD
SOUTHFIELD ROAD
ALBERT DRIVE
ALEXANDRA DR.
VICTORIA DRIVE
ROSS LANE
NORTHFIELD ROAD
LINACRE LANE
WINDSOR RD
MIDLAND RAILWAY
Walton Gaol
MUNICIPAL
HORNBY ROAD
Footpath
Copyright
0 100 200 300 400 440 Yards
0 100 200 300 400 Metres

Continued

7

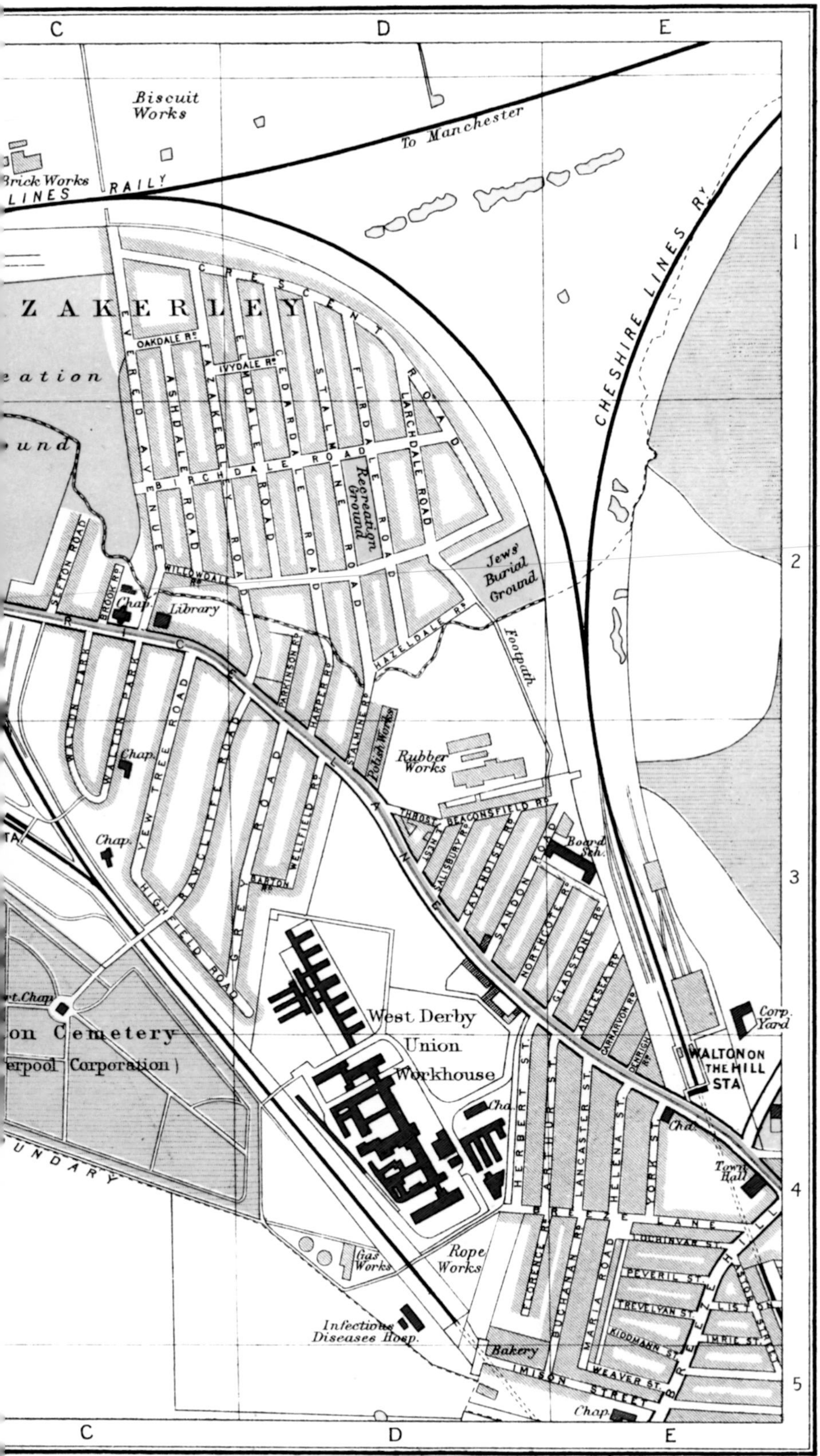

C
D
E
Biscuit Works
Brick Works
LINES
RAILY
To Manchester
CHESHIRE LINES RY
1
2
3
4
5
FAZAKERLEY
Recreation Ground
CRESCENT ROAD
OAKDALE RD
IVYDALE RD
EVERED AVENUE
ASHDALE
FAZAKERLEY ROAD
ELMDALE
CEDARDALE
STALMINE ROAD
FIRDALE ROAD
LARCHDALE ROAD
BIRCHDALE ROAD
Recreation Ground
WILLOWDALE RD
HAZELDALE RD
Jews' Burial Ground
Footpath
SEFTON ROAD
BROOK RD
Chap.
Library
WALTON PARK
YEW TREE ROAD
HIGHFIELD ROAD
RAWCLIFFE ROAD
GREY ROAD
WELLFIELD RD
BARTON RD
PARKINSON RD
HARPER RD
STALMINE RD
Polish Works
Rubber Works
BEACONSFIELD RD
SALISBURY RD
CAVENDISH RD
SANDON ROAD
NORTHCOTE RD
GLADSTONE RD
ANGLESEA RD
CARNARVON RD
DENBIGH RD
Board Sch.
West Derby Union Workhouse
Cemetery
Corporation
BOUNDARY
Corp. Yard
WALTON ON THE HILL STA
Cha.
HERBERT ST
ARTHUR ST
LANCASTER ST
HELENA ST
YORK ST
Town Hall
BREEZE LANE
Gas Works
Rope Works
Infectious Diseases Hosp.
Bakery
FLORENCE ST
BUCHANAN RD
MARIA ROAD
DUCHINVAR ST
PEVERIL ST
TREVELYAN ST
KIDDMANN ST
WEAVER ST
IMRIE ST
IMISON STREET
Chap.


Continued on 8

6 & 17

*Tramway Routes shown thus*

*The Plan is divided into Quarter-mile Squares*

John Bartholomew & Son Ltd Edinburgh

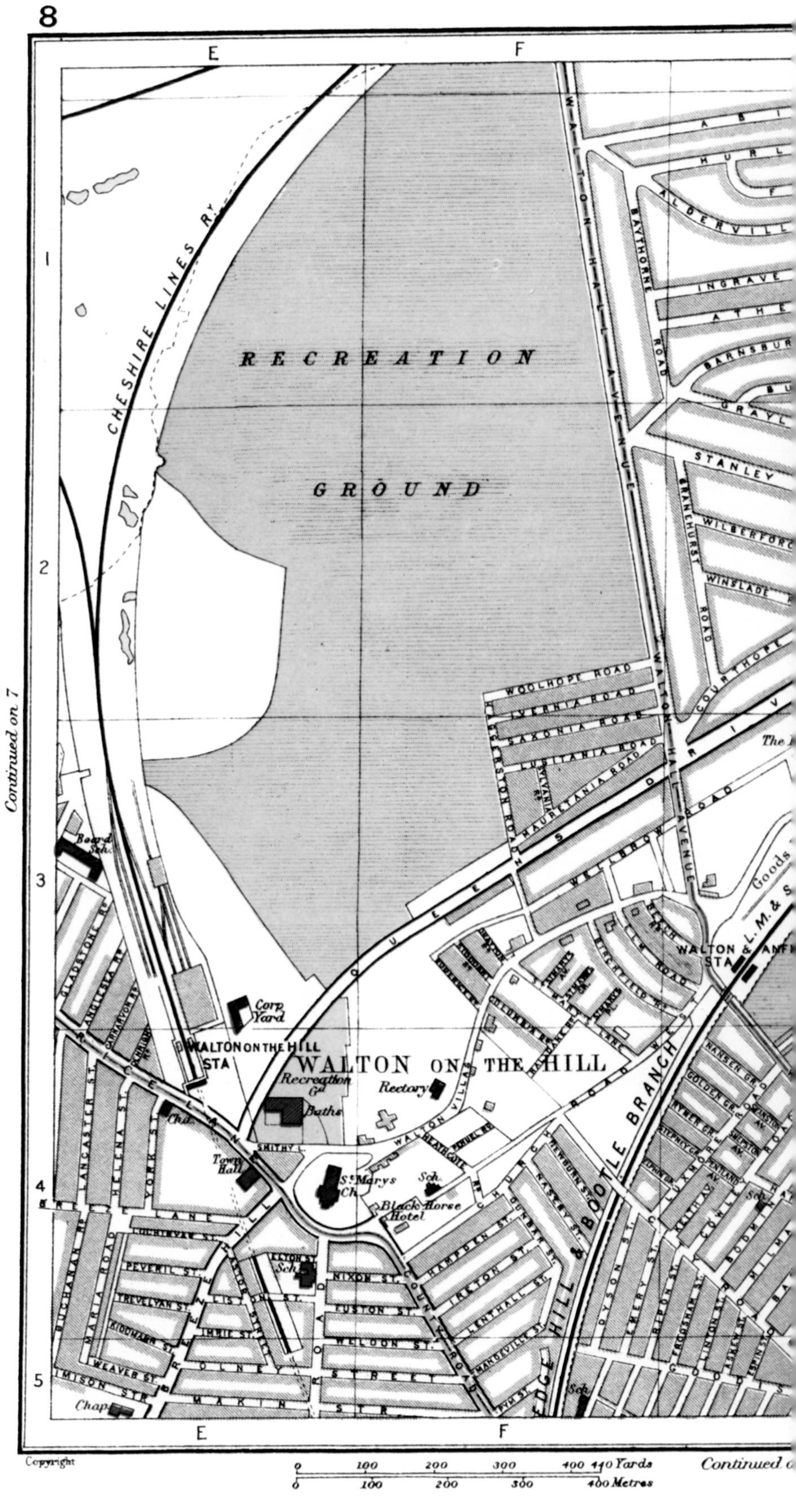
8
E
F
Continued on 7
CHESHIRE LINES RY.
RECREATION
GROUND
WALTON HALL AVENUE
BAYTHORNE ROAD
ALDERVILLE
INGRAVE
STANLEY
WILBERFORCE
WINSLADE
CRANEHURST ROAD
COURTHOPE
WOOLHOPE ROAD
VERNIA ROAD
SAXONIA ROAD
LUSITANIA ROAD
MAURITANIA ROAD
QUEENS DRIVE
WELBROW ROAD
Board Sch.
GLADSTONE RD
Corp Yard
WALTON ON THE HILL STA
WALTON ON THE HILL
Recreation Gd
Rectory
Baths
Town Hall
St. Marys Ch.
Sch.
Black Horse Hotel
WALTON VILLAS
SMITHY L.
RICE LANE
WALTON & ANFIELD STA
L.M. & S.
Goods
EDGE HILL & BOOTLE BRANCH
LANCASTER ST.
HELENA ST.
YORK ST.
BUCHANAN RD
PEVERIL ST.
TREVELYAN ST.
WEAVER ST.
ELTON ST.
NIXON ST.
EUSTON ST.
WELDON ST.
HAMPDEN ST.
LENTHALL ST.
MANDEVILLE ST.
DYSON ST.
Chap.
Sch.
Copyright
0 100 200 300 400 440 Yards
0 100 200 300 400 Metres
Continued

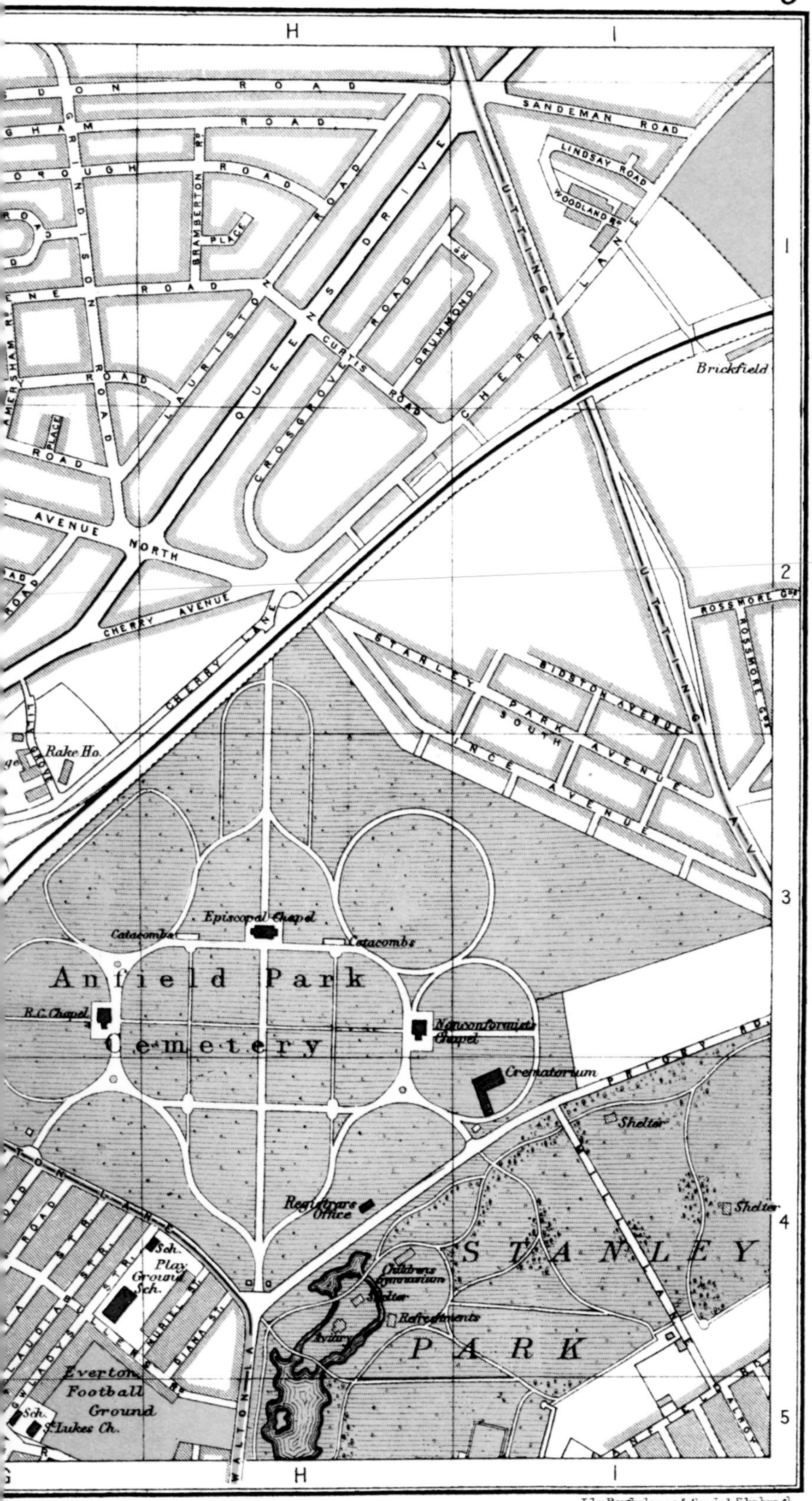
H
I
1
2
3
4
5
G
SANDEMAN ROAD
LINDSAY ROAD
WOODLAND Rd.
UTTING AVE
CHERRY LANE
Brickfield
ROAD
GRINDISON
BRAMBERTON Rd.
PLACE
ROAD
LAURISTON ROAD
QUEENS DRIVE
CROSGROVE ROAD
CURTIS ROAD
DRUMMOND Rd.
AMERSHAM Rd.
PLACE
ROAD
AVENUE NORTH
CHERRY AVENUE
CHERRY LANE
ROSSMORE Gds.
ROSSMORE Gds.
STANLEY PARK
BIDSTON AVENUE
SOUTH AVENUE
AVENUE
UTTING AVE
Rake Ho.
Episcopal Chapel
Catacombs
Catacombs
Anfield Park Cemetery
R.C. Chapel
Nonconformists Chapel
Crematorium
PRIORY RD.
Shelter
Shelter
Registrars Office
STANLEY PARK
Childrens Gymnasium
Shelter
Refreshments
Aviary
Sch.
Play Ground
Sch.
Everton Football Ground
Sch.
St. Lukes Ch.
WALTON LANE
DIANA ST.

Continued on 10

8 & 19 — *Tramway Routes shown thus* ═══

*The Plan is divided into Quarter-mile Squares*

John Bartholomew & Son Ltd Edinburgh

10

Continued on 9

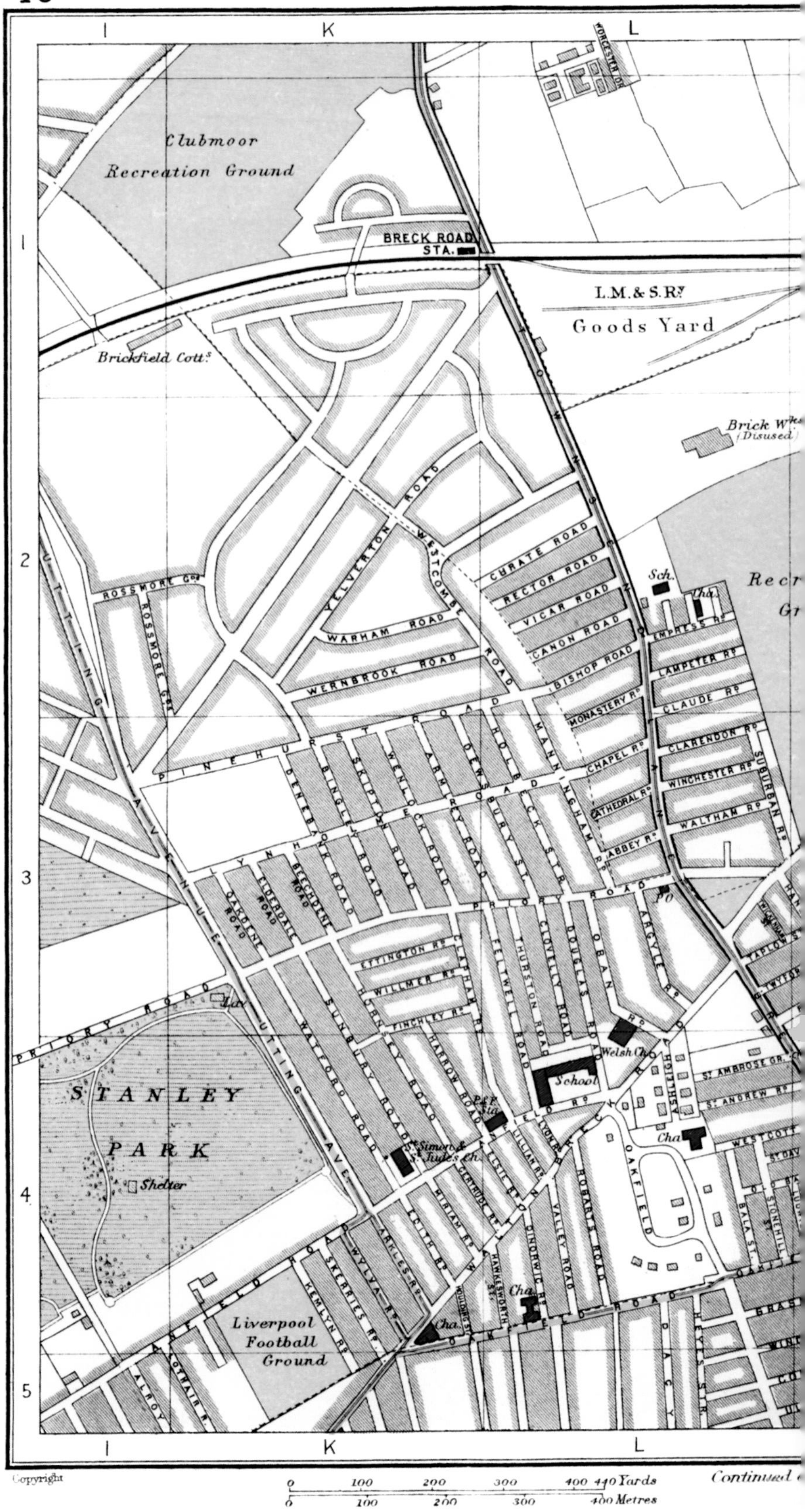
I
K
L
1
2
3
4
5
Clubmoor
Recreation Ground
BRECK ROAD STA.
L.M.& S.Ry
Goods Yard
Brickfield Cotts
Brick Wks (Disused)
ROSSMORE GDS
ROSSMORE GDS
YELVERTON ROAD
WESTCOMBE ROAD
WARHAM ROAD
WERNBROOK ROAD
CURATE ROAD
RECTOR ROAD
VICAR ROAD
CANON ROAD
BISHOP ROAD
Sch.
Cha.
EMPRESS RD
LAMPETER RD
CLAUDE RD
CLARENDON RD
WINCHESTER RD
SUBURBAN RD
WALTHAM RD
MONASTERY RD
CHAPEL RD
CATHEDRAL RD
ABBEY RD
PINEHURST ROAD
LYNHOLME ROAD
PRIORY ROAD
MANNINGHAM
ARGYLE RD
OBAN
CLOVELLY ROAD
THURSTON ROAD
ETTINGTON RD
WILLMER RD
FINCHLEY RD
HARROW ROAD
SUNBURY ROAD
WALFORD ROAD
UTTING AVE.
OAKTREE ROAD
ELDERDALE ROAD
BEECHDENE ROAD
PO
Welsh Ch.
School
P&P Sta.
St Simon & St Judes Ch.
LILLIAN RD
OAKFIELD
ROBARTS ROAD
VALLEY ROAD
Cha.
ST AMBROSE GR.
ST ANDREW RD
WESTCOTT
STANLEY
PARK
Shelter
Lav.
ANFIELD ROAD
SKERRIES RD
KEMLYN RD
ARKLES RD
WYLVA RD
Liverpool
Football
Ground
ALROY
Cha.
Cha.
Recr
Gr
0 100 200 300 400 440 Yards
0 100 200 300 400 Metres
Continued

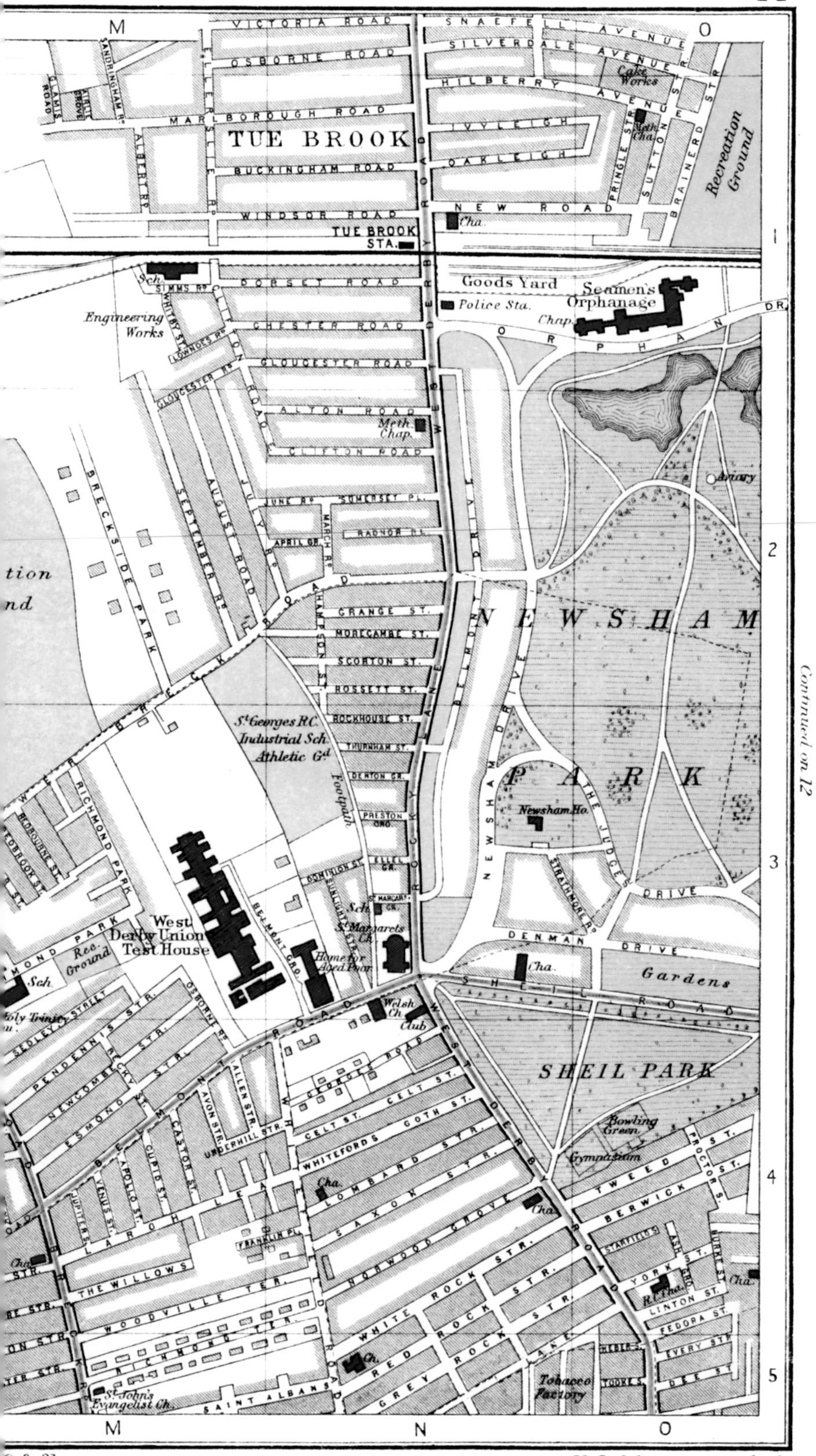
TUE BROOK
TUE BROOK STA.
Victoria Road
Osborne Road
Marlborough Road
Buckingham Road
Windsor Road
Snaefell Avenue
Silverdale Avenue
Hilberry Avenue
Ivyleigh
Oakleigh
New Road
Cake Works
Recreation Ground
Goods Yard
Seamen's Orphanage
Police Sta.
Orphan Dr.
Engineering Works
Dorset Road
Chester Road
Gloucester Road
Alton Road
Clifton Road
West Derby Road
Rocky Lane
Newsham Drive
Belmont Drive
NEWSHAM PARK
Newsham Ho.
Judge Drive
Denman Drive
Gardens
Sheil Road
SHEIL PARK
Bowling Green
Gymnasium
Breckside Park
Breck Road
St. Georges R.C. Industrial Sch. Athletic Gd.
Footpath
Grange St.
Morecambe St.
Scorton St.
Rossett St.
Rockhouse St.
West Derby Union Test House
Home for Aged Poor
St. Margarets Ch.
Welsh Ch.
Club
Rec. Ground
Belmont Road
Richmond Park
Whitefords St.
Lombard Str.
Saxon Str.
Norwood Grove
White Rock Str.
Red Rock Str.
Grey Rock Str.
Tweed St.
Berwick St.
Tobacco Factory
The Willows
Woodville Ter.
Saint Albans
St. John's Evangelist Ch.
M
N
O
1
2
3
4
5
Continued on 12

9 & 21 *Tramway Routes shown thus* ——— *The Plan is divided into Quarter-mile Squares*

John Bartholomew & Son, Ltd. Edinburgh

12

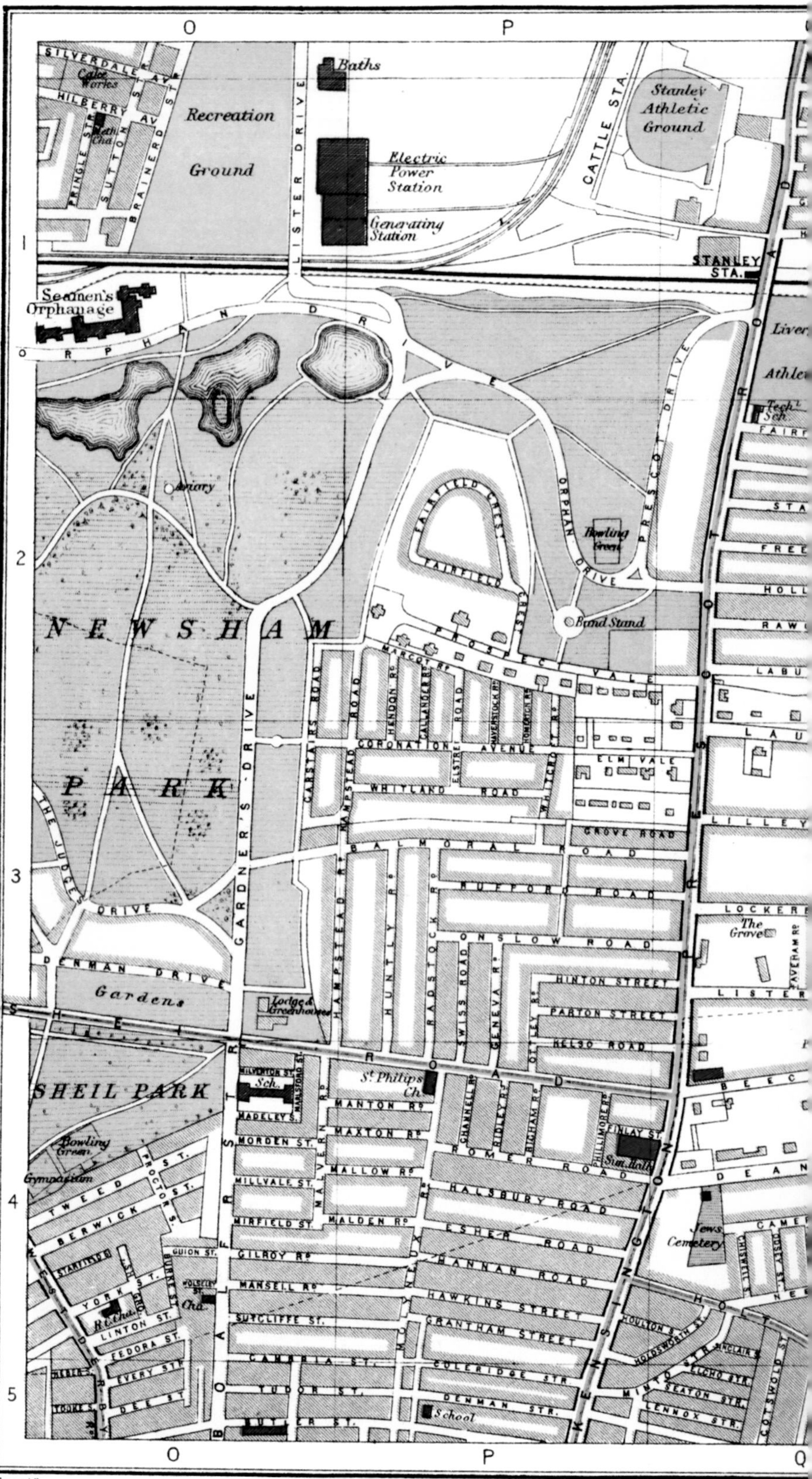
O
P
Q
1
2
3
4
5
Silverdale Av
Cake Works
Hilberry Av
Pringle St
Sutton St
Brainerd St
Recreation Ground
Lister Drive
Baths
Electric Power Station
Generating Station
Cattle Sta.
Stanley Athletic Ground
Stanley Sta.
Seamen's Orphanage
Orphan Drive
Aviary
Fairfield Cres
Fairfield
Orphan Drive
Prescot Drive
Bowling Green
Band Stand
Newsham Park
Prospect Vale
Marcot Rd
Carstairs Road
Hampstead Road
Hendon Rd
Callander Rd
Elstree Road
Coronation Avenue
Elm Vale
Whitland Road
Grove Road
Balmoral Road
Rufford Road
Onslow Road
Hinton Street
Parton Street
Kelso Road
Huntly Rd
Radstock Rd
Swiss Road
Geneva Rd
Gardner's Drive
The Judges Drive
Denman Drive
Gardens
Lodge & Greenhouses
Sheil Road
Sheil Park
St Philips Ch.
Sch.
Manton Rd
Maxton Rd
Mallow Rd
Malden Rd
Morden St.
Millvale St.
Mirfield St.
Madeley St.
Malvern Rd
Channell Rd
Ridley Rd
Bicham Rd
Phillimore Rd
Finlay St
Romer Road
Halsbury Road
Esher Road
Hannan Road
Hawkins Street
Grantham Street
Coleridge Str
Denman Str.
School
Gilroy Rd
Mansell Rd
Sutcliffe St.
Cambria St.
Tudor St.
Butler St.
Boaler Street
Holywell
Kensington
Jews Cemetery
Bowling Green
Gymnasium
Tweed St.
Berwick St.
Proctor St.
York St.
Linton St.
Fedora St.
Every St.
Dee St.
Tookes
West Derby Rd
R.C. Ch.
Ch.
Guion St.
Burgess St.
Liver
Athle
Tech. Sch.
Fairf
Sta
Free
Holl
Rawl
Labu
Lau
Lilley
Lockerby
The Grove
Faversham Rd
Lister
Beech
Dean
Came
Houlton St
Holdsworth St
Elcho Str.
Seaton Str.
Lennox Str.
Cotswold St.

Continued on 11

Copyright

0 100 200 300 400 440 Yards
0 100 200 300 400 Metres

Continued on

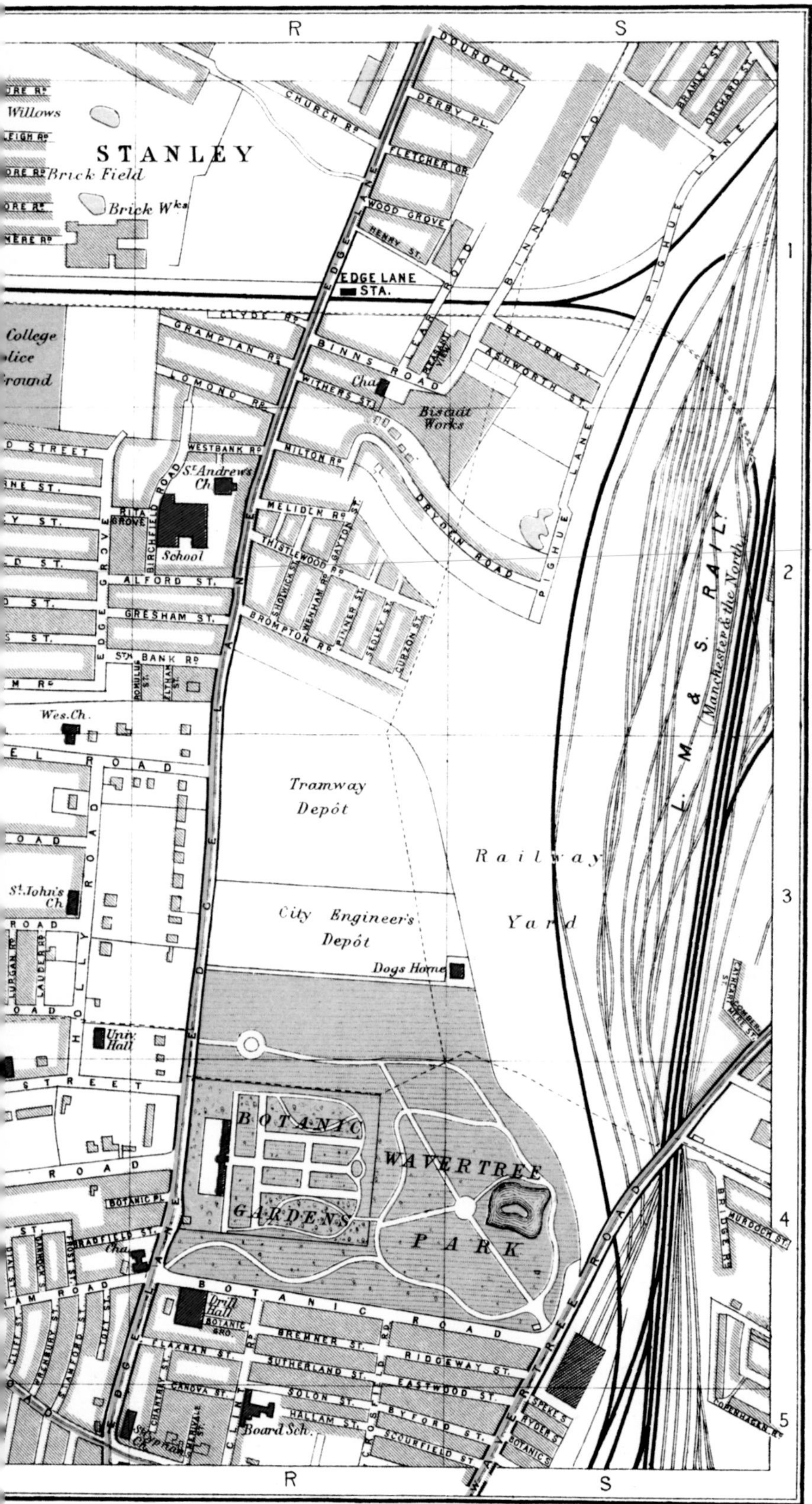
R
S
STANLEY
Willows
Brick Field
Brick Wks
CHURCH Rd
DOURO PL.
DERBY PL.
FLETCHER GR.
WOOD GROVE
HENRY ST.
BINNS ROAD
BRAMLEY ST.
ORCHARD ST.
PIGHUE LANE
EDGE LANE STA.
CLYDE Rd
GRAMPIAN Rd
LOMOND Rd
BINNS ROAD
WITHERS ST.
REFORM ST.
ASHWORTH ST.
Cha.
Biscuit Works
College
Police
Ground
WESTBANK Rd
St Andrews Ch.
MILTON Rd
MELIDEN Rd
THISTLEWOOD Rd
DRYDEN ROAD
RITA GROVE
BIRCHFIELD ROAD
School
EDGE GROVE
ALFORD ST.
GRESHAM ST.
BROMPTON Rd
WENHAM Rd
PINNER ST.
SEDLEY ST.
CURZON ST.
St. BANK Rd
L. M. & S. RAILY.
Manchester & the North
Wes. Ch.
Tramway Depôt
Railway Yard
St. John's Ch.
HOLLY ROAD
City Engineer's Depôt
Dogs Home
Univ. Hall
EDGE LANE
BOTANIC GARDENS
WAVERTREE PARK
BOTANIC PL.
Cha.
WAVERTREE ROAD
MURDOCH ST.
Drill Hall
BOTANIC ROAD
BREMNER ST.
RIDGEWAY ST.
FLAXMAN ST.
SUTHERLAND ST.
EASTWOOD ST.
CANOVA ST.
SOLON ST.
BYFORD ST.
HALLAM ST.
Board Sch.
SCOURFIELD ST.
SPEKE ST.
RYDER ST.
BOTANIC ST.
COPENHAGEN ST.
1
2
3
4
5

Continued on 13

& 23.

Tramway Routes shown thus
The Plan is divided into Quarter-mile Squares

John Bartholomew & Son Ltd. Edinburgh

14

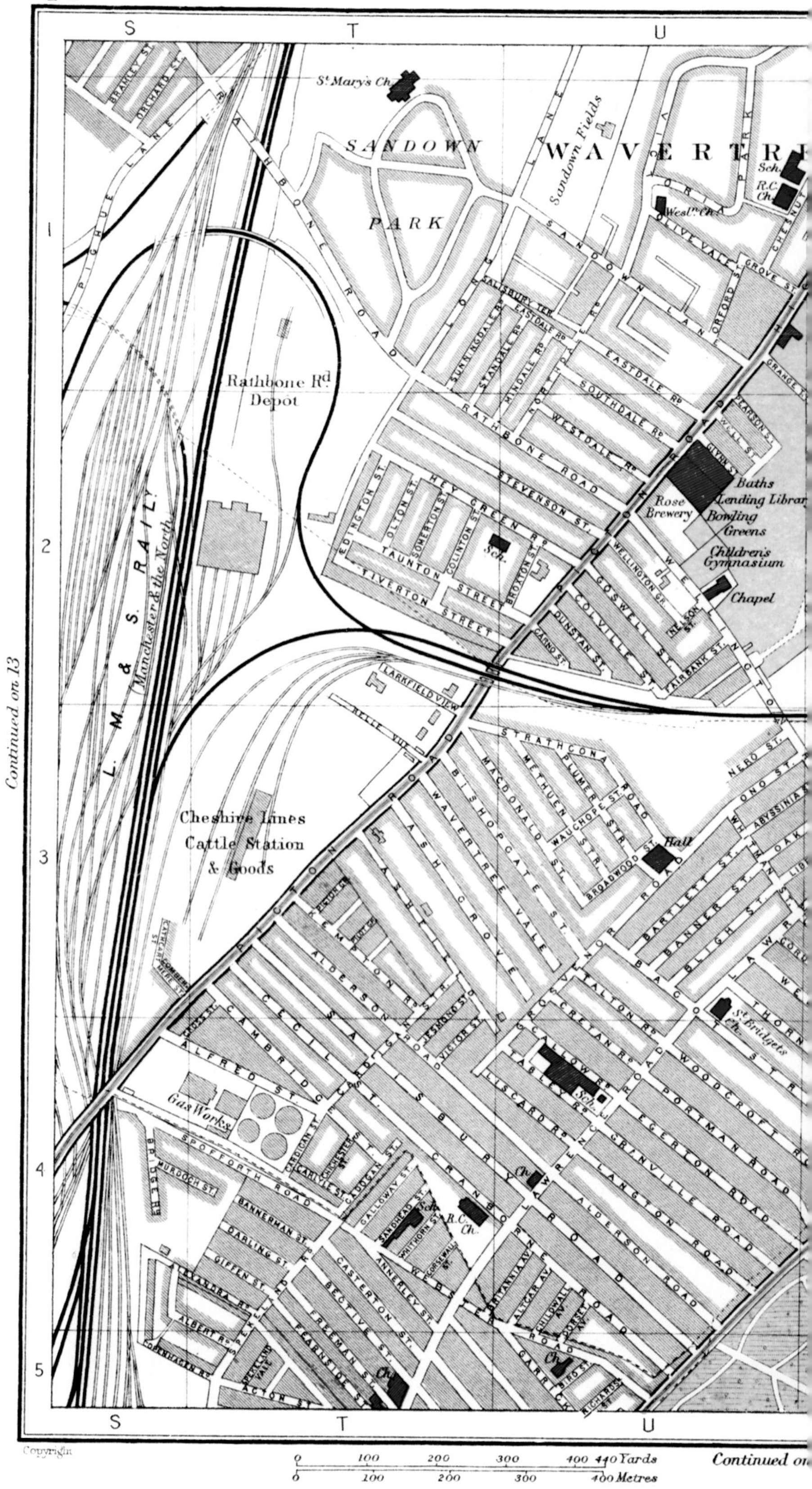
S
T
U
1
2
3
4
5
St. Mary's Ch.
SANDOWN
PARK
WAVERTR
Sandown Fields
Sch.
R.C. Ch.
Wesl<sup>n</sup> Ch.
Rathbone Rd. Depot
L. M. & S. RAILY.
Manchester & the North
Cheshire Lines Cattle Station & Goods
RATHBONE ROAD
SANDOWN LANE
SALISBURY TER.
EASTDALE RD.
SOUTHDALE RD.
WESTDALE RD.
STEVENSON ST.
HEY GREEN RD.
TAUNTON ST.
TIVERTON STREET
EDINGTON ST.
OLTON ST.
SOMERTON ST.
COLINTON ST.
Sch.
Rose Brewery
Baths
Lending Library
Bowling Greens
Children's Gymnasium
Chapel
WELLINGTON RD.
GOSWELL ST.
COLVILLE ST.
DUNSTAN ST.
FAIRBANK ST.
LARKFIELD VIEW
STRATHCONA ROAD
BISHOPGATE ST.
WAVERTREE VALE
MACDONALD ST.
ASH GROVE
BROADWOOD ST.
Hall
PICTON ROAD
NERO ST.
ONO ST.
ABYSSINIA
OAK
BARTLETT ST.
BANNER ST.
HIGH ST.
St. Bridgets Ch.
WOODCROFT
PORTMAN ROAD
EGERTON ROAD
GRANVILLE ROAD
LANGTON ROAD
ALDERSON ROAD
CRETAN RD.
GALLOWAY ST.
ISCARD RD.
TALTON RD.
Sch.
ALFRED ST.
CAMBRIDGE ST.
CECIL ST.
Gas Works
SPOFFORTH ROAD
MURDOCH ST.
BANNERMAN ST.
DARLING ST.
GIFFEN ST.
ALBERT RD.
COPENHAGEN RD.
CASTERTON ST.
BECTIVE ST.
FREEMAN ST.
PEARNSIDE ST.
ANNERLEY ST.
ACTON ST.
Sch.
R.C. Ch.
Ch.
BRITANNIA AV.
ALCAR AV.
CARRICK ST.
Ch.
Continued on 13
S
T
U
Copyright
0 100 200 300 400 440 Yards
0 100 200 300 400 Metres
Continued on

V
W
X
Clock Tower
Town Hall
Waterloo St.
Cong! Cha.
Sch.
Tramway Depot
Old Quarry
Charles Berrington Road
Brereton Av.
Beverley Rd
Bristol Rd
Hereford Rd
Norwich Rd
Peterborough Rd
Truro Rd
Newcastle Rd
Coventry Rd
Church Road
Holy Trinity Ch.
Blue Coat Sch.
Prince Alfred Road
Springfield
Barnhill Rd
Richmond Lo.
Tramway Depot
Glenfield Rd
Pagefield Rd
Edenfield Rd
Freshfield Rd
Brierfield Rd
Micklefield Rd
Winchfield Rd
Grant Avenue
Dust Destructor & Electric Power Sta.
Dudley Rd
Ramilies Rd
Russell Road
Crawford Av.
Shelter
Wavertree Playground
L. M. & S. Raily (Runcorn Crewe & London)
Wavertree Sta.
Sefton Park Sta.
Nicander Rd
R.C. Sch.
Sch.
Mossley Av.
Arlington Av.
Green Bank Road
Holly Bank Rd
Elm Bank Rd
Oak Bank Rd
Beech Bank Rd
Gorsebank Rd
Brookdale Rd
Ferndale Rd
Langdale Rd
Borrowdale Rd
Idderdale Rd
Patterdale Rd
Withsdale Rd
Weardale Rd
Avondale Road
Kenmare Road
Claremont Road
Barrington Road
Blantyre Road
Garmoyle Road
Brookdale Road
Ferndale Road
Langdale Road
Borrowdale Road
Idderdale Road
Smithdown Road
St. Columba's Ch.
Cha.
Wellington Fields
Sch.
Asylum
Hosp.
Toxteth Park Workhouse
Rosset Av.
Gresford Av.
Hawarden Av.
Halkyn Avenue
Cumberland Avenue
Rutland Av.
York Av.
St. Clare's R.C.Ch.
Ullet Road
Greenbank Drive
Drive
Croxteth Drive
Cricket Ground
Sefton Park
Toxteth Park Cemetery
1
2
3
4
5

24 & 25

*Tramway Routes shown thus*

*The Plan is divided into Quarter-mile Squares*

John Bartholomew & Son, Ltd. Edinburgh

Continued

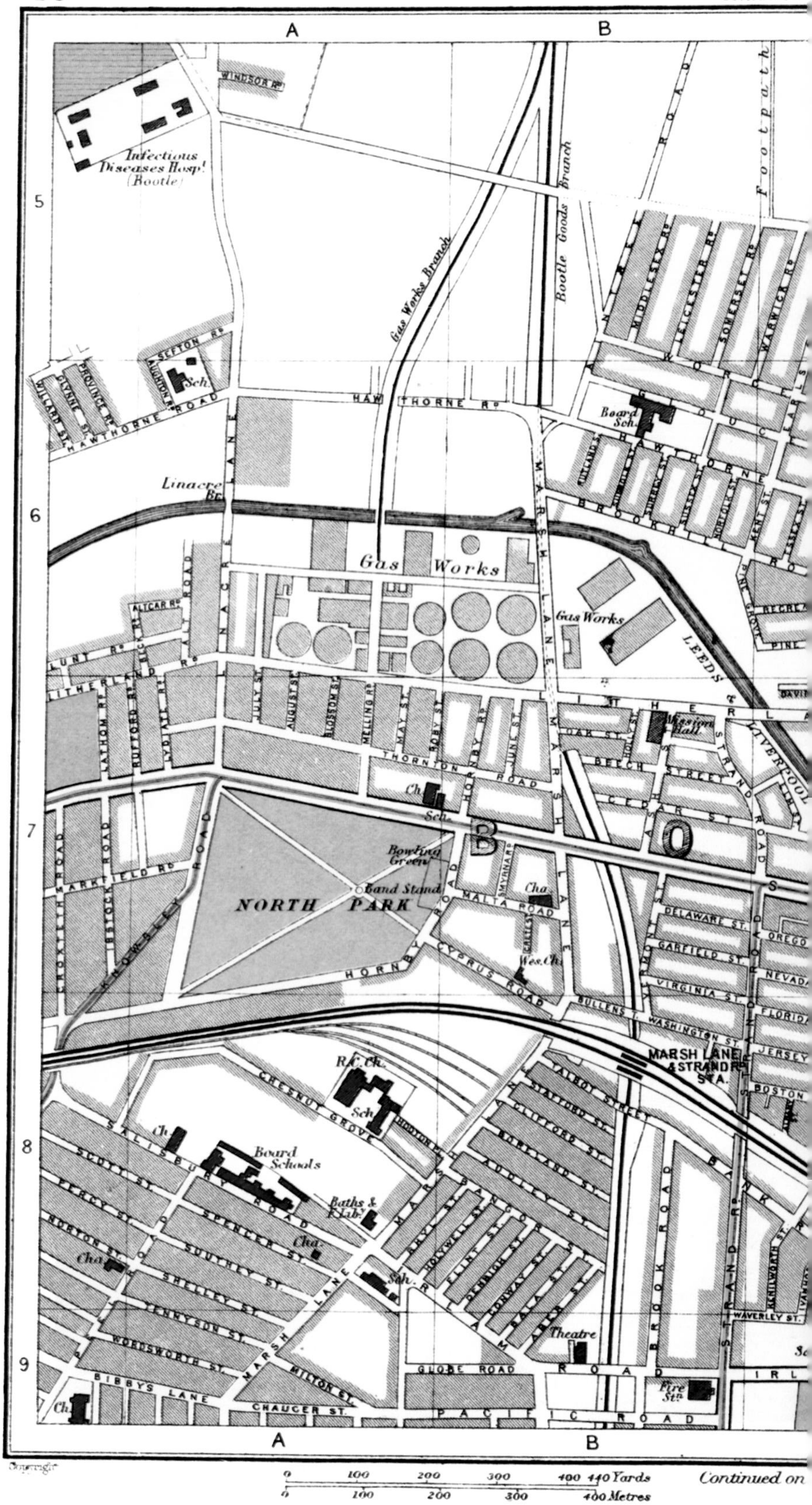
A
B
5
6
7
8
9
Windsor Rd
Infectious Diseases Hosp! (Bootle)
Sefton Rd
Sch.
Hawthorne Road
Haw Thorne Rd
Gas Works Branch
Bootle Goods Branch
Footpath
Road
Middlesex Rd
Leicester Rd
Somerset Rd
Warwick Rd
Board Sch.
Linacre Br.
Linacre Lane
Gas Works
Leeds
Altcar Rd
Lunt Rd
Litherland Rd
Thornton Road
Ch.
Sch.
Mission Hall
Beech Street
Strand Road
Liverpool
Marsh Lane
Bowling Green
Band Stand
NORTH PARK
Knowsley Road
Markfield Rd
Malta Road
Cha.
Wes. Ch.
Cyprus Road
Hornby
B
O
Delaware St.
Garfield St.
Virginia St.
Washington St.
Bullens
Oregon
Nevada
Florida
Jersey
Boston
MARSH LANE & STRAND Rd STA.
R.C. Ch.
Sch.
Chesnut Grove
Ch.
Salisbury Road
Board Schools
Baths & F. Lib.
Scott St.
Percy St.
Norton St.
Spenser St.
Southey St.
Shelley St.
Tennyson St.
Wordsworth St.
Bibbys Lane
Milton St.
Chaucer St.
Marsh Lane
Cha.
Sch.
Theatre
Globe Road
Pacific Road
Fire Stn
Brook Road
Strand Rd
Waverley St.
Talbot Street
Stafford St.
Clifford St.
Copyright
0 100 200 300 400 440 Yards
0 100 200 300 400 Metres

Continued on

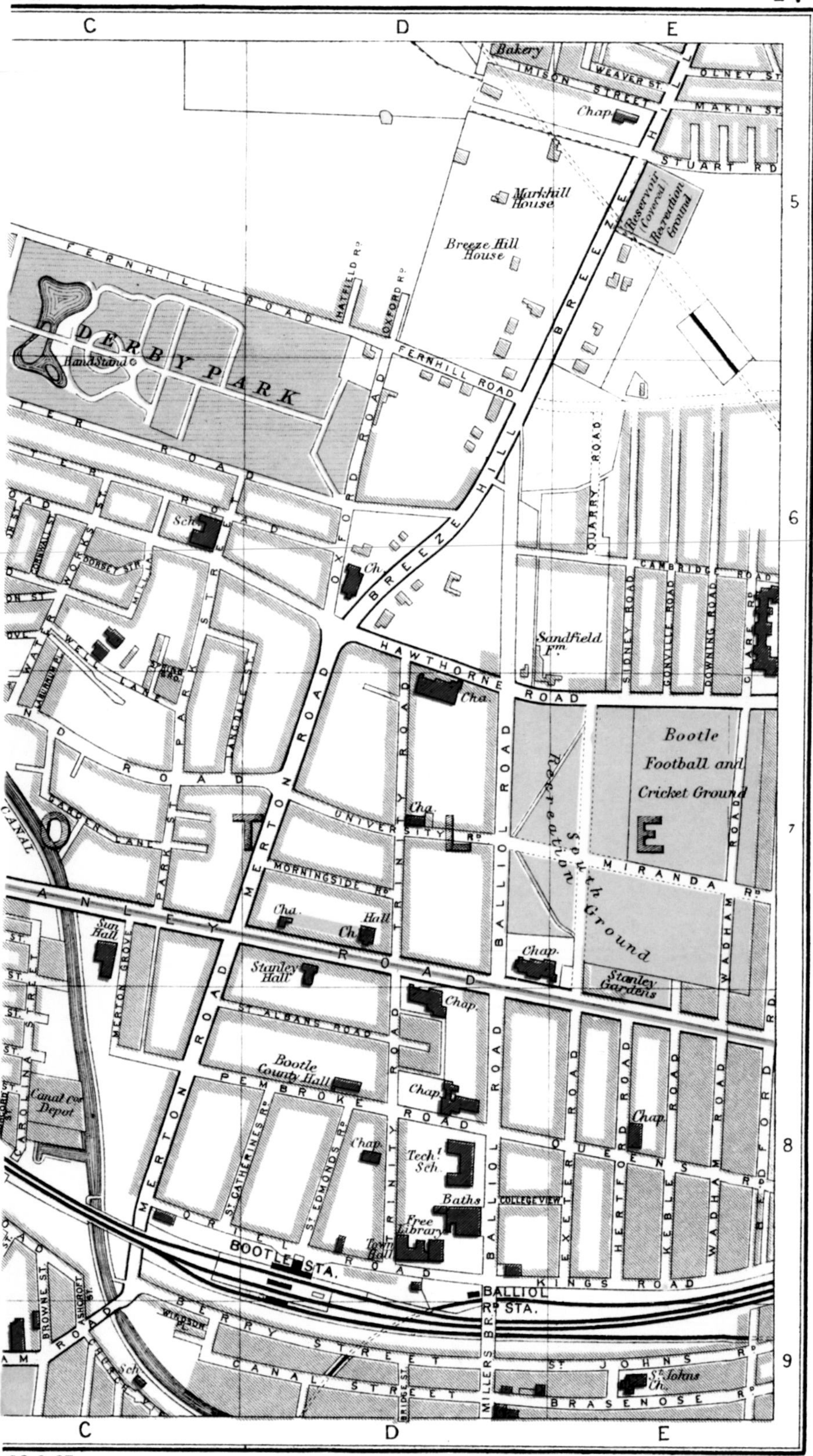
C
D
E
5
6
7
8
9
Bakery
IMISON STREET
WEAVER ST.
OLNEY ST.
MAKIN ST.
STUART RD.
Chap.
Markhill House
Breeze Hill House
Reservoir (Covered) Recreation Ground
FERNHILL ROAD
HATFIELD RD.
OXFORD RD.
DERBY PARK
Band Stand
OXFORD ROAD
BREEZE HILL
QUARRY ROAD
CAMBRIDGE ROAD
SIDNEY ROAD
GONVILLE ROAD
DOWNING ROAD
CLARE RD.
Sandfield Fm.
HAWTHORNE ROAD
Sch.
Ch.
DORSET ST.
CORNWALL ST.
WORCESTER ST.
PARK ST.
MERTON ROAD
TRINITY ROAD
UNIVERSITY RD.
MORNINGSIDE RD.
BALLIOL ROAD
Cha.
Bootle Football and Cricket Ground
Recreation South Ground
MIRANDA RD.
WADHAM RD.
CANAL
STANLEY ROAD
Sun Hall
MERTON GROVE
Stanley Hall
Hall
Stanley Gardens
ST. ALBANS ROAD
Bootle County Hall
PEMBROKE ROAD
ST. CATHERINES RD.
ST. EDMONDS RD.
Tech.l Sch.
Baths
Free Library
Town Hall
COLLEGE VIEW
EXETER ROAD
HERTFORD ROAD
KEBLE ROAD
QUEENS RD.
BEDFORD RD.
Canal Cos Depot
ORIEL ROAD
BOOTLE STA.
BALLIOL RD. STA.
KINGS ROAD
BERRY STREET
WINDSOR PL.
BROWNE ST.
ASHCROFT ST.
CANAL STREET
BRIDGE ST.
MILLERS BR.
ST. JOHNS RD.
St. Johns Ch.
BRASENOSE RD.

Continued on 18

26 & 27

*Tramway Routes shown thus* ═══

*The Plan is divided into Quarter-mile Squares*

John Bartholomew & Son, Ltd. Edinburgh.

18

Continued on

Continued on 17

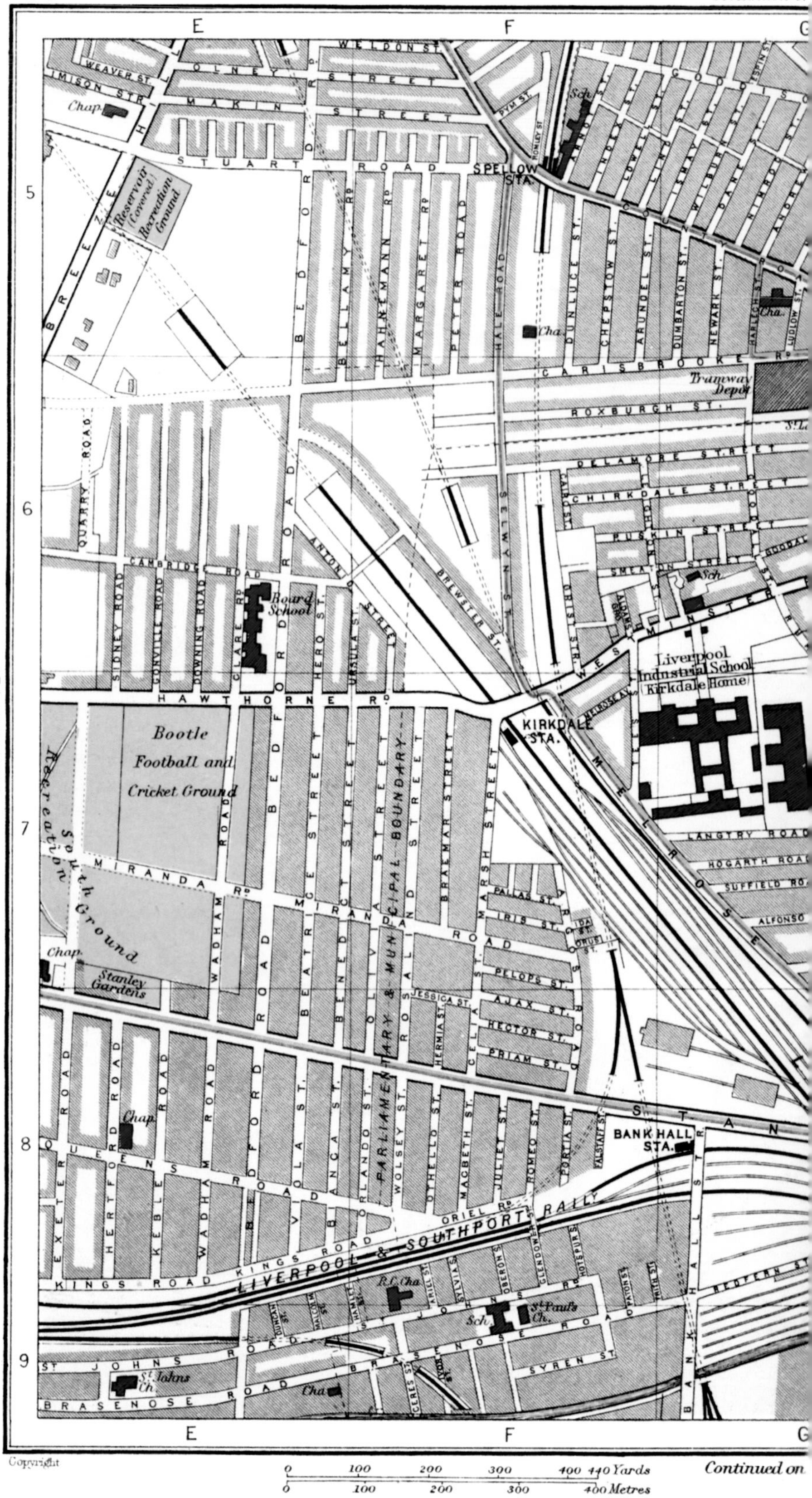
E
F
G
5
6
7
8
9
WELDON ST.
WEAVER ST.
IMISON STR.
OLNEY STREET
MAKIN STREET
STUART ROAD
Chap.
Sch.
PYM ST.
SPELLOW STA.
Reservoir (Covered) Recreation Ground
BREEZE
BEDFORD RD.
BELLAMY RD.
HAHNEMANN RD.
MARGARET RD.
PETER ROAD
HALE ROAD
DUNLUCE ST.
CHEPSTOW ST.
ARUNDEL ST.
DUMBARTON ST.
NEWARK ST.
HARLECH ST.
LUDLOW ST.
Cha.
CARISBROOKE RD.
Tramway Depot
ROXBURGH ST.
DELAMORE STREET
CHIRKDALE STREET
RUSKIN STREET
SMEATON STREET
QUARRY ROAD
CAMBRIDGE ROAD
ANTON
BREWSTER ST.
SELWYN ST.
Board School
SIDNEY ROAD
TONVILLE ROAD
DOWNING ROAD
CLARE RD.
HERO ST.
URSULA ST.
STREET
WESTMINSTER
Liverpool Industrial School
Kirkdale Home
HAWTHORNE RD.
KIRKDALE STA.
MELROSE
Bootle Football and Cricket Ground
Recreation
South Ground
MIRANDA RD.
MIRANDA ROAD
BEATRICE STREET
BENEDICT STREET
PARLIAMENTARY & MUNICIPAL BOUNDARY
BRAEMAR STREET
MARSH STREET
LANGTRY ROAD
HOGARTH ROAD
SUFFIELD ROAD
ALFONSO
PALLAS ST.
IRIS ST.
PELOPS ST.
AJAX ST.
HECTOR ST.
PRIAM ST.
JESSICA ST.
HERMIA ST.
Chap.
Stanley Gardens
WADHAM
ROAD
EXETER ROAD
HERTFORD ROAD
KEBLE ROAD
WADHAM ROAD
BEDFORD ROAD
VIOLA ST.
BIANCA ST.
ORLANDO ST.
WOLSEY ST.
OTHELLO ST.
MACBETH ST.
JULIET ST.
ROMEO ST.
PORTIA ST.
FALSTAFF ST.
STANLEY
BANK HALL STA.
QUEENS ROAD
ORIEL RD.
KINGS ROAD
LIVERPOOL & SOUTHPORT RAILY
R.C.Cha.
ST JOHNS ROAD
Sch.
St. Paul's Ch.
SYREN ST.
BRASENOSE ROAD
St. Johns Ch.
Cha.
CERES ST.
BANK HALL STR.
REDFERN ST.
0 100 200 300 400 440 Yards
0 100 200 300 400 Metres



Continued on

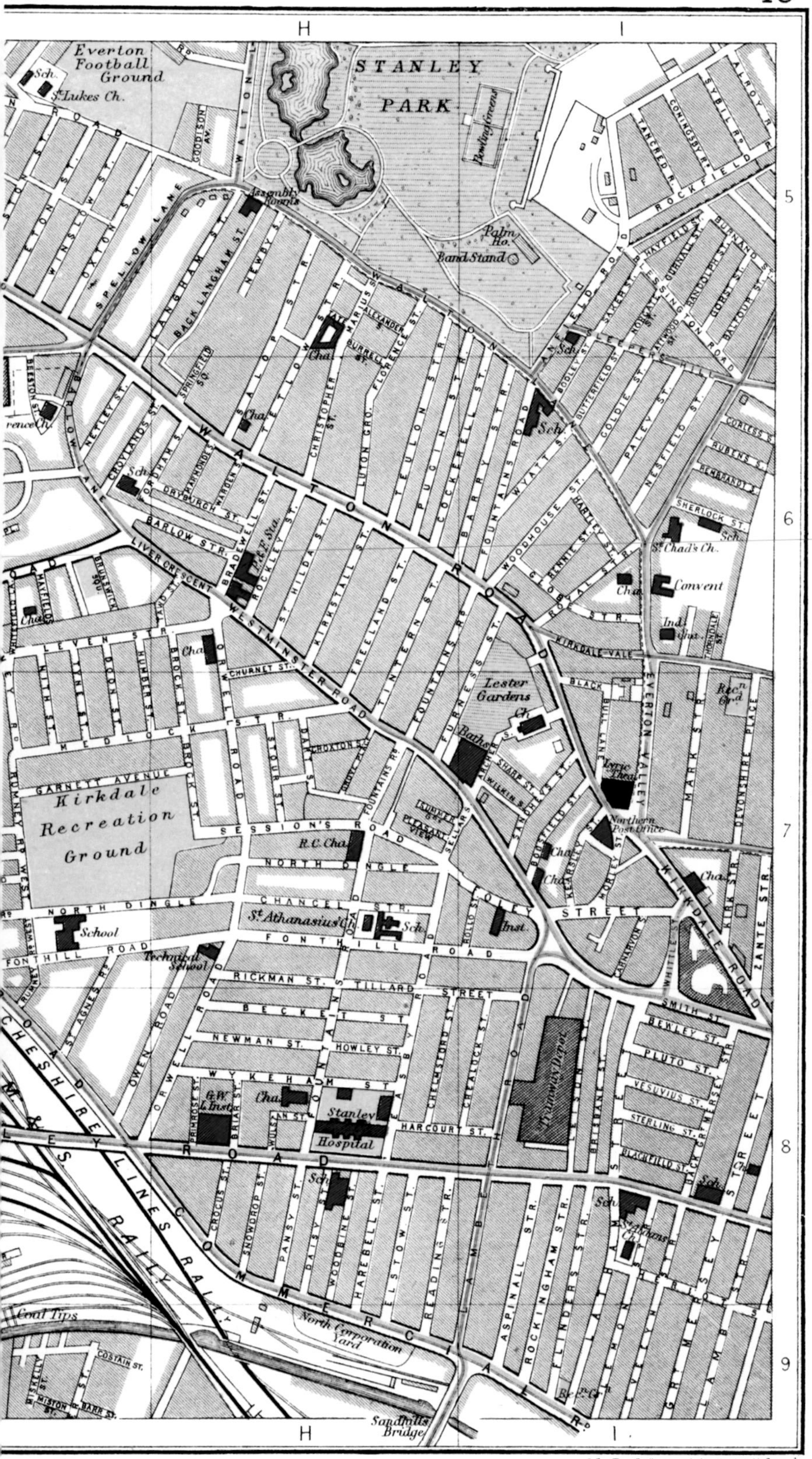
H
I
Everton Football Ground
St. Lukes Ch.
STANLEY PARK
Bowling Greens
Assembly Rooms
Palm Ho.
Band Stand
WALTON ROAD
SPELLOW LANE
LANGHAM ST.
BACK LANGHAM ST.
NEWBY ST.
GOODISON AV.
ANFIELD ROAD
ROCKFIELD RD.
LESSINGTON ROAD
WESTMINSTER ROAD
BARLOW LANE
BARLOW STR.
LIVER CRESCENT
Liv. & E. Sta.
ROCKLEY ST.
KIRKSTALL ST.
TREELAND ST.
TINTERN ST.
FOUNTAINS RD.
FURNESS ST.
Lester Gardens
Baths
KIRKDALE VALE
EVERTON VALLEY
Lyric Thea.
Northern Post Office
St. Chad's Ch.
Convent
Ind. Sch.
MARK STR.
DEVONSHIRE PLACE
LEVEN STR.
GARNETT AVENUE
Kirkdale Recreation Ground
SESSION'S ROAD
NORTH DINGLE
R.C. Cha.
St. Athanasius' Ch.
CHANCEL STR.
FONTHILL ROAD
School
Technical School
RICKMAN ST.
TILLARD STREET
BECKET ST.
NEWMAN ST.
HOWLEY ST.
WYKEHAM ST.
G.W. L. Inst.
Stanley Hospital
HARCOURT ST.
Tramway Depot
KIRKDALE ROAD
SMITH ST.
BEWLEY ST.
PLUTO ST.
VESUVIUS ST.
STERLING ST.
BLACKFIELD ST.
STANLEY ROAD
CHESHIRE LINES RAILY.
L. & Y. RAILY.
COMMERCIAL RD.
LAMBETH ROAD
ASPINALL STR.
ROCKINGHAM STR.
FLINDERS ST.
Coal Tips
North Corporation Yard
Sandhills Bridge
5
6
7
8
9

Continued on 20



*Tramway Routes shown thus*
*The Plan is divided into Quarter-mile Squares*

John Bartholomew & Son, Ltd. Edinburgh

Continued

Continued on 19

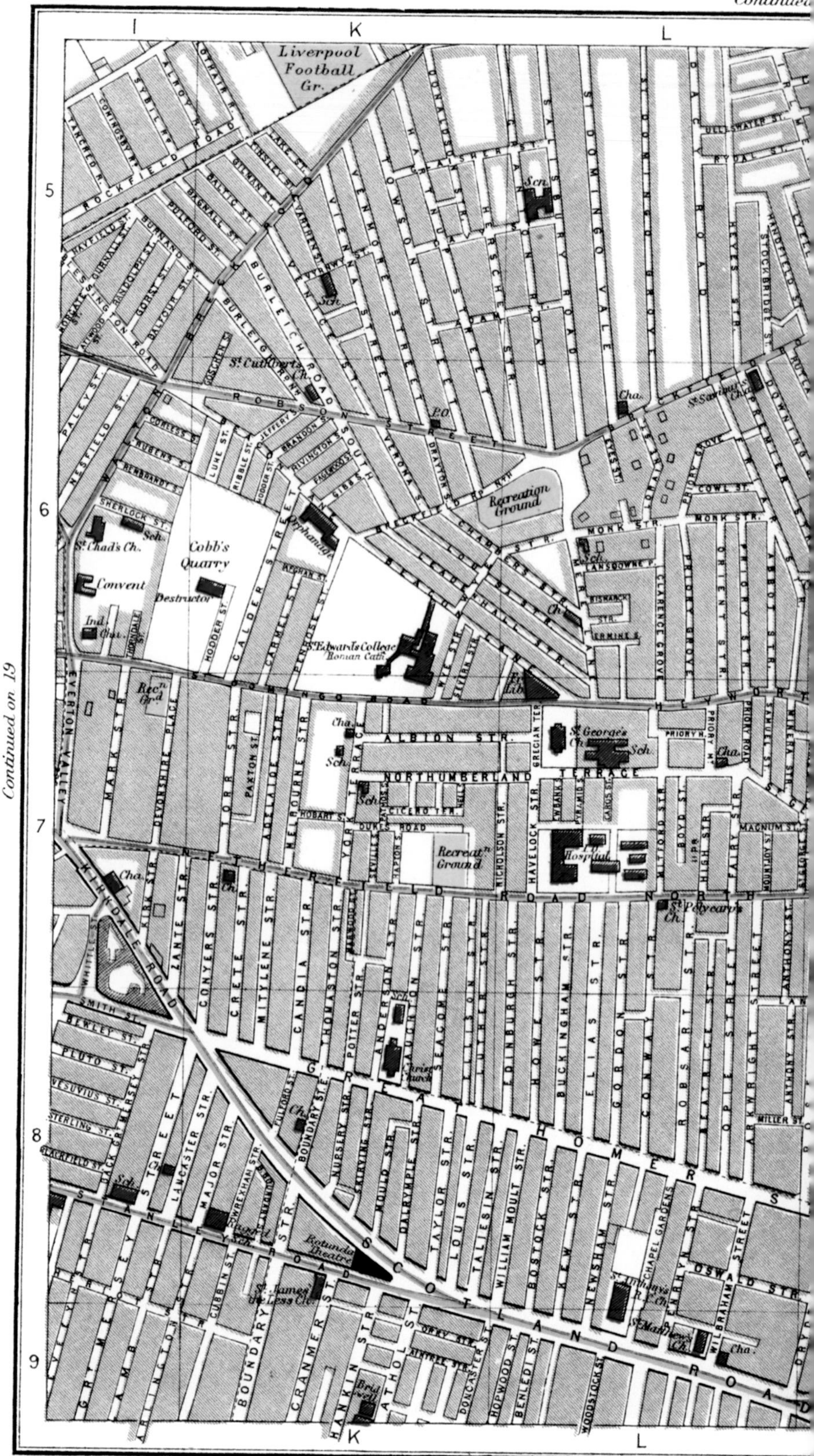
I
K
L
5
6
7
8
9
Liverpool Football Gr.
ROCKFIELD ROAD
BRECK ROAD
BURLEIGH ROAD
ROBSON STREET
St. Cuthbert's Ch.
Sch.
Cha.
St. Saviour's Ch.
DOMINGO VALE
Recreation Ground
MONK STR.
COWL ST.
St. Chad's Ch.
Convent
Cobb's Quarry
Destructor
Orphanage
St. Edward's College Roman Cath.
CALDER STREET
HODDER ST.
Ind. Cha.
EVERTON VALLEY
MARK STR.
DEVONSHIRE PLACE
DOMINGO ROAD
Recn Grd
ALBION STR.
NORTHUMBERLAND TERRACE
St. George's Ch.
Sch.
PRIORY RD.
Recreatn Ground
Hospital
NETHERFIELD ROAD NORTH
St. Polycarp's Ch.
KIRKDALE ROAD
ZANTE STR.
CONYERS STR.
CRETE STR.
MITYLENE STR.
CANDIA STR.
HOMASTON STR.
POTTER STR.
EDINBURGH STR.
BUCKINGHAM STR.
ELIAS STR.
GORDON STR.
ROBSART STR.
Christ Church
GREAT HOMER STR.
PLUTO ST.
VESUVIUS ST.
STERLING ST.
LANCASTER STR.
MAJOR STR.
BOUNDARY ST. E.
MOULD STR.
DALRYMPLE STR.
TAYLOR STR.
LOUIS STR.
TALIESIN STR.
WILLIAM MOULT STR.
BOSTOCK STR.
KEW STR.
NEWSHAM STR.
Rotunda Theatre
SCOTLAND ROAD
St. James the Less Ch.
St. Anthony's R.C. Ch.
St. Matthew's Ch.
OSWALD STR.
WILBRAHAM STREET
BOUNDARY STR.
CRANMER STR.
HANKIN STR.
ATHOL ST.
Brid well
DONCASTER ST.
HOPWOOD ST.
BENLEDI ST.
WOODSTOCK ST.
CUBBIN ST.
MILLER ST.
ANTHONY STR.
ARKWRIGHT STR.

Copyright

| | | | | | |
|---|---|---|---|---|---|
| 0 | 100 | 200 | 300 | 400 | 440 Yards |
| 0 | 100 | 200 | 300 | 400 Metres | |

Continued o

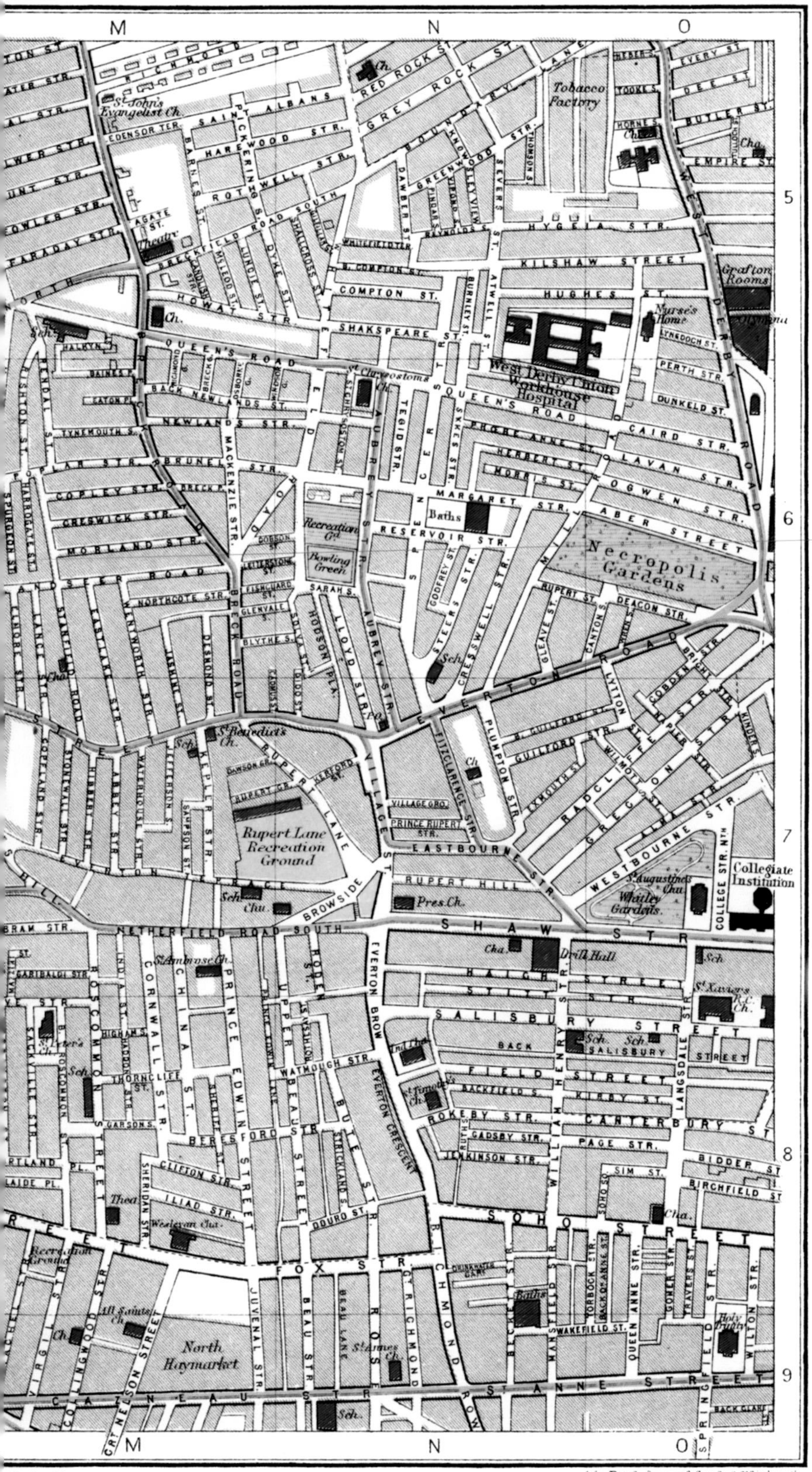
M
N
O
5
6
7
8
9
Tobacco Factory
St. John's Evangelist Ch.
Theatre
Grafton Rooms
Nurse's Home
West Derby Union Workhouse Hospital
Baths
Recreation Gd.
Bowling Green
Necropolis Gardens
Rupert Lane Recreation Ground
Collegiate Institution
St. Augustine's Chu.
Whitley Gardens
Drill Hall
St. Xavier's R.C. Ch.
Pres. Ch.
St. Ambrose Ch.
St. Benedict's Ch.
Wesleyan Chu.
North Haymarket
All Saints Ch.
Holy Trinity
SHAW STR.
NETHERFIELD ROAD SOUTH
EVERTON ROAD
WEST DERBY ROAD
BRECK ROAD
QUEEN'S ROAD
KILSHAW STREET
HUGHES ST.
COMPTON ST.
SHAKSPEARE ST.
HYGEIA STR.
SALISBURY STREET
SOHO STREET
ST. ANNE STREET
FOX STR.
WESTBOURNE STR.
EVERTON BROW
EVERTON CRESCENT
WILLIAM HENRY STR.
PRINCE EDWIN STREET
CORNWALL STR.
RICHMOND ROW
MISSOURI ROAD

Continued on 22

40 & 31

Tramway Routes shown thus

The Plan is divided into Quarter mile Squares

John Bartholomew & Son, Ltd. Edinburgh

22

Continued o

Continued on 21

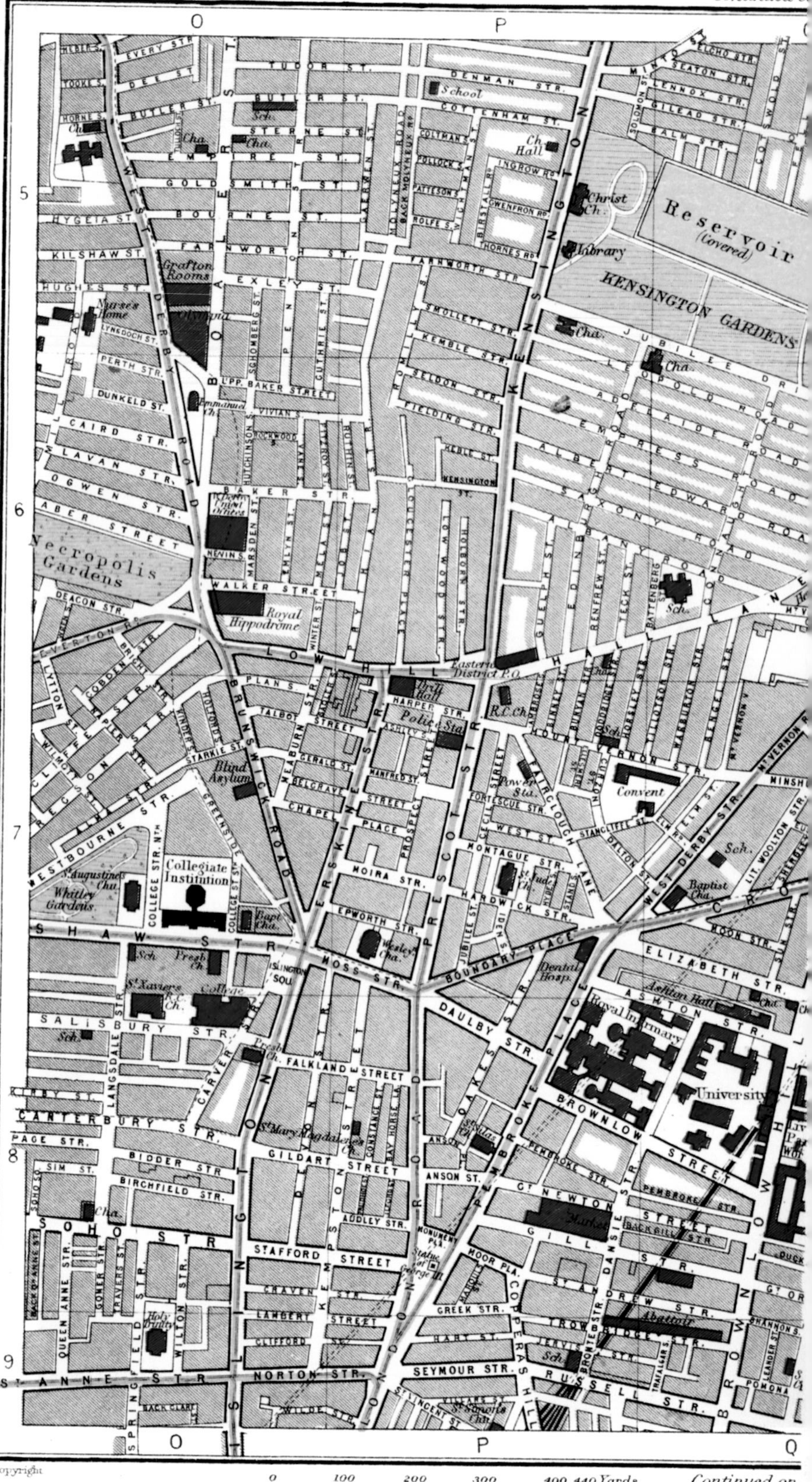
O
P
Q
5
6
7
8
9
West Derby Road
Kensington
Reservoir (Covered)
Kensington Gardens
Christ Ch.
Library
Grafton Rooms
Olympia
Nurse's Home
Necropolis Gardens
Royal Hippodrome
Low Hill
Eastern District P.O.
Brunswick Road
Erskine Str.
Prescot Str.
Blind Asylum
Police Sta.
Drill Hall
Convent
Collegiate Institution
St. Augustine's Chu.
Whitley Gardens
Shaw Str.
Moss Str.
Boundary Place
Dental Hosp.
Royal Infirmary
University
Ashton Hall
Elizabeth Str.
St. Xavier's R.C. Ch.
College
Salisbury Str.
Islington
Falkland Street
Canterbury Str.
St. Mary Magdalene's Ch.
Gildart Street
Pembroke Place
Daulby Str.
Brownlow Street
Market
Soho Str.
Stafford Street
London Road
Statue of George III
Abattoir
Trowbridge Str.
Seymour Str.
Russell Str.
Norton Str.
St. Anne Str.
Copperas Hill
St. Simon's Chu.
Holy Trinity
Tudor St.
Denman Str.
Cottenham St.
Goldsmith St.
Bourne St.
Farnworth St.
Kilshaw St.
Hygeia St.
Exley St.
Baker Str.
Walker Street
Westbourne Str.
Epworth Str.
Moira Str.
Montague Str.
Hardwick Str.
Fairclough Lane
Mount Vernon Str.
Wesley Cha.
Baptist Cha.
Craven Str.
Lambert Street
Clifford
Greek Str.
Hart St.
Birchfield Str.
Bidder Str.
Page Str.
Kirby St.
Queen Anne Str.
Gill Str.
St. Andrew Str.
Dansie Str.
Anson St.

Copyright

0 100 200 300 400 440 Yards
0 100 200 300 400 Metres

Continued on

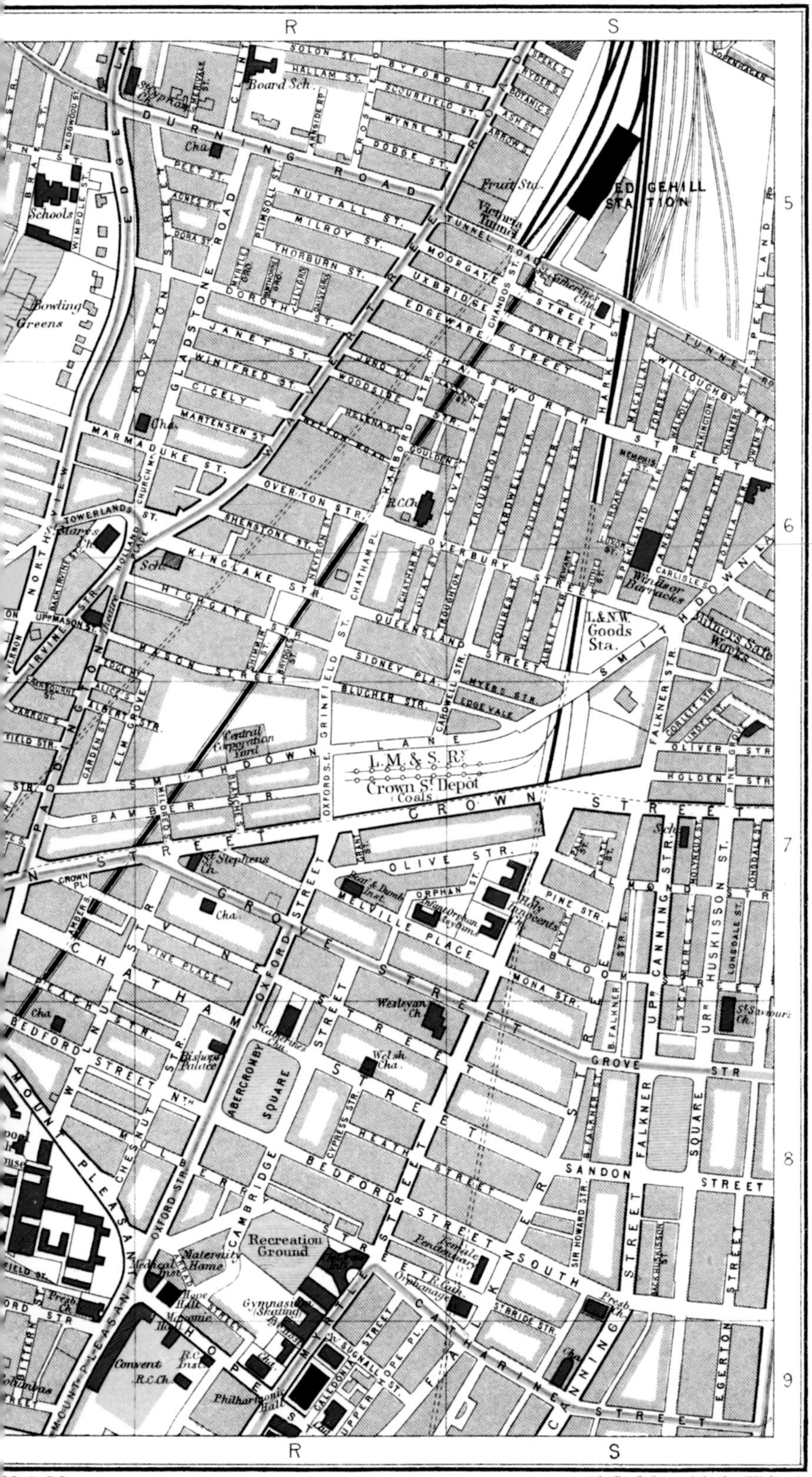
R
S
5
6
7
8
9
SOLON ST.
HALLAM ST.
BYFORD ST.
SCOURFIELD ST.
WYNNE ST.
DODGE ST.
Board Sch.
DURNING ROAD
EDGE LANE
PEET ST.
AGNES ST.
DORA ST.
Schools
WIMPOLE ST.
Bowling Greens
NUTTALL ST.
MILROY ST.
THORBURN ST.
PLIMSOLL ST.
DOROTHY ST.
JANET ST.
WINIFRED ST.
CICELY ST.
MARTENSEN ST.
MARMADUKE ST.
GLADSTONE ROAD
ROYSTON STREET
Fruit Sta.
Victoria Tunnel
EDGEHILL STATION
TUNNEL ROAD
MOORGATE ST.
UXBRIDGE ST.
EDGEWARE STREET
CHANDOS ST.
St. Catherines Ch.
CHATSWORTH STREET
WILLOUGHBY ST.
SPEKELAND RD.
MACAULAY ST.
WOODSIDE ST.
HELENA ST.
OVERTON STR.
SHENSTONE ST.
KINGLAKE STR.
HIGHGATE ST.
MASON STREET
R.C.Ch.
OVERBURY STREET
QUEENSLAND STREET
SIDNEY PLA.
BLUCHER STR.
MYERS STR.
EDGE VALE
CHATHAM PL.
Windsor Barracks
CARLISLE ST.
L.&N.W. Goods Sta.
SMITHDOWN LANE
Milners Safe Works
FALKNER STR.
OLIVER STR.
HOLDEN STR.
TOWERLANDS ST.
St. Marys Ch.
IRVINE STR.
PADDINGTON
GRINFIELD ST.
Central Corporation Yard
SMITHDOWN LANE
L.M.&S. Ry.
Crown St. Depot
Coals
CROWN STREET
BAMBER STR.
St. Stephens Ch.
OLIVE STR.
Deaf & Dumb Inst.
Infant Orphan Asylums
MELVILLE PLACE
PINE STR.
Holy Innocents Ch.
GROVE STREET
CHATHAM STREET
VINE PLACE
BEDFORD STREET
WALNUT STR.
Bishops Palace
ABERCROMBY SQUARE
OXFORD STREET
Wesleyan Ch.
Welsh Cha.
MONA STR.
UPR. CANNING STR.
HUSKISSON ST.
St. Saviours Ch.
GROVE STR.
FALKNER SQUARE
SANDON STREET
BEDFORD STREET
HEATH ST.
CYPRESS ST.
CAMBRIDGE ST.
Recreation Ground
Maternity Home
Medical Inst.
Gymnasium (Skating)
Female Penitentiary
Orphanage
NSOUTH
SIR HOWARD STR.
CANNING STREET
ST. BRIDE STR.
Presb. Ch.
EGERTON ST.
CATHARINE ST.
MOUNT PLEASANT
Convent
R.C.Ch.
Philharmonic Hall
SIGNALL ST.
HOPE PL.
CALEDONIA STREET
HOPE STREET
MYRTLE ST.

Continued on 24

32 & 33

*Tramway Routes shown thus*
*The Plan is divided into Quarter-mile Squares*

John Bartholomew & Son Ltd. Edinburgh

Continued o

Continued on 23

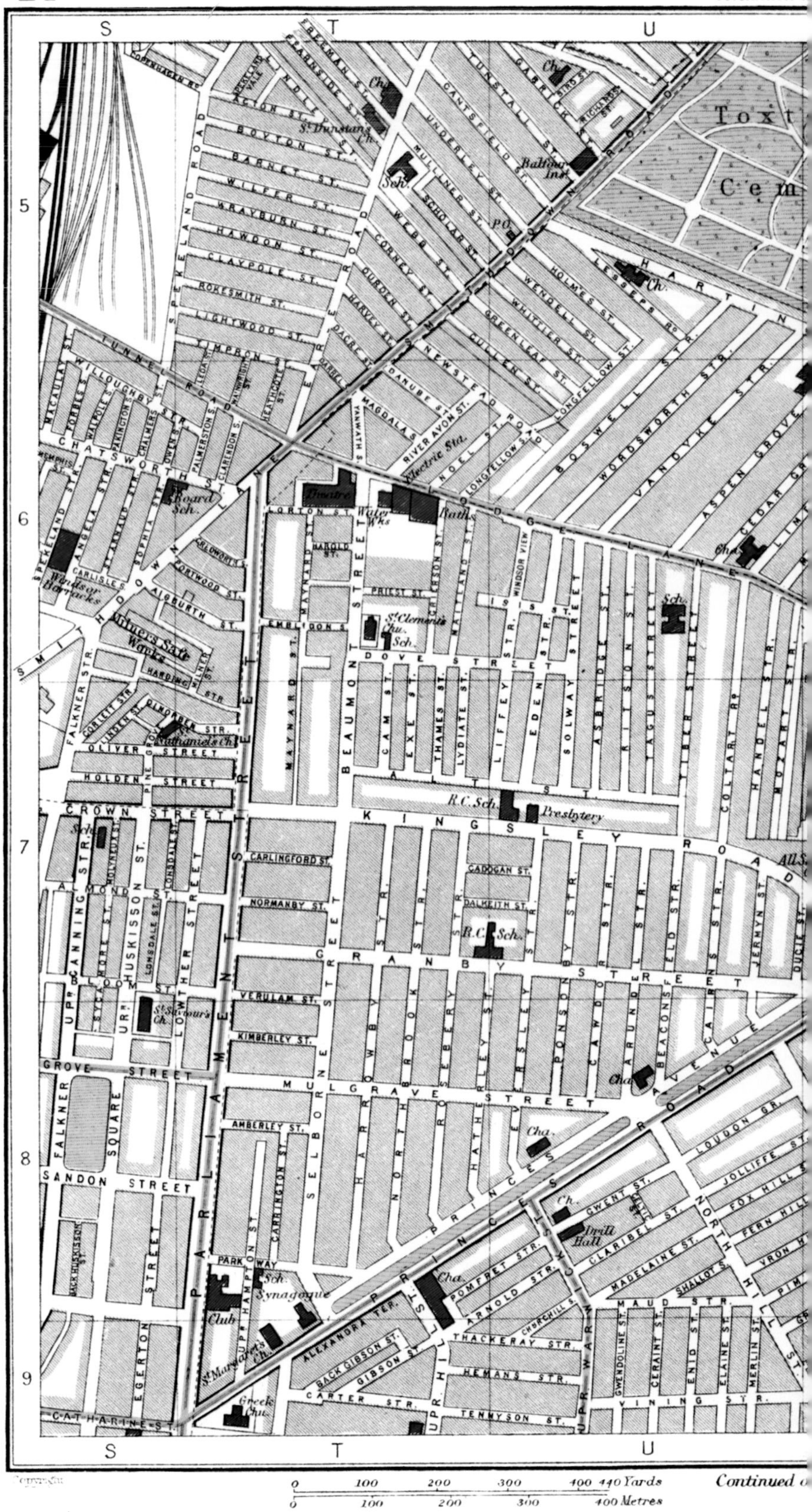
S
T
U
5
6
7
8
9
Toxt
Cem
TUNNEL ROAD
SMITHDOWN ROAD
SMITHDOWN LANE
SPEKELAND ROAD
ACTON ST.
BOYTON ST.
BARNET ST.
WILFER ST.
KRAYBURN ST.
HAWDON ST.
CLAYPOLE ST.
ROKESMITH ST.
LIGHTWOOD ST.
St. Dunstan's Ch.
Sch.
Ch.
Balfour Inst.
P.O.
MULLINER ST.
SCHOLAR ST.
WEBB ST.
CORNEY ST.
DURDEN ST.
HARVEY ST.
DACRE ST.
NEWSTEAD
DANUBE ST.
MAGDALA ST.
RIVER AVON ST.
Electric Sta.
NOEL ST.
LONGFELLOW ST.
HOLMES ST.
WENDELL ST.
WHITTIER ST.
GREENLEAF ST.
LESSEPS RD.
HARTINGTON
BOSWELL
WORDSWORTH STR.
VANDYKE STR.
ASPEN GROVE
CEDAR
EDGE LANE
MACAULAY
WILLOUGHBY STR.
CHATSWORTH ST.
Board Sch.
Theatre
Water Wks.
Baths
LORTON ST.
HAROLD ST.
PRIEST ST.
St. Clement's Chu.
Sch.
EMBLEDON S.
DOVE STREET
WINDSOR VIEW
Windsor Barracks
Millers Safe Works
AIGBURTH ST.
HARDING ST.
FALKNER STR.
St. Nathaniel's Ch.
OLIVER STREET
HOLDEN STREET
CROWN STREET
MAYNARD ST.
BEAUMONT STREET
CAM ST.
EXE ST.
THAMES ST.
LYDIATE ST.
LIFFEY STR.
EDEN ST.
SOLWAY STR.
ASBRIDGE ST.
TAGUS STREET
TIBER STREET
COLTART RD.
HANDEL STR.
MOZART STR.
R.C. Sch.
Presbytery
KINGSLEY ROAD
All S.
Sch.
CANNING STR.
HUSKISSON ST.
LOWTHER ST.
ALMOND ST.
CARLINGFORD ST.
NORMANBY ST.
CADOGAN ST.
DALKEITH ST.
R.C. Sch.
GRANBY STREET
JERMYN ST.
DUCIE ST.
BLOOM ST.
St. Saviour's Ch.
VERULAM ST.
KIMBERLEY ST.
PARLIAMENT STREET
SELBORNE STREET
GROVE STREET
MULGRAVE STREET
AVENUE
Cha.
FALKNER SQUARE
AMBERLEY ST.
SANDON STREET
CARRINGTON ST.
SELBORNE ST.
HARROWBY ST.
NORTHBROOK ST.
PRINCES ROAD
Cha.
Ch.
GWENT ST.
Drill Hall
CLARIBEL ST.
MADELAINE ST.
LOUDON GR.
JOLLIFFE ST.
FOX HILL
FERN HILL
VRON HILL
NORTH HILL ST.
SHALLOT ST.
BACK HUSKISSON ST.
PARK WAY
Sch.
Synagogue
Club
St. Margaret's Ch.
ALEXANDRA TER.
BACK GIBSON ST.
GIBSON ST.
POMFRET STR.
ARNOLD STR.
THACKERAY STR.
HEMANS STR.
TENNYSON ST.
CARTER STR.
Greek Chu.
EGERTON
CATHARINE ST.
UPPER HILL ST.
UPPER WARWICK
MAUD STR.
GWENDOLINE ST.
GERAINT ST.
ENID ST.
ELAINE ST.
MERLIN ST.
VINING STR.
0 100 200 300 400 440 Yards
0 100 200 300 400 Metres

Continued o

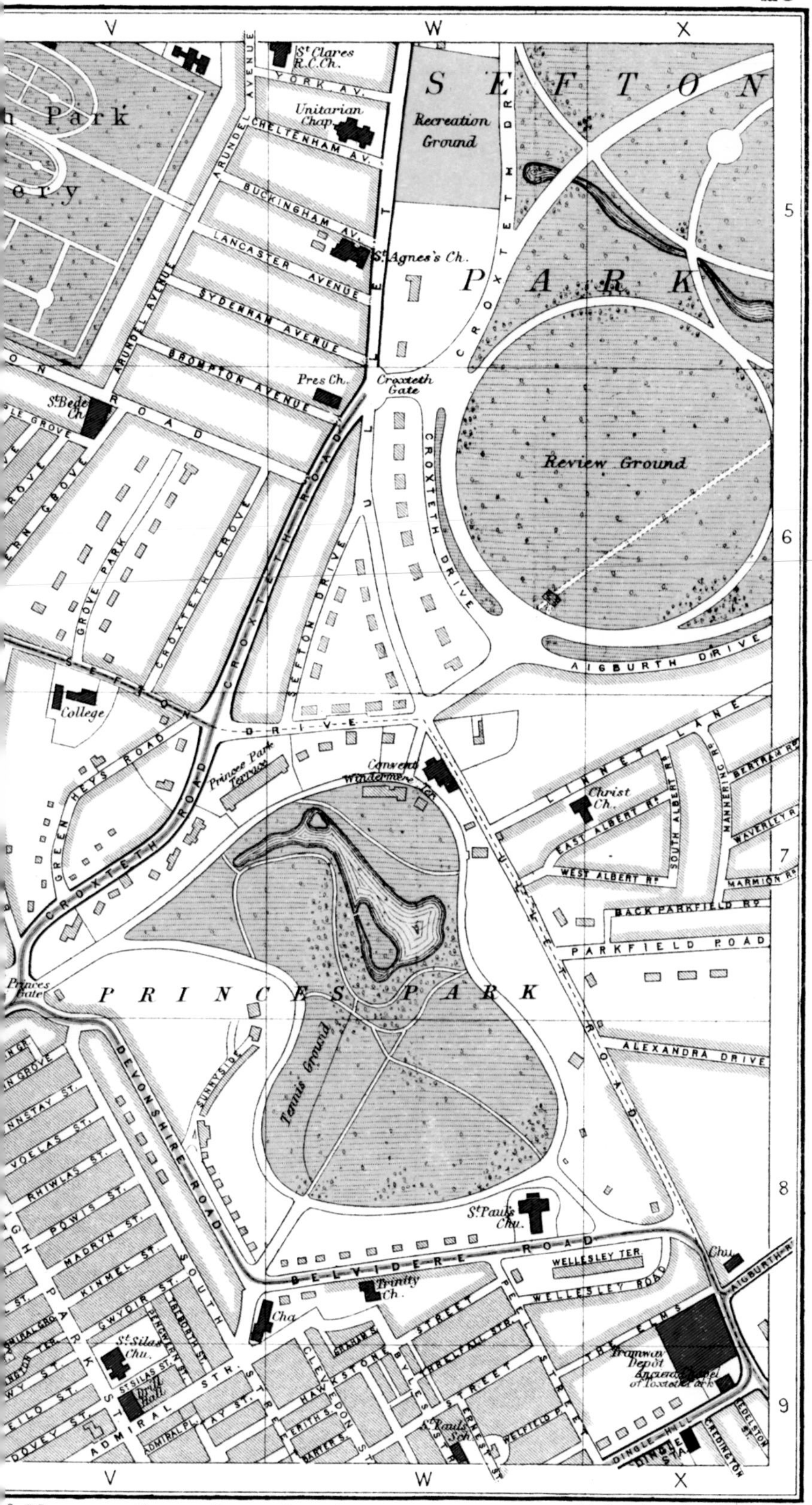
V
W
X
St Clares R.C.Ch.
YORK AV.
Unitarian Chap.
CHELTENHAM AV.
BUCKINGHAM AV.
LANCASTER AVENUE
SYDENHAM AVENUE
BROMPTON AVENUE
ARUNDEL AVENUE
St Agnes's Ch.
Pres Ch.
S E F T O N
P A R K
Recreation Ground
CROXTETH DR.
Croxteth Gate
CROXTETH DRIVE
Review Ground
AIGBURTH DRIVE
St Bedes Ch.
GROVE PARK
CROXTETH GROVE
CROXTETH ROAD
SEFTON DRIVE
College
GREEN HEYS ROAD
Princes Park Terrace
Convent
Windermere Ter.
LINNET LANE
Christ Ch.
EAST ALBERT RD
SOUTH ALBERT RD
WEST ALBERT RD
MANNERING RD
BERTRAM RD
WAVERLEY RD
MARMION RD
BACK PARKFIELD RD
PARKFIELD ROAD
Princes Gate
P R I N C E S P A R K
ALEXANDRA DRIVE
Tennis Ground
SUNNYSIDE
DEVONSHIRE ROAD
St Paul's Chu.
BELVIDERE ROAD
WELLESLEY TER.
WELLESLEY ROAD
Trinity Ch.
Cha.
Chu.
AIGBURTH RD
THE ELMS
Tramway Depot
Ancient Chapel of Toxteth Park
DINGLE HILL
DINGLE STA.
CREDINGTON ST.
KEDLESTON ST.
HAWKSTONE ST.
CLEVEDON ST.
BYLES ST.
PEEL STREET
St Silas Chu.
ST SILAS ST.
ADMIRAL ST.
ADMIRAL PL.
PARK ST.
POWIS ST.
MADRYN ST.
KINMEL ST.
GWYDIR ST.
RHIWLAS ST.
VOELAS ST.
St Pauls Sch.
5
6
7
8
9



*Tramway Routes shown thus*

*The Plan is divided into Quarter-mile Squares*

John Bartholomew & Son, Ltd. Edinburgh

Continued

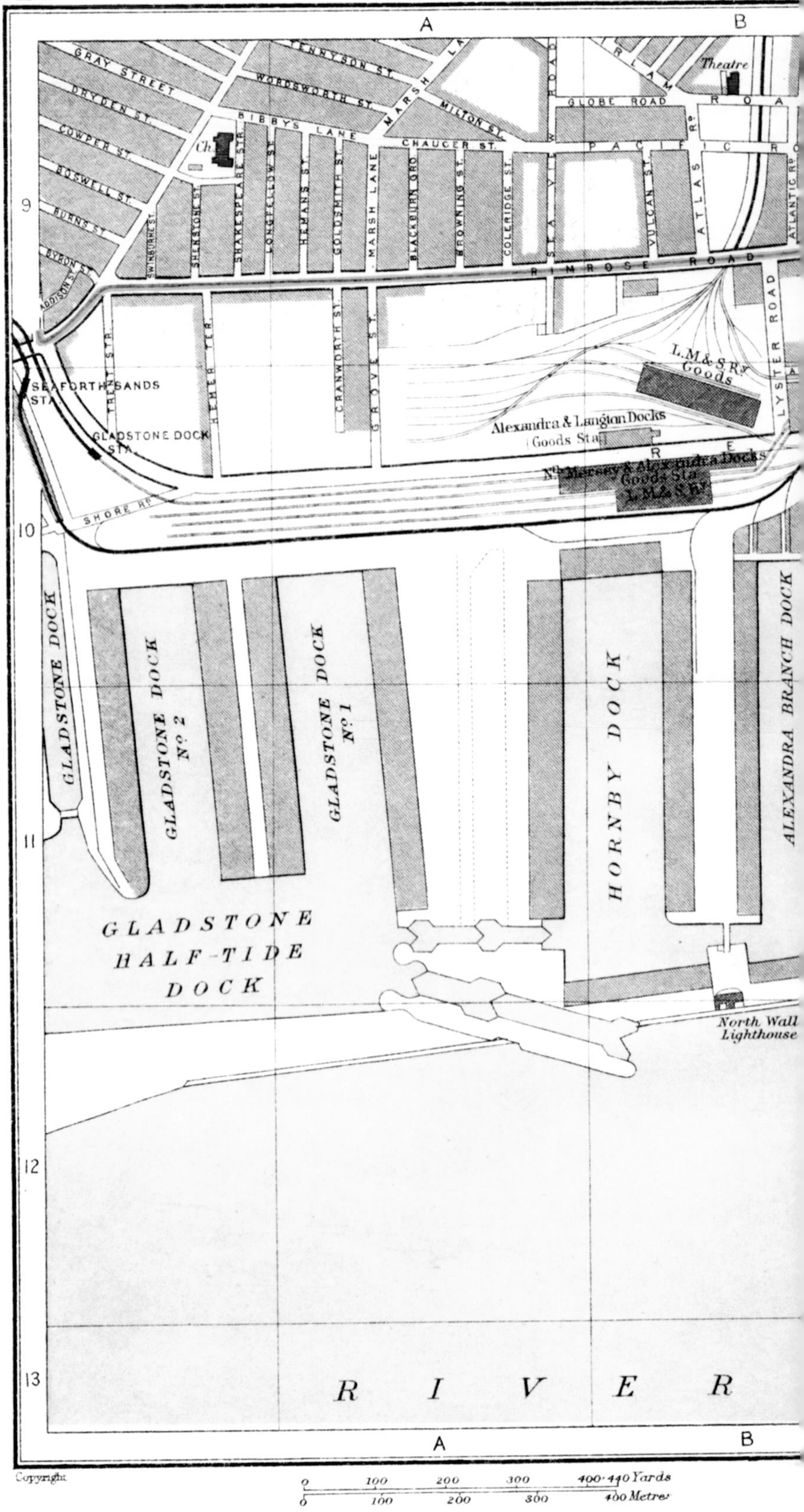
A
B
9
10
11
12
13
GRAY STREET
DRYDEN ST.
COWPER ST.
BOSWELL ST.
BURNS ST.
BYRON ST.
ADDISON ST.
TENNYSON ST.
WORDSWORTH ST.
BIBBYS LANE
MARSH LANE
MILTON ST.
CHAUCER ST.
GLOBE ROAD
Theatre
PACIFIC ROAD
ATLANTIC RD.
ATLAS
VULCAN ST.
COLERIDGE ST.
BROWNING ST.
BLACKBURN GRO.
GOLDSMITH ST.
HEMANS ST.
LONGFELLOW ST.
SHAKESPEARE STR.
SHENSTONE ST.
SWINBURNE ST.
Ch.
RIMROSE ROAD
LYSTER ROAD
TRENT STR.
HEMER TER.
CRANWORTH ST.
GROVE ST.
SEAFORTH SANDS STA.
GLADSTONE DOCK STA.
L.M.& S.Ry. Goods
Alexandra & Langton Docks (Goods Sta.)
Nth. Mersey & Alexandra Docks Goods Sta. L.M.& S.Ry.
SHORE RD.
GLADSTONE DOCK
GLADSTONE DOCK No. 2
GLADSTONE DOCK No. 1
HORNBY DOCK
ALEXANDRA BRANCH DOCK
GLADSTONE HALF-TIDE DOCK
North Wall Lighthouse
RIVER
Copyright
0 100 200 300 400 440 Yards
0 100 200 300 400 Metres

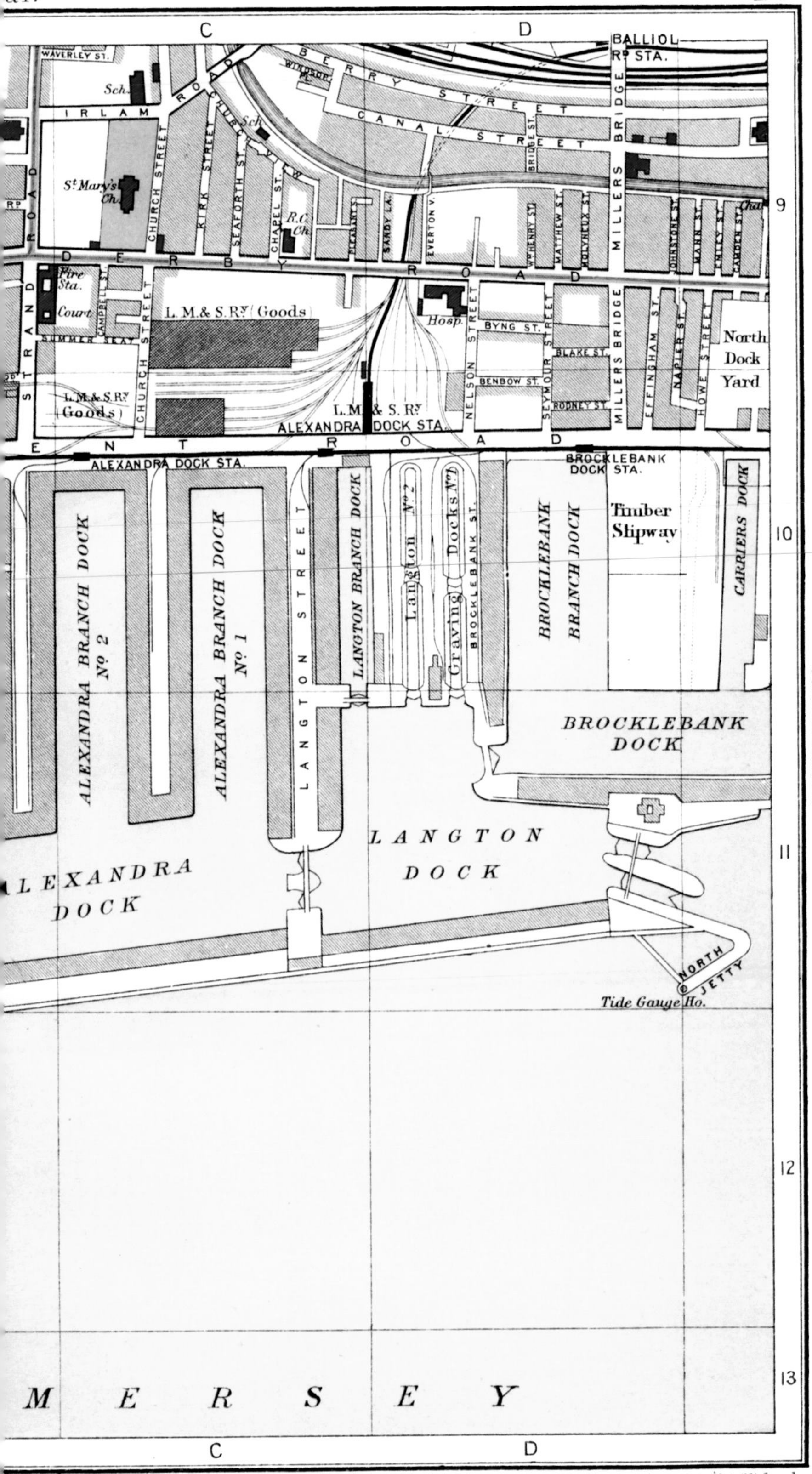
C
D
BALLIOL Rd STA.
WAVERLEY ST.
Sch.
IRLAM
ROAD
BERRY STREET
CANAL STREET
St Mary's Ch.
CHURCH STREET
KIRK STREET
SEAFORTH ST.
CHAPEL ST.
R.C. Ch.
SANDY LA.
EVERTON V.
W. HENRY ST.
MATHEW ST.
MOLYNEUX ST.
MILLERS BRIDGE
JOHNSTONE ST.
MANN ST.
CAMDEN ST.
Chap.
9
DERBY ROAD
Fire Sta.
Court
CAMPBELL ST.
SUMMER SEAT
STRAND ROAD
L. M.& S. Ry (Goods)
L. M.& S. Ry (Goods)
Hosp.
NELSON STREET
BYNG ST.
SEYMOUR STREET
BLAKE ST.
BENBOW ST.
RODNEY ST.
EFFINGHAM ST.
NAPIER ST.
HOWE STREET
North Dock Yard
L. M. & S. Ry ALEXANDRA DOCK STA.
REGENT ROAD
ALEXANDRA DOCK STA.
BROCKLEBANK DOCK STA.
Timber Slipway
CARRIERS DOCK
10
ALEXANDRA BRANCH DOCK No 2
ALEXANDRA BRANCH DOCK No 1
LANGTON STREET
LANGTON BRANCH DOCK
Langton No 2
Graving Docks No 1
BROCKLEBANK ST.
BROCKLEBANK BRANCH DOCK
BROCKLEBANK DOCK
11
LANGTON DOCK
ALEXANDRA DOCK
NORTH JETTY
Tide Gauge Ho.
12
13
MERSEY
C
D

Continued on 28

Tramway Routes shown thus
The Plan is divided into Quarter-mile Squares

John Bartholomew & Son Ltd Edinburgh

Continued

Continued on 27

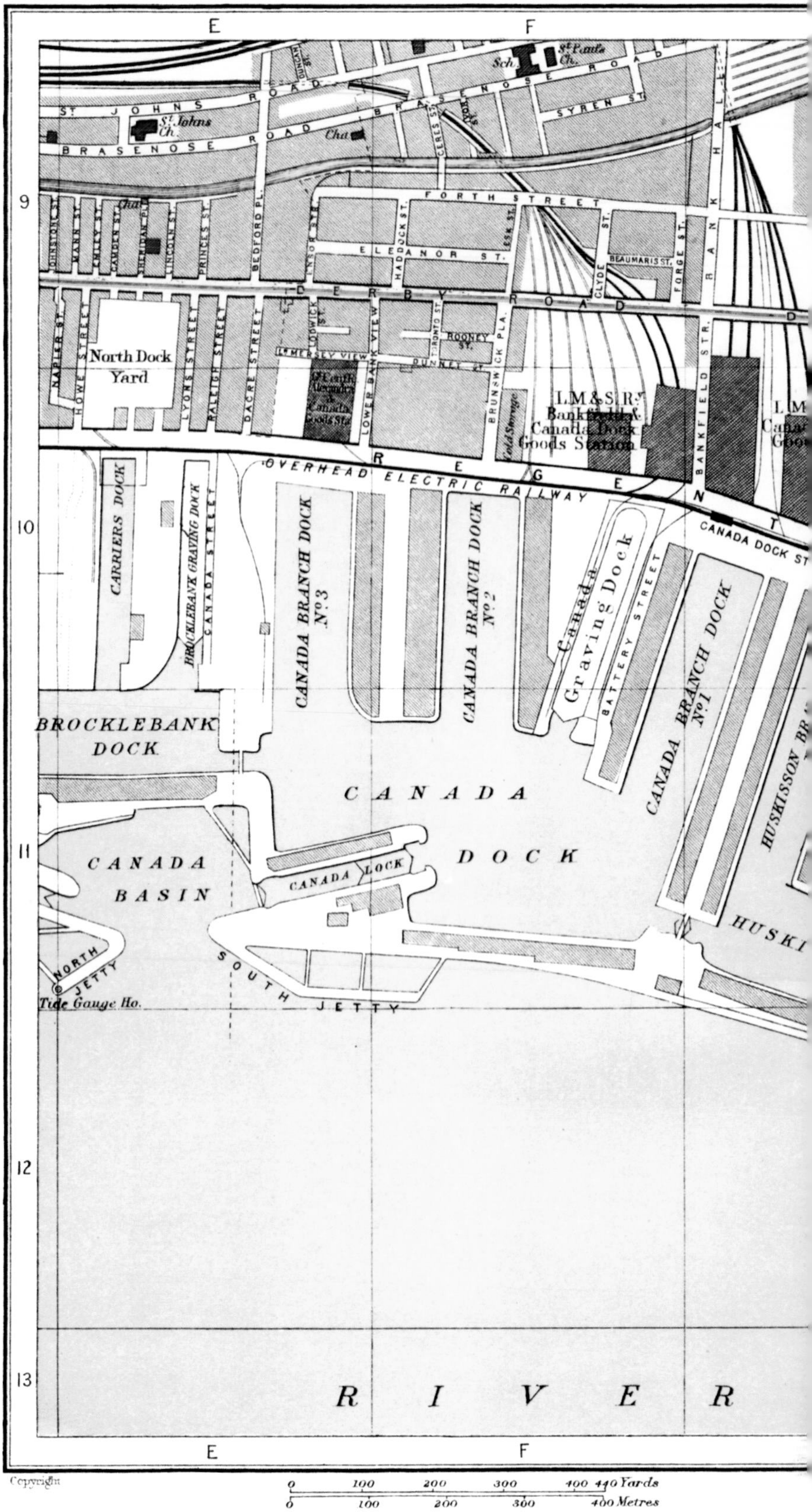
E
F
9
10
11
12
13
ST JOHNS ROAD
St Johns Ch.
BRASENOSE ROAD
Chat
Sch.
St Pauls Ch.
SYREN ST.
CERES ST.
FORTH STREET
JOHNSON ST.
MANN ST.
EMILY ST.
CAMDEN ST.
SHERIDAN PL.
LINCOLN ST.
PRINCES ST.
BEDFORD PL.
ELEANOR ST.
HADDOCK ST.
ESK ST.
CLYDE ST.
BEAUMARIS ST.
FORGE ST.
DERBY ROAD
NAPIER ST.
HOWE STREET
North Dock Yard
LYONS STREET
RALEIGH STREET
DACRE STREET
BOSWICK ST.
MERSEY VIEW
LOWER BANK VIEW
TORONTO ST.
ROONEY ST.
DUNNEY ST.
BRUNSWICK PLA.
BANKFIELD STR.
BANK HALL
L.M.&S.Ry. Bankfield & Canada Dock Goods Station
Cold Storage
REGENT
OVERHEAD ELECTRIC RAILWAY
CANADA DOCK ST.
CARRIERS DOCK
BROCKLEBANK GRAVING DOCK
CANADA STREET
CANADA BRANCH DOCK No.3
CANADA BRANCH DOCK No.2
Canada Graving Dock
BATTERY STREET
CANADA BRANCH DOCK No.1
HUSKISSON BR
BROCKLEBANK DOCK
CANADA DOCK
CANADA BASIN
CANADA LOCK
NORTH JETTY
Tide Gauge Ho.
SOUTH JETTY
HUSKI
R I V E R
Copyright
0 100 200 300 400 440 Yards
0 100 200 300 400 Metres

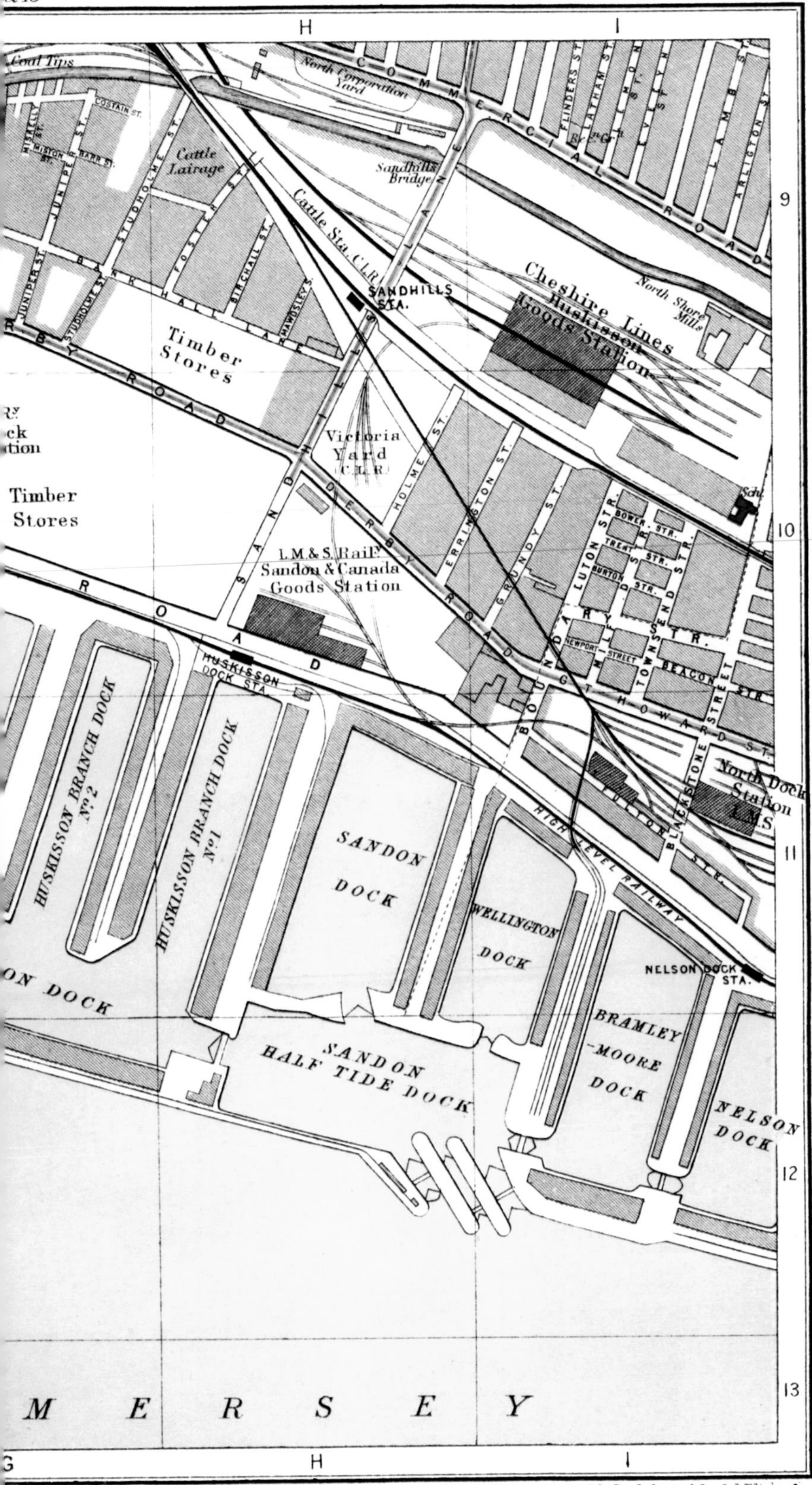
H
I
Coal Tips
North Corporation Yard
COMMERCIAL ROAD
FLINDERS ST.
LATHAM ST.
LAMB ST.
ARLIGTON ST.
COSTAIN ST.
Cattle Lairage
Sandhills Bridge
Cattle Sta. C.L.R.
SANDHILLS STA.
Cheshire Lines Huskisson Goods Station
North Shore Mills
Timber Stores
Victoria Yard (C.L.R.)
HOLME ST.
ERRINGTON ST.
GRUNDY ST.
BOWER STR.
TRENT STR.
BURTON STR.
LUTON STR.
DERBY ROAD
SANDHILLS LANE
L.M.&S. Railʸ Sandon & Canada Goods Station
HUSKISSON DOCK STA.
BOUNDARY STR.
NEWPORT STREET
TOWNSEND STR.
BEACON STR.
HOWARD ST.
BLACKSTONE STREET
North Dock Station L.M.S.
FULTON STR.
HIGH LEVEL RAILWAY
HUSKISSON BRANCH DOCK Nº2
HUSKISSON BRANCH DOCK Nº1
SANDON DOCK
WELLINGTON DOCK
NELSON DOCK STA.
BRAMLEY-MOORE DOCK
NELSON DOCK
SANDON HALF TIDE DOCK
Timber Stores
9
10
11
12
13
MERSEY
G
H
I

Continued on 30

Tramway Routes shown thus
The Plan is divided into Quarter-mile Squares

John Bartholomew & Son, Ltd. Edinburgh

Continued

Continued on 29

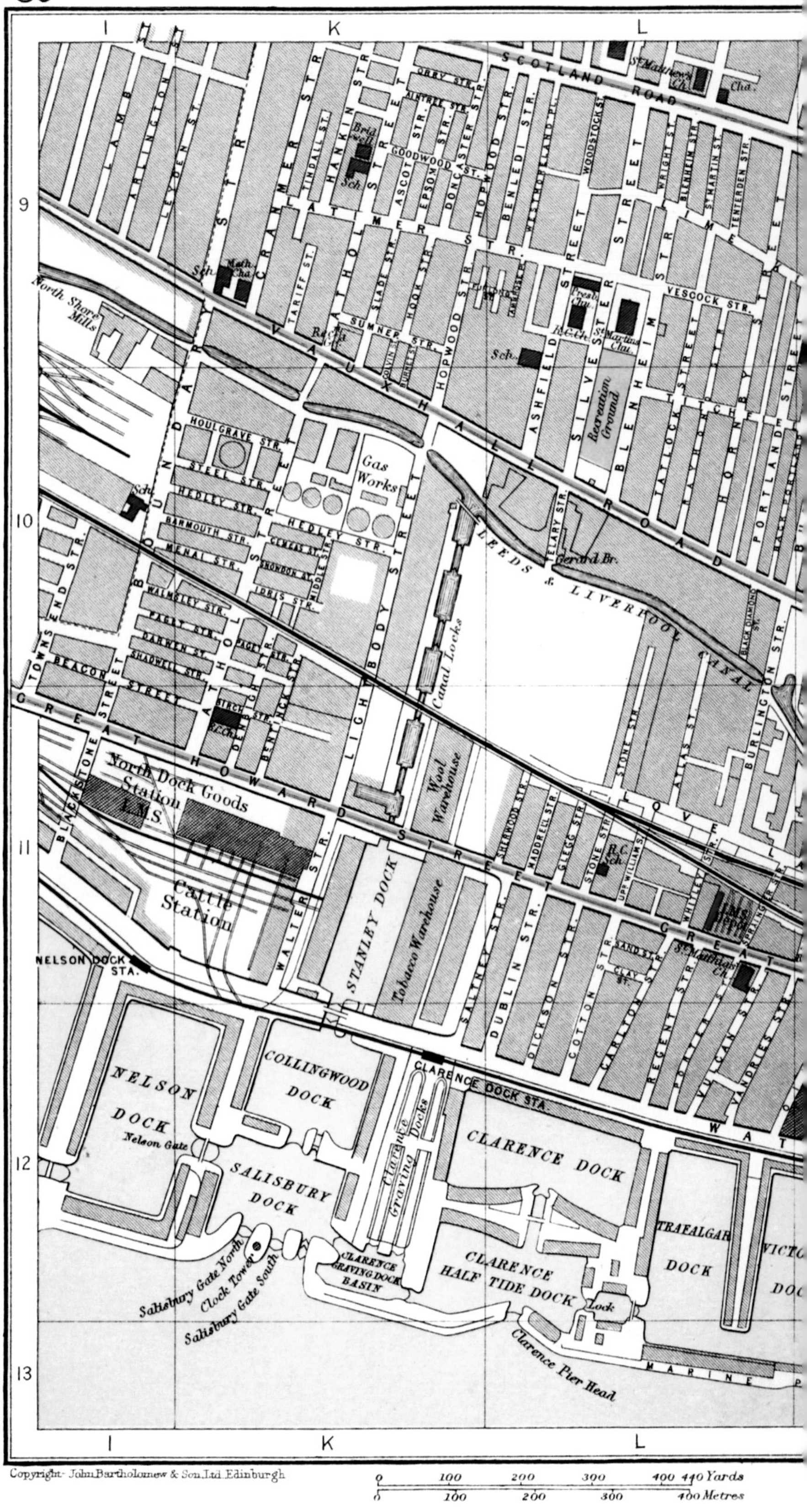
I
K
L
9
10
11
12
13
SCOTLAND ROAD
VAUXHALL ROAD
GREAT HOWARD STREET
LEEDS & LIVERPOOL CANAL
Canal Locks
Gas Works
North Shore Mills
North Dock Goods Station L.M.S.
Cattle Station
NELSON DOCK STA.
CLARENCE DOCK STA.
STANLEY DOCK
Tobacco Warehouse
Wool Warehouse
Recreation Ground
NELSON DOCK
Nelson Gate
COLLINGWOOD DOCK
SALISBURY DOCK
Salisbury Gate North
Clock Tower
Salisbury Gate South
Clarence Graving Docks
CLARENCE GRAVING DOCK BASIN
CLARENCE DOCK
CLARENCE HALF TIDE DOCK
Lock
Clarence Pier Head
TRAFALGAR DOCK
LAMB
ARLINGTON
LEYDEN ST.
CRANMER STR.
TINDALL ST.
HANKIN STR.
GOODWOOD ST.
ASCOT STR.
EPSOM ST.
DONCASTER STR.
HOPWOOD STR.
BENLEDI STR.
WOODSTOCK ST.
SUMNER STR.
HOULGRAVE STR.
STEEL STR.
HEDLEY STR.
BARMOUTH STR.
MENAI STR.
SNOWDON ST.
IDRIS STR.
WALMSLEY STR.
PAGET STR.
DARWEN ST.
SHADWELL STR.
BEACON STREET
TOWNSEND STR.
BLACKSTONE STREET
BOUNDARY STR.
LIGHTBODY STREET
WALTER STR.
SALTNEY STR.
DUBLIN STR.
DICKSON STR.
COTTON STR.
SHERWOOD STR.
MADDRELL STR.
GLEGG STR.
STONE STR.
VESCOCK STR.
ASHFIELD STREET
SILVESTER STREET
BLENHEIM STREET
PORTLANDE STREET
BURLINGTON STR.
HORNBY STREET
REGENT
WATERLOO
VANDRIES STR.
Gerard Br.
Sch.
Chu.
R.C. Ch.
L.M.S. Depot
MARINE
Copyright - John Bartholomew & Son Ltd. Edinburgh
0 100 200 300 400 440 Yards
0 100 200 300 400 Metres

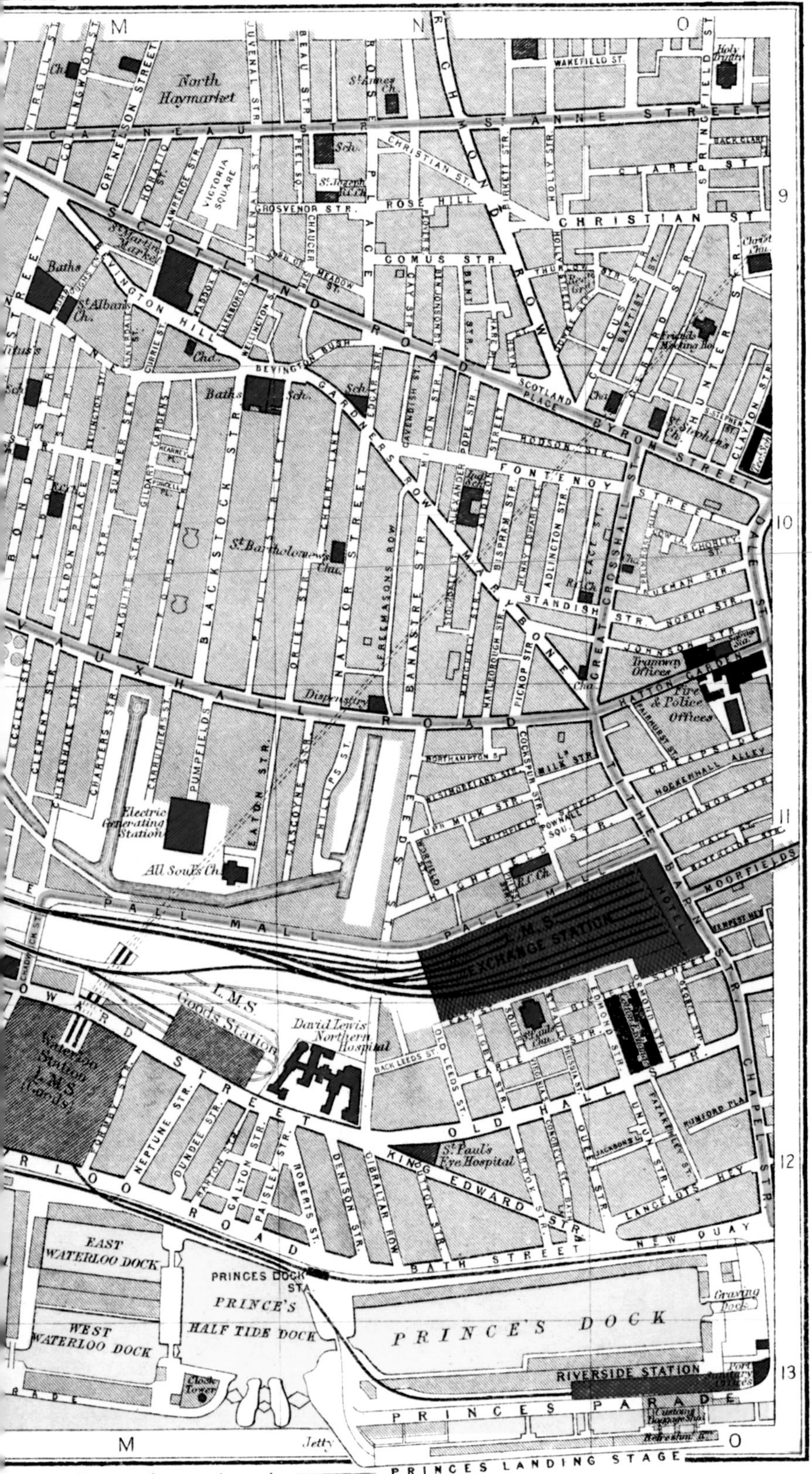
M
N
O
North Haymarket
St. Annes Ch.
WAKEFIELD ST.
Holy Trinity
ST. ANNE STREET
CAZNEAU STR.
VICTORIA SQUARE
CHRISTIAN ST.
ROSE HILL
CHRISTIAN ST.
GROSVENOR STR.
COMUS STR.
St. Martins Market
Baths
St. Albans Ch.
BEVINGTON HILL
SCOTLAND ROAD
SCOTLAND PLACE
BYROM STREET
Friends Meeting Ho.
St. Stephens Ch.
HUNTER STR.
GARDNERS ROW
HODSON STR.
FONTENOY STR.
St. Bartholomews Chu.
BLACKSTOCK STR.
NAYLOR STREET
FREEMASONS ROW
BANASTRE STR.
STANDISH STR.
GREAT CROSSHALL ST.
NORTH STR.
JOHNSON STR.
Tramway Offices
Fire & Police Offices
HATTON GARDEN
DALE ST.
VAUXHALL ROAD
Dispensary
PUMPFIELDS
EATON STR.
Electric Generating Station
All Souls Ch.
NORTHAMPTON ST.
MILK STR.
HOCKENHALL ALLEY
TITHEBARN STR.
MOORFIELDS
PALL MALL
L.M.S. EXCHANGE STATION
HOTEL
L.M.S. Goods Station
David Lewis Northern Hospital
Waterloo Station L.M.S. (Goods)
GREAT HOWARD STREET
OLD HALL STR.
St. Pauls Eye Hospital
KING EDWARD STR.
CHAPEL STR.
LANCELOTS HEY
NEW QUAY
WATERLOO ROAD
BATH STREET
EAST WATERLOO DOCK
WEST WATERLOO DOCK
PRINCES DOCK STA.
PRINCE'S HALF TIDE DOCK
PRINCE'S DOCK
Graving Dock
RIVERSIDE STATION
Clock Tower
PRINCES PARADE
Jetty
PRINCES LANDING STAGE
9
10
11
12
13

Tramway Routes shown thus

The Plan is divided into Quarter mile Squares

Continued on 32

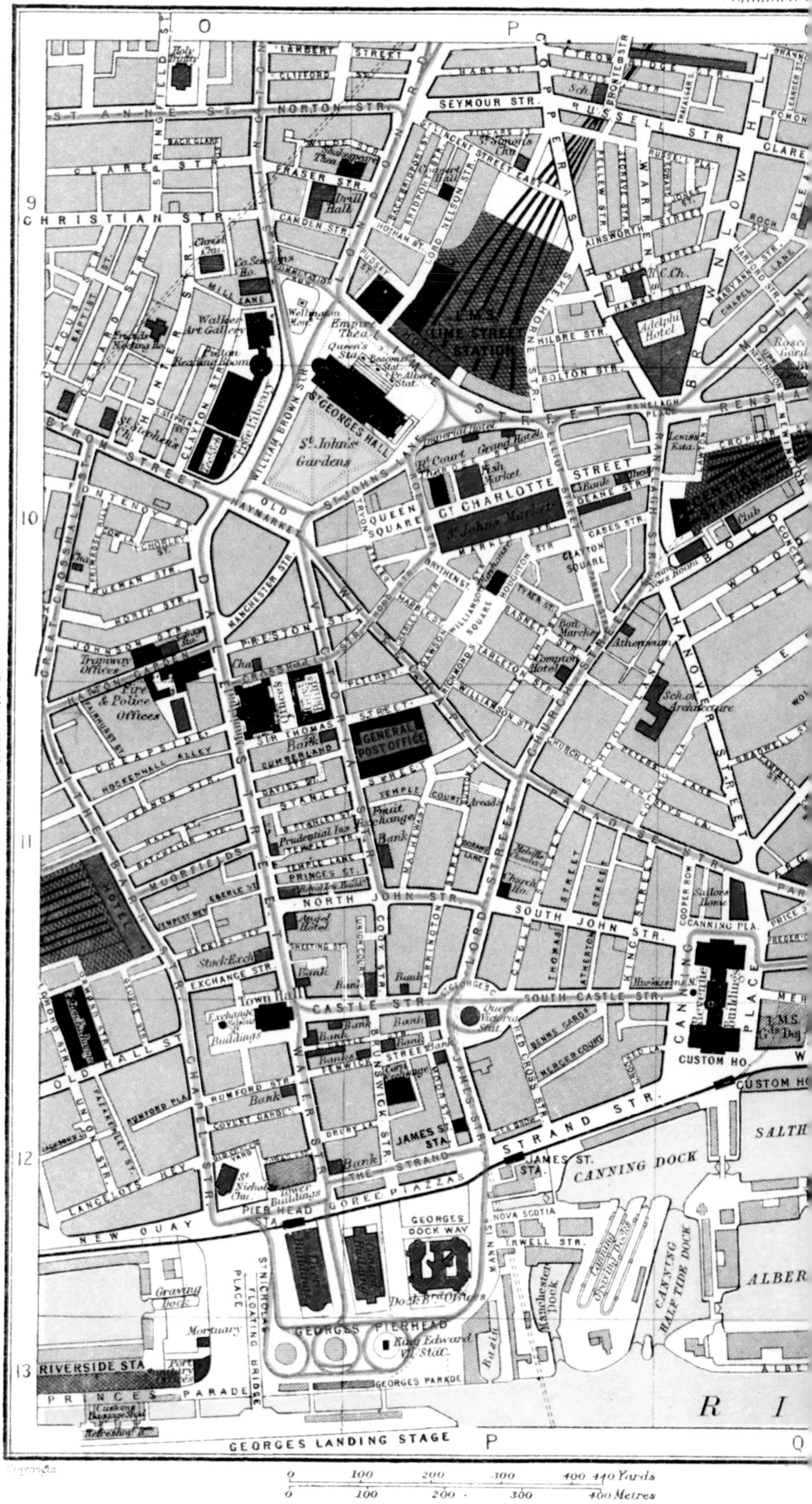
O
P
Q
9
10
11
12
13
ST. ANNE ST.
NORTON STR.
SEYMOUR STR.
RUSSELL STR.
CLARE STR.
CHRISTIAN STR.
LAMBERT STREET
CLIFFORD
HART ST.
FRASER STR.
CAMDEN STR.
Drill Hall
Shakespeare Thea.
Holy Trinity
Christ Chu.
Co. Sessions Ho.
MILL LANE
Wellington Mont.
Walker Art Gallery
Picton Reading Room
Free Library
Museum
Empire Theat.
Queen's Stat.
Lord Nelson St.
LIME STREET STATION
HILBRE STR.
BOLTON STR.
Adelphi Hotel
AINSWORTH ST.
BROWNLOW HILL
RENSHAW
RANELAGH PLACE
CIRCUS ST.
BAPTIST ST.
HUNTER STR.
CLAYTON STR.
ST. Stephen's Ch.
BYRON STREET
WILLIAM BROWN STR.
ST. GEORGES HALL
St. John's Gardens
OLD HAYMARKET
ST. JOHNS LANE
FONTENOY ST.
GREAT CROSSHALL ST.
QUEEN SQUARE
GT. CHARLOTTE ST.
St. John's Market
Fish Market
Imperial Hotel
Grand Hotel
STREET
CLAYTON SQUARE
HOUGHTON
WILLIAMSON SQUARE
Bon Marche
Athenaeum
Compton Hotel
MANCHESTER STR.
PRESTON ST.
VICTORIA
DALE STREET
Tramway Offices
Fire & Police Offices
Municipal Offices
STR. THOMAS
CUMBERLAND
Bank
GENERAL POST OFFICE
HOCKENHALL ALLEY
STANLEY ST.
Fruit Exchange
Prudential Ins.
PRINCES ST.
Royal Ins. Bldgs.
NORTH JOHN STR.
SOUTH JOHN STR.
MOORFIELDS
TEMPLE
LORD STREET
CHURCH STREET
School of Architecture
HANOVER STREET
PARADISE STR.
School
Sailors Home
CANNING PLA.
Angel Hotel
Stock Exch.
EXCHANGE STR.
Town Hall
Exchange Buildings
CASTLE STR.
SOUTH CASTLE STR.
Queen Victoria Stat.
Revenue Buildings
CUSTOM HO.
CANNING PLACE
L.M.S. Gds. Dep.
TITHEBARN
HOTEL
OLD HALL STR.
UNION STR.
RUMFORD PLA.
RUMFORD STR.
COVENT GARDEN
WATER STR.
BRUNSWICK STR.
JAMES ST. STA.
JAMES STR.
REDCROSS STR.
STRAND STR.
THE STRAND
JAMES ST. STA.
CANNING DOCK
SALTH
Tower Buildings
St. Nicholas Chu.
LANCELOTS HEY
NEW QUAY
GOREE PIAZZAS
PIER HEAD
GEORGES DOCK WAY
Dock Bd. Offices
NOVA SCOTIA
IRWELL STR.
Manchester Dock
Canning Graving Docks
CANNING HALF TIDE DOCK
ALBERT
Graving Dock
Mortuary
ST. NICHOLAS PLACE
FLOATING BRIDGE
GEORGES PIERHEAD
King Edward VII Stat.
GEORGES PARADE
RIVERSIDE STA.
PRINCES PARADE
GEORGES LANDING STAGE
R I
0 100 200 300 400 440 Yards
0 100 200 300 400 Metres

Continued on 31

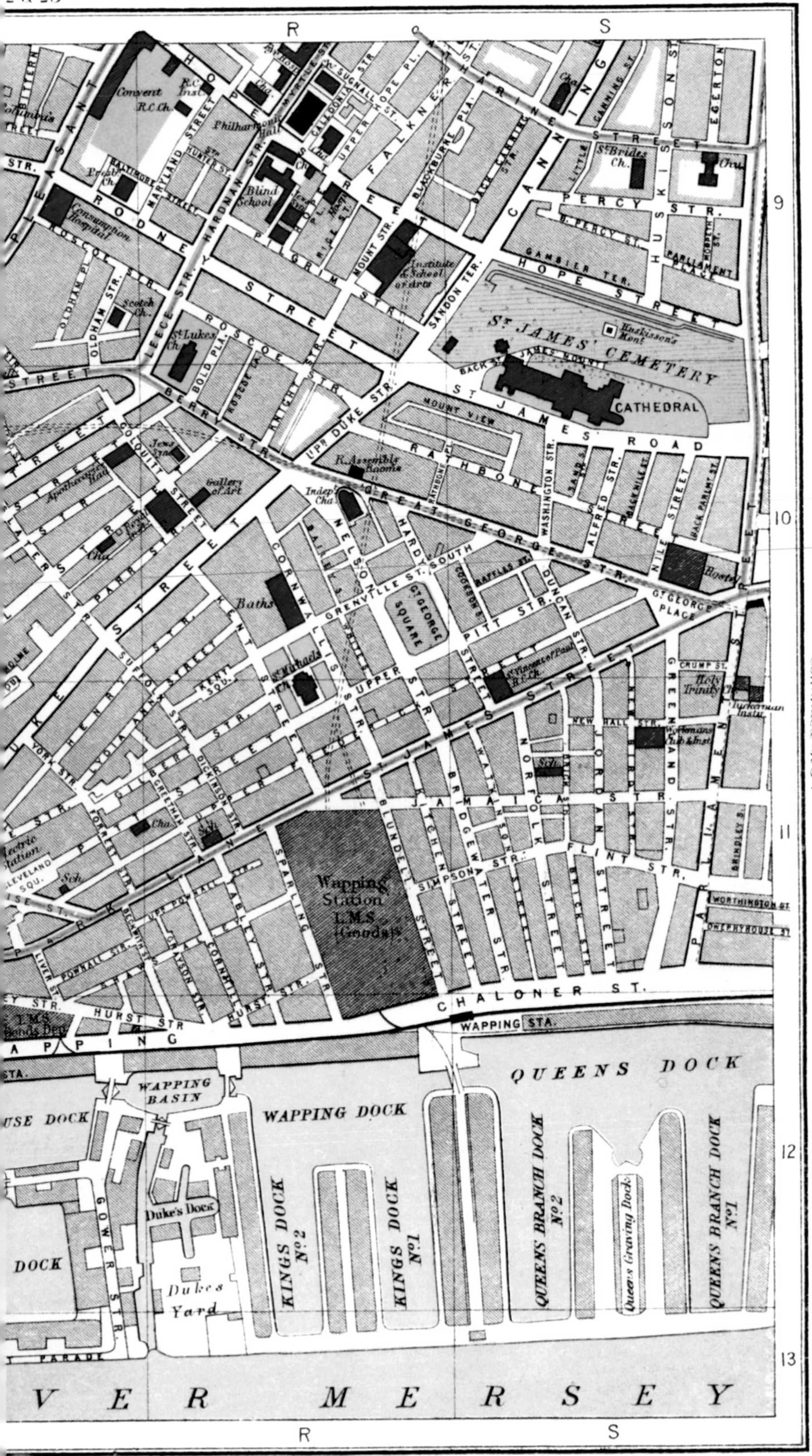
R
S
9
10
11
12
13
Convent R.C.Ch.
Philharmonic Hall
Blind School
Consumption Hospital
RODNEY STREET
HOPE STREET
PILGRIM STR.
MOUNT STR.
Institute & School of Arts
FALKNER ST.
CANNING ST.
HUSKISSON ST.
EGERTON ST.
St Brides Ch.
PERCY STR.
HOPE STREET
GAMBIER TER.
PARLIAMENT PLACE
SANDON TER.
St JAMES' CEMETERY
Huskisson's Mont
CATHEDRAL
ST JAMES' ROAD
MOUNT VIEW
RATHBONE ST.
UPR DUKE STR.
LEECE STR.
St Lukes Ch.
ROSCOE STR.
BOLD PLA.
BERRY STR.
COLQUITT STREET
Gallery of Art
R. Assembly Rooms
Indep't Cha.
GREAT GEORGE STR.
NELSON ST.
HARDY ST.
WASHINGTON STR.
ALFRED STR.
NILE STREET
Hostel
GRENVILLE ST. SOUTH
Gt GEORGE SQUARE
PITT STR.
DUNCAN STR.
Gt GEORGE PLACE
Baths
CORNWALLIS STREET
St Michaels Ch.
UPPER STR.
ST JAMES STREET
St Vincent of Paul R.C.Ch.
GREENLAND STR.
CRUMP ST.
Holy Trinity Ch.
NEW HALL STR.
Workmans Club & Inst.
NORFOLK STR.
JAMAICA STR.
FLINT STR.
BRINDLEY S.
WORTHINGTON ST.
DUKE STREET
PARR STREET
SUFFOLK STREET
KENT SQU.
YORK STR.
DICKINSON STR.
GREETHAM ST.
Cha.
Sch.
LANE
SPARLING STR.
Wapping Station L.M.S. (Goods)
BUNDELL STREET
KITCHEN STREET
BRIDGEWATER STR.
SIMPSON STR.
BRICK STREET
JORDAN STREET
PARK LANE
POWNALL STR.
HURST STR.
CORNHILL
CHALONER ST.
WAPPING STA.
WAPPING
QUEENS DOCK
WAPPING BASIN
WAPPING DOCK
Duke's Dock
Dukes Yard
GOWER STR.
DOCK
KINGS DOCK No2
KINGS DOCK No1
QUEENS BRANCH DOCK No2
Queens Graving Dock
QUEENS BRANCH DOCK No1
PARADE
VER MERSEY

Continued on 34

Tramway Routes shown thus

The Plan is divided into Quarter mile Squares

2A

John Bartholomew & Son Ltd. Edinburgh

Continued on

Continued on 33

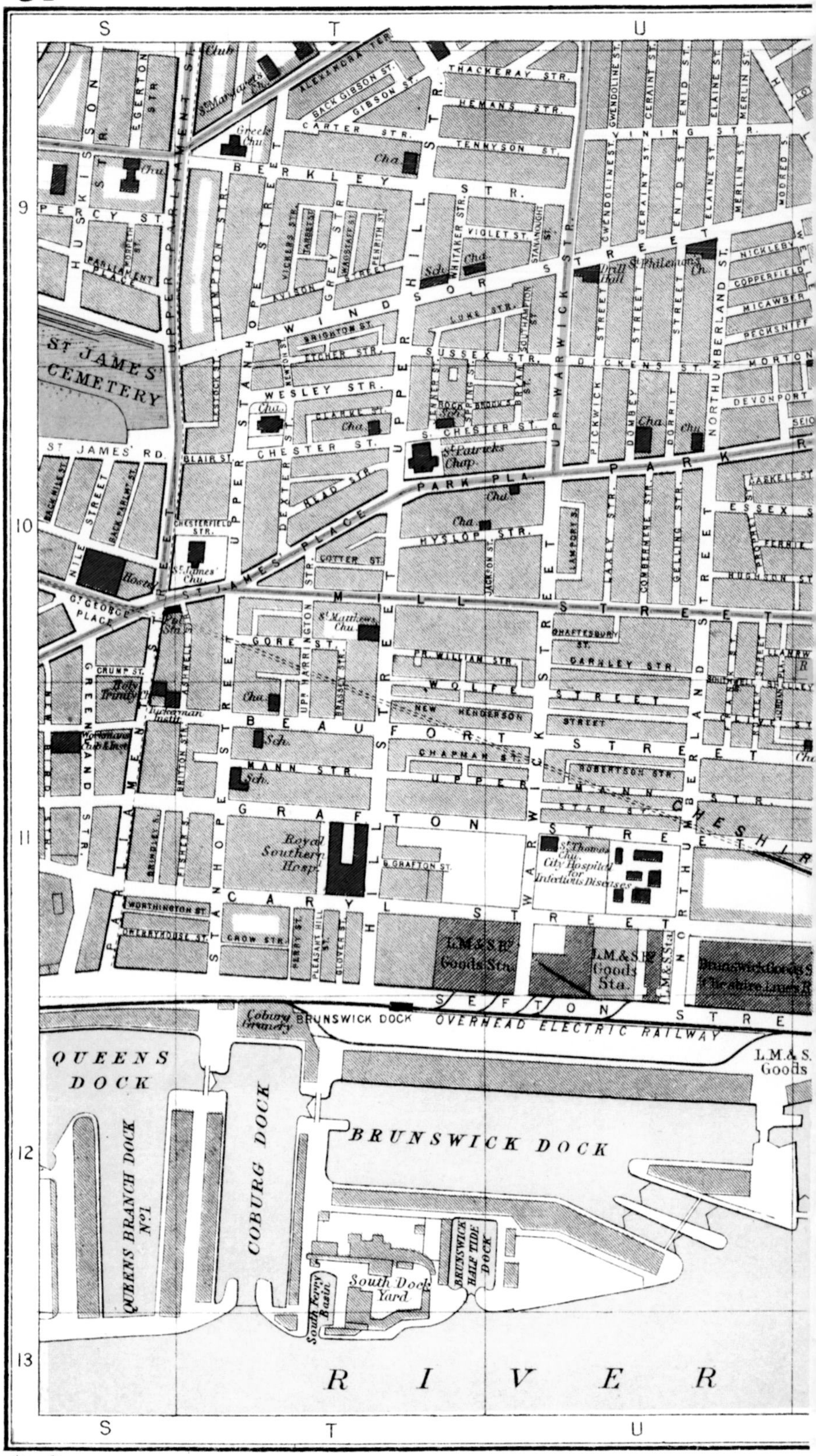
S
T
U
9
10
11
12
13
ST JAMES' CEMETERY
ST JAMES' RD.
UPPER PARLIAMENT ST.
BERKLEY ST.
PERCY ST.
HUSKISSON ST.
EGERTON ST.
PARLIAMENT PLACE
HAMPTON ST.
UPPER STANHOPE STREET
WINDSOR STREET
UPPER HILL ST.
UPR. WARWICK ST.
NORTHUMBERLAND ST.
THACKERAY STR.
HEMANS STR.
TENNYSON ST.
VINING ST.
CARTER STR.
GIBSON ST.
BACK GIBSON ST.
ALEXANDRA TER.
WHITAKER STR.
VIOLET ST.
LUKE STR.
SUSSEX STR.
DICKENS ST.
PICKWICK
DOMBEY
DORRIT
NICKLEBY
COPPERFIELD
MICAWBER
PECKSNIFF
MORTON
DEVONPORT
BRIGHTON ST.
WESLEY STR.
CHESTER ST.
S. CHESTER ST.
St. Patricks Chap.
PARK PLA.
PARK RD.
ESSEX ST.
HYSLOP STR.
COTTER ST.
ST JAMES' PLACE
St. James' Chu.
MILL STREET
CHESTERFIELD STR.
BLAIR ST.
NILE STREET
Hostel
St. GEORGE PLACE
CRUMP ST.
GREENLAND ST.
Holy Trinity Chu.
St. Matthews Chu.
GORE ST.
UPR. HARRINGTON
PR. WILLIAM STR.
WOLFE STREET
NEW HENDERSON STREET
SHAFTESBURY ST.
CARNLEY STR.
BEAUFORT STREET
CHAPMAN ST.
ROBERTSON STR.
MANN STR.
GRAFTON STREET
Royal Southern Hosp.
S. GRAFTON ST.
St. Thomas Chu.
City Hospital for Infectious Diseases
CARYL STREET
WORTHINGTON ST.
CROW STR.
L.M.&S.Ry. Goods Sta.
SEFTON STREET
CHESHIRE
Coburg Granary
BRUNSWICK DOCK
OVERHEAD ELECTRIC RAILWAY
QUEENS DOCK
QUEENS BRANCH DOCK No. 1
COBURG DOCK
BRUNSWICK DOCK
South Dock Yard
BRUNSWICK HALF TIDE DOCK
South Ferry Basin
L.M.&S. Goods
RIVER



0 100 200 300 400 440 Yards
0 100 200 300 400 Metres

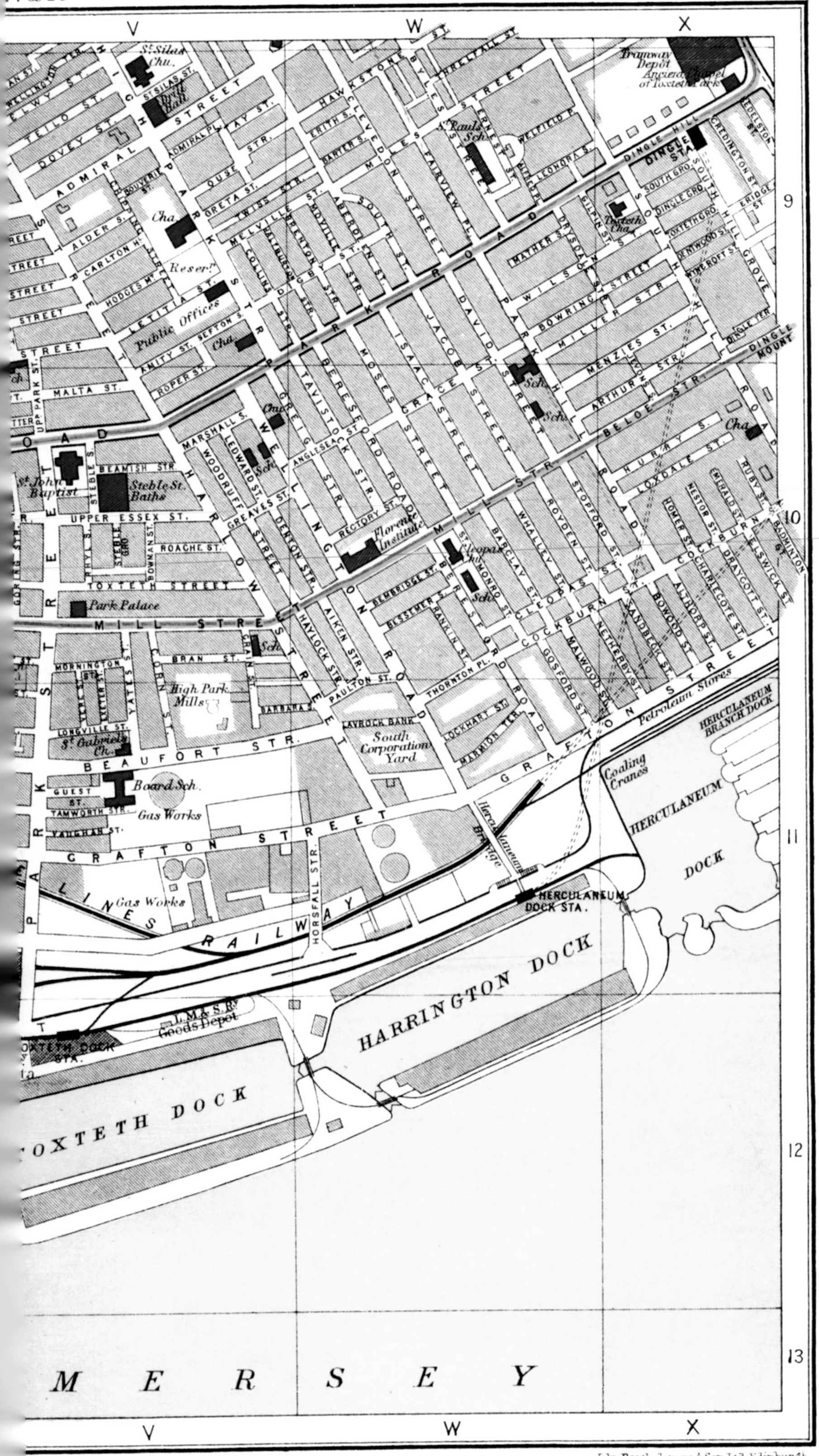
V
W
X
9
10
11
12
13
St. Silas Chu.
Drill Hall
Tramway Depot
Ancient Chapel of Toxteth Park
HAWKSTONE
ADMIRAL ST.
PARK STREET
DINGLE HILL
DINGLE STA.
St. Pauls Sch.
Cha.
Reser.
Public Offices
PARK ROAD
Toxteth Cha.
MATHER S.
BOWRING STREET
MILLER STR.
MENZIES ST.
ARTHUR STR.
BELOE STR.
DINGLE MOUNT
DINGLE TER.
GROVE
LOXDALE ST.
HURRY S.
Cha.
MALTA ST.
UPP. PARK ST.
ROAD
St. John Baptist
Steble St. Baths
BEAMISH STR.
UPPER ESSEX ST.
ROACHE ST.
TOXTETH STREET
Park Palace
MILL STREET
HARLOW STREET
WELLINGTON ROAD
Florence Institute
Cleopas Chu.
Sch.
JACOB STREET
DAVID ST.
ISAAC STREET
MOSES ST.
TAVISTOCK STR.
BERESFORD ROAD
STOPFORD ST.
ROYDEN ST.
WHALLEY ST.
BARCLAY ST.
CLEOPAS ST.
COCKBURN ST.
BESSEMER ST.
PEMBRIDGE ST.
GOSFORD ST.
MALWOOD ST.
NETHERBY ST.
HOMER ST.
NESTOR ST.
DRAYCOTT ST.
BADMINTON ST.
BOWOOD ST.
SANDBECK ST.
GRAFTON STREET
Petroleum Stores
HERCULANEUM BRANCH DOCK
Coaling Cranes
HERCULANEUM DOCK
Herculaneum Bridge
HERCULANEUM DOCK STA.
THORNTON PL.
LOCKHART ST.
MARMION TER.
PAULTON ST.
HAYLOCK STR.
AIKEN STR.
LAYROCK BANK
South Corporation Yard
BRAN ST.
High Park Mills
BARBARA S.
MORNINGTON ST.
YATES ST.
LONGVILLE ST.
St. Gabriel's Ch.
BEAUFORT STR.
Board Sch.
GUEST ST.
TAMWORTH STR.
VAUGHAN ST.
Gas Works
GRAFTON STREET
HORSFALL STR.
Gas Works
LINES RAILWAY
L.M.& S.Ry. Goods Depot
TOXTETH DOCK STA.
HARRINGTON DOCK
TOXTETH DOCK
M E R S E Y

*Tramway Routes shown thus*
*The Plan is divided into Quarter mile Squares*

John Bartholomew & Son Ltd. Edinburgh

36

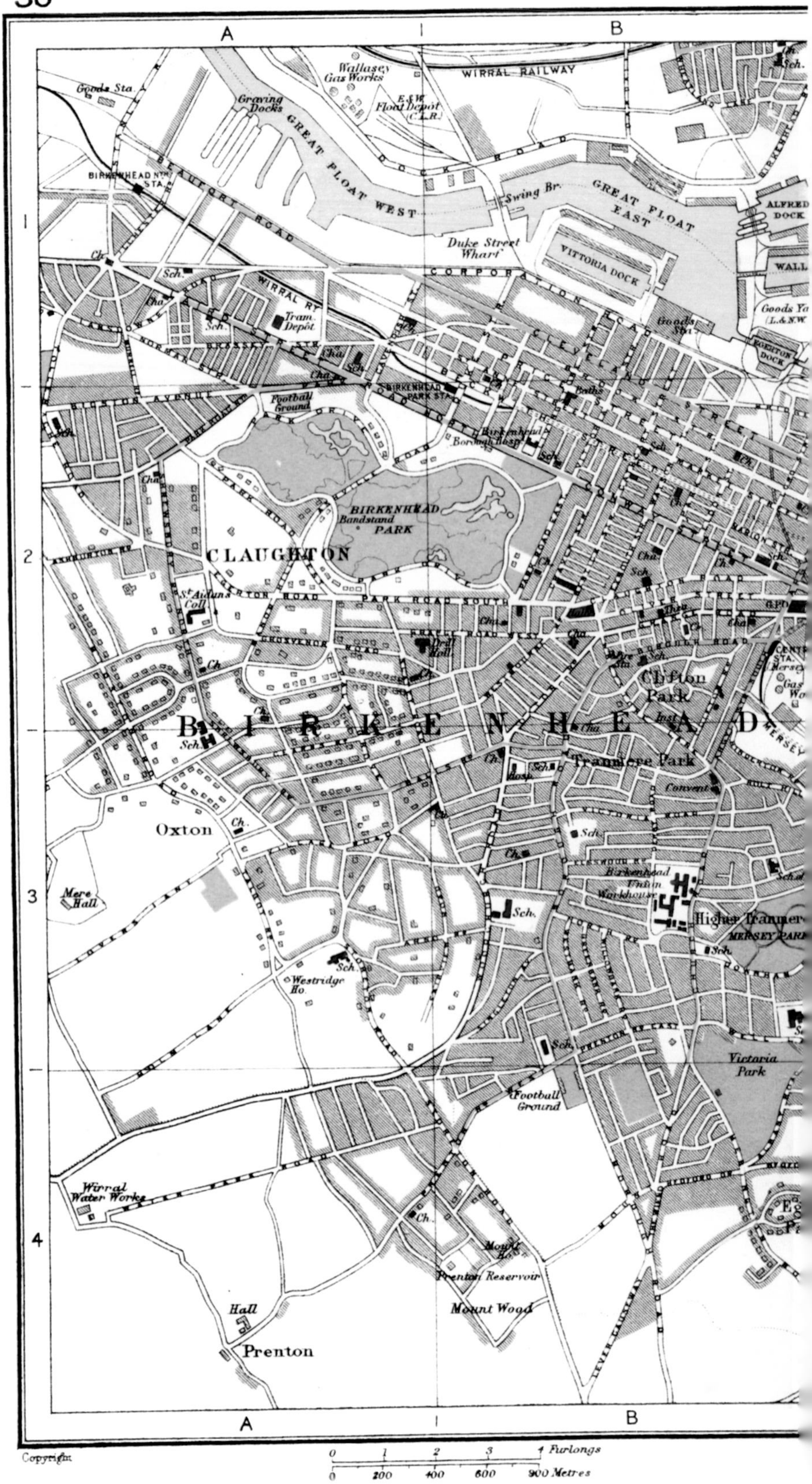
A
B
1
2
3
4
Goods Sta.
Wallasey Gas Works
WIRRAL RAILWAY
Graving Docks
GREAT FLOAT WEST
BIRKENHEAD NTH STA.
BEAUFORT ROAD
Swing Br.
GREAT FLOAT EAST
ALFRED DOCK
Duke Street Wharf
VITTORIA DOCK
CORPORATION ROAD
WIRRAL RY
Tram Depôt
Goods Sta.
Baths
Football Ground
BIRKENHEAD PARK STA.
Birkenhead Borough Hosp.
BIRKENHEAD PARK
Bandstand
CLAUGHTON
St Aidan's Coll
PARK ROAD SOUTH
Drill Hall
Clifton Park
BIRKENHEAD
Tranmere Park
Convent
Oxton
Birkenhead Union Workhouse
Higher Tranmere
MERSEY PARK
Mere Hall
Westridge Ho.
Victoria Park
Football Ground
Wirral Water Works
Prenton Reservoir
Mount Wood
Hall
Prenton
0 1 2 3 4 Furlongs
0 200 400 600 800 Metres

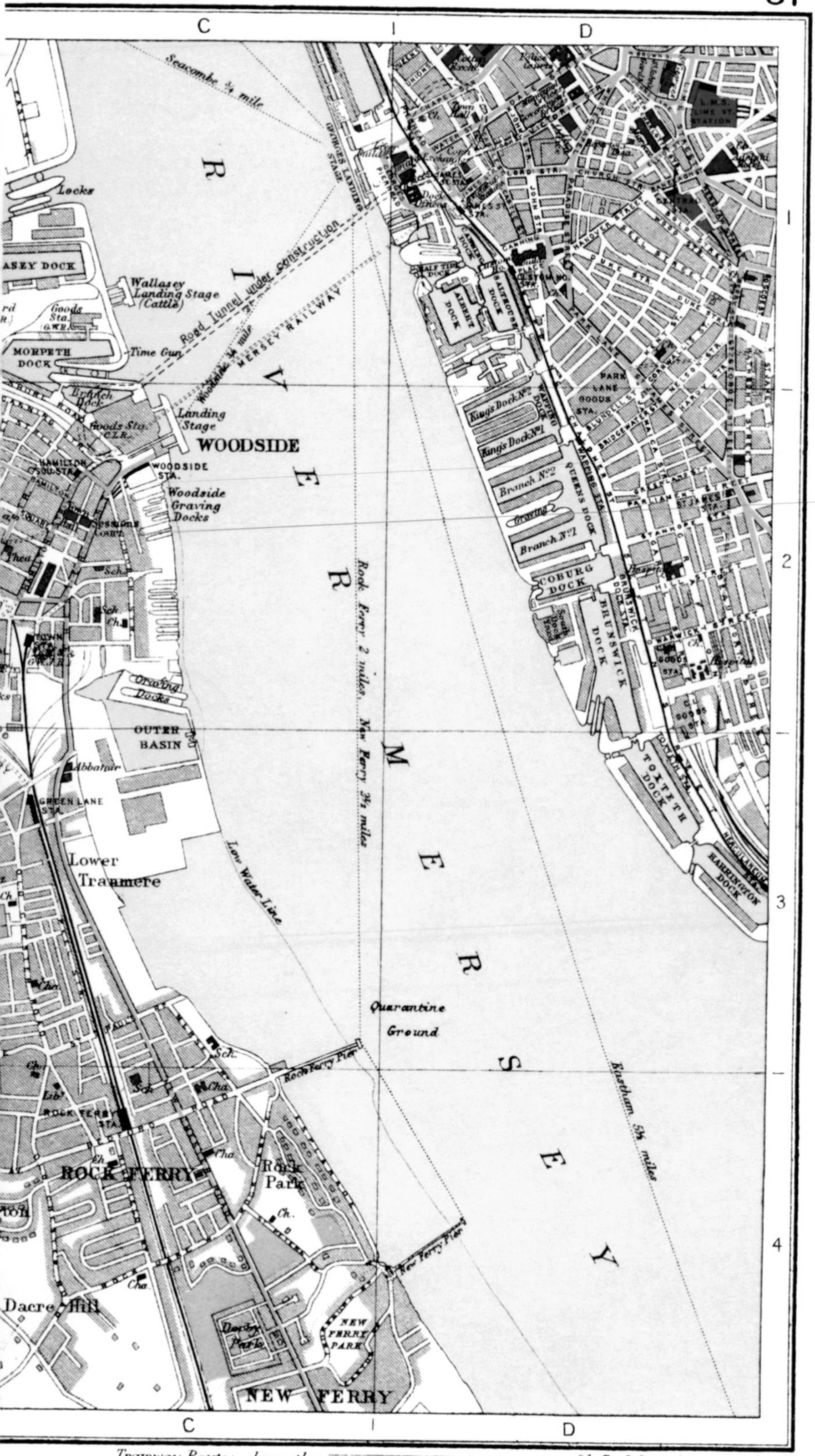
C
D
1
2
3
4
Seacombe ¾ mile
RIVER
MERSEY
Locks
Wallasey Landing Stage (Cattle)
Goods Sta.
G.W.R.
MORPETH DOCK
Time Gun
Road Tunnel under construction
MERSEY RAILWAY
Branch Dock
Landing Stage
Goods Sta. C.L.R.
WOODSIDE
WOODSIDE STA.
Woodside Graving Docks
HAMILTON SQU. STA.
Sessions Court
Thea.
Sch.
Ch.
Graving Docks
OUTER BASIN
Abbatoir
GREEN LANE STA.
Lower Tranmere
Low Water Line
Rock Ferry 2 miles. New Ferry 3¼ miles
Quarantine Ground
Rock Ferry Pier
Lib.
ROCK FERRY STA.
ROCK FERRY
Rock Park
New Ferry Pier
Dacre Hill
Derby Park
NEW FERRY PARK
NEW FERRY
Garston 5¼ miles
L.M.S. LIME ST. STATION
CENTRAL STA.
CHURCH STA.
HANOVER STA.
DUKE STA.
ALBERT DOCK
SALTHOUSE DOCK
HALF TIDE DOCK
PARK LANE GOODS STA.
King's Dock No. 2
King's Dock No. 1
Branch No. 2
Graving
Branch No. 1
QUEENS DOCK
COBURG DOCK
BRUNSWICK DOCK
South Dock
TOXTETH DOCK
HARRINGTON DOCK
Hospital
GOODS STA.

Tramway Routes shown thus

The Plan is divided into Quarter mile Squares

John Bartholomew & Son Ltd. Edinburgh

38

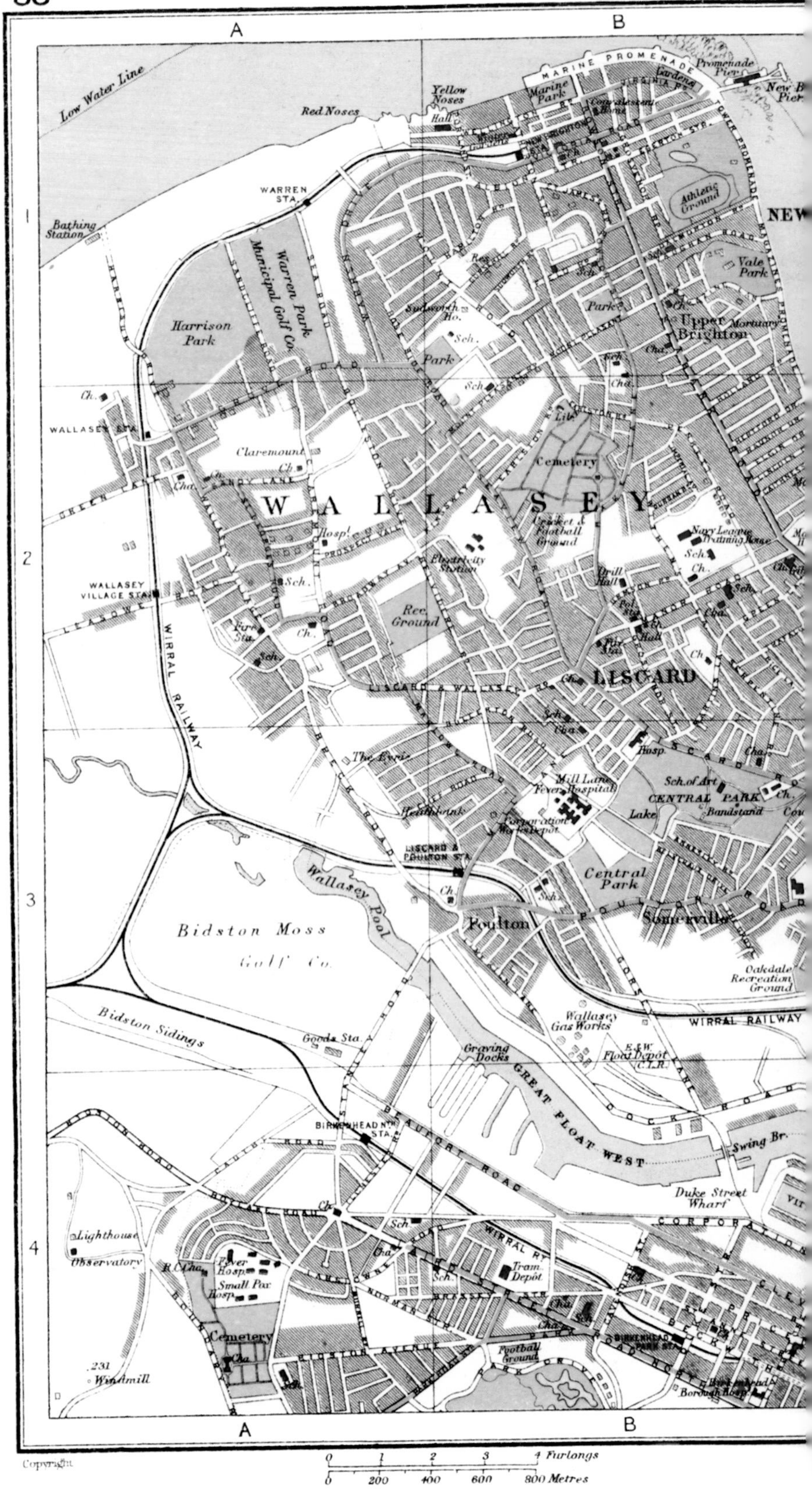
A
B
1
2
3
4
Low Water Line
Red Noses
Yellow Noses
Marine Park
MARINE PROMENADE
Promenade Pier
New B Pier
WARREN STA.
Bathing Station
Warren Park Municipal Golf Co.
Harrison Park
Athletic Ground
Vale Park
Upper Brighton
Mortuary
Sudworth Ho.
Sch.
Park
Ch.
Cha.
WALLASEY STA.
Claremount
Cemetery
W A L L A S E Y
Cricket & Football Ground
Navy League Training House
Hosp.
Electricity Station
WALLASEY VILLAGE STA.
Rec. Ground
Drill Hall
Fire Sta.
LISCARD
WIRRAL RAILWAY
The Eyrie
Mill Lane Fever Hospital
Sch. of Art
CENTRAL PARK
Bandstand
Lake
Heathbank
Corporation Works Depot
LISCARD & POULTON STA.
Wallasey Pool
Central Park
Poulton
Somerville
Bidston Moss
Golf Co.
Oakdale Recreation Ground
Bidston Sidings
Goods Sta.
Wallasey Gas Works
Graving Docks
GREAT FLOAT WEST
Swing Br.
BIRKENHEAD NTH STA.
BEAUFORT ROAD
Duke Street Wharf
Lighthouse
Observatory
R.C. Cha.
Fever Hosp.
Small Pox Hosp.
Tram Depot
WIRRAL RY.
Cemetery
Football Ground
BIRKENHEAD PARK STA.
Birkenhead Borough Hosp.
231
Windmill
Copyright
0 1 2 3 4 Furlongs
0 200 400 600 800 Metres

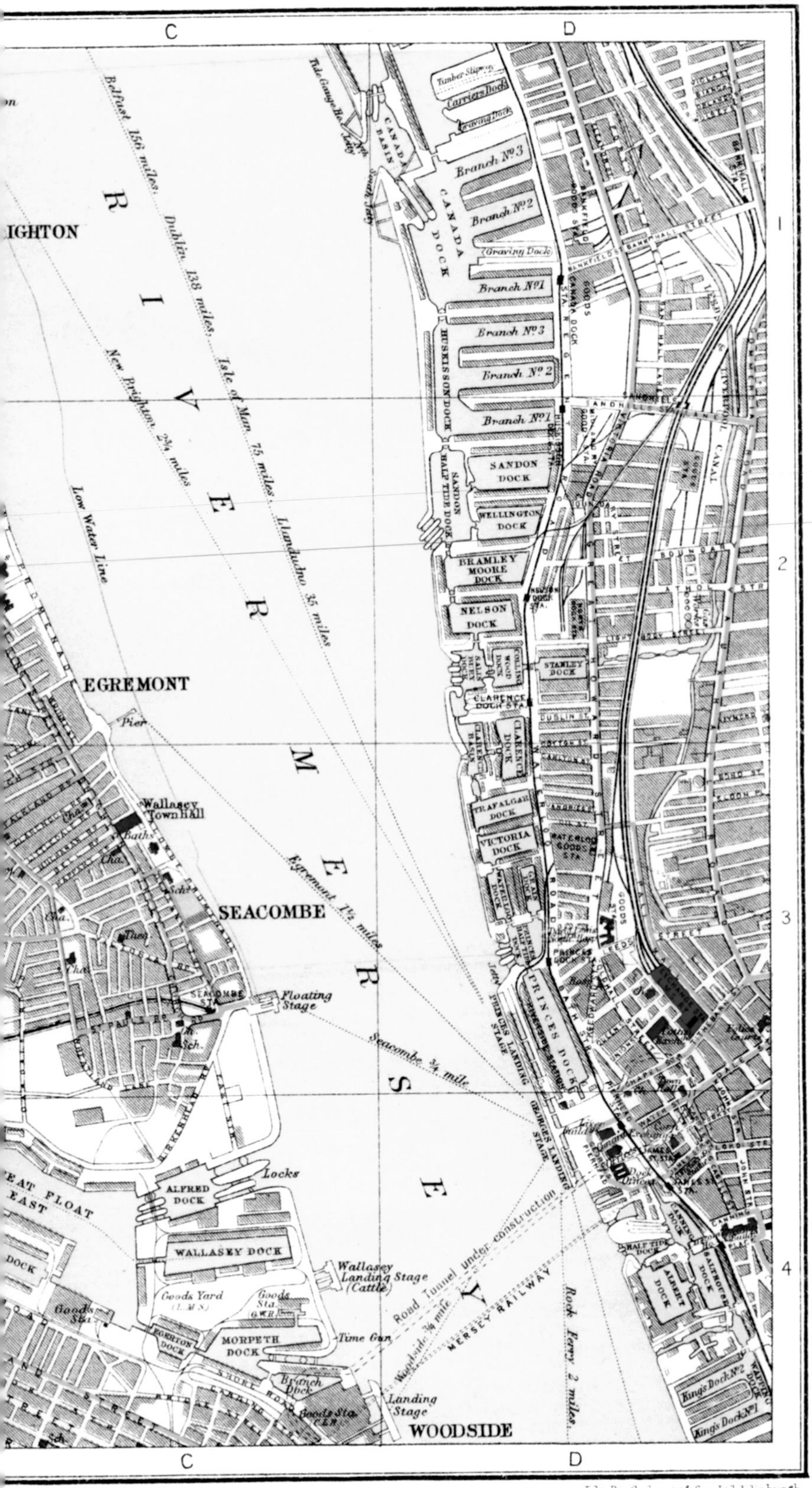
C
D
RIVER MERSEY
Belfast 156 miles.
Dublin 138 miles.
Isle of Man 75 miles.
Llandudno 35 miles
New Brighton 2¾ miles
Low Water Line
Egremont 1½ miles
Seacombe ¾ mile
Woodside ¾ mile
Rock Ferry 2 miles
Road Tunnel under construction
MERSEY RAILWAY
Timber Slip
Carriers Dock
Graving Dock
CANADA BASIN
CANADA DOCK
Branch Nº3
Branch Nº2
Graving Dock
Branch Nº1
HUSKISSON DOCK
Branch Nº3
Branch Nº2
Branch Nº1
SANDON HALF TIDE DOCK
SANDON DOCK
WELLINGTON DOCK
BRAMLEY MOORE DOCK
NELSON DOCK
STANLEY DOCK
CLARENCE DOCK STA.
CLARENCE DOCK
TRAFALGAR DOCK
VICTORIA DOCK
WATERLOO GOODS STA.
PRINCES DOCK
PRINCES LANDING STAGE
GEORGES LANDING STAGE
LEEDS STREET
CANAL
HALF TIDE DOCK
ALBERT DOCK
SALTHOUSE DOCK
Kings Dock Nº2
Kings Dock Nº1
IGHTON
EGREMONT
Pier
Wallasey Town Hall
Baths
SEACOMBE
Floating Stage
EAT FLOAT
EAST
Locks
ALFRED DOCK
WALLASEY DOCK
Wallasey Landing Stage (Cattle)
Goods Yard (L.M.S.)
Goods Sta. G.W.R.
Goods Sta.
EGERTON DOCK
MORPETH DOCK
Time Gun
Branch Dock
Goods Sta.
Landing Stage
WOODSIDE
1
2
3
4

*Tramway Routes shown thus*

John Bartholomew & Son, Ltd. Edinburgh

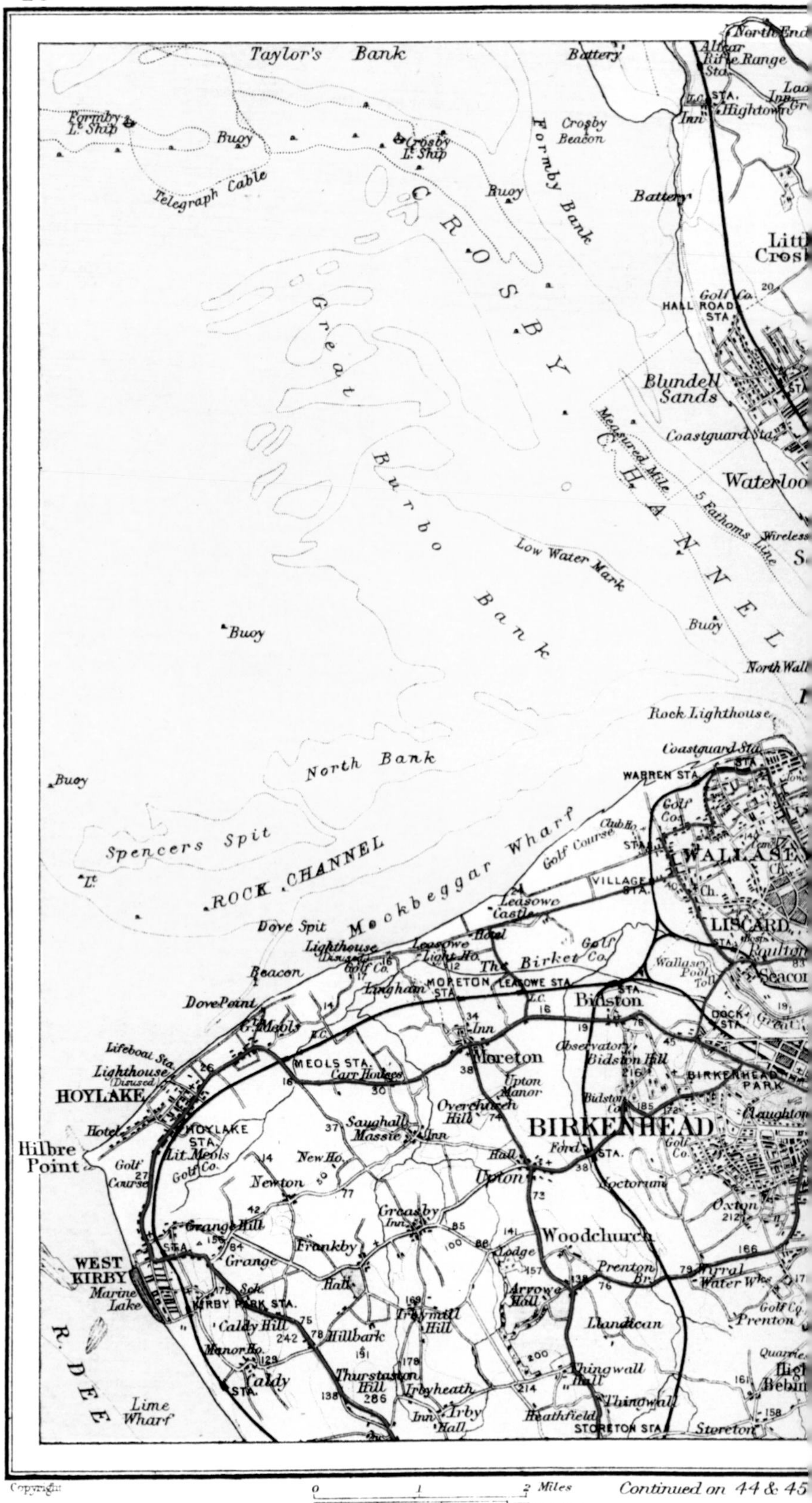
Taylor's Bank
Battery
Formby Lt. Ship
Buoy
Crosby Lt. Ship
Telegraph Cable
Crosby Beacon
Formby Bank
C R O S B Y
Great
Burbo
Bank
Measured Mile
C H A N N E L
Low Water Mark
5 Fathoms Line
Buoy
North Wall
Rock Lighthouse
Coastguard Sta.
North Bank
Spencers Spit
ROCK CHANNEL
Mockbeggar Wharf
Golf Course
Leasowe Castle
Dove Spit
Lighthouse
Beacon
Dove Point
Lifeboat Sta.
Lighthouse (Disused)
HOYLAKE
Hotel
Hilbre Point
Golf Course
WEST KIRBY
Marine Lake
R. DEE
Lime Wharf
Caldy
Caldy Hill
Grange Hill
Grange
Frankby
Newton
Saughall Massie
Moreton
Upton Manor
Overchurch Hill
BIRKENHEAD
Upton
Woodchurch
Greasby
Arrowe Hall
Irby
Irby Hall
Irbyheath
Thurstaston Hill
Hillbark
Landican
Prenton
Oxton
Bidston
Bidston Hill
Observatory
WALLASEY
LISCARD
Poulton
Seacombe
BIRKENHEAD PARK
Claughton
Waterloo
Blundell Sands
Coastguard Sta.
HALL ROAD STA.
Little Crosby
Hightown
Altcar Rifle Range
North End
Thingwall
Storeton
STORETON STA.
Heathfield
Noctorum
Tranmere
Bebington
Wireless
WARREN STA.
MORETON STA.
LEASOWE STA.
MEOLS STA.
HOYLAKE STA.
KIRBY PARK STA.
DOCK STA.
VILLAGE STA.



0 1 2 Miles
0 1 2 3 Kilometres

Continued on 44 & 45

 Continued on 42 & 43 

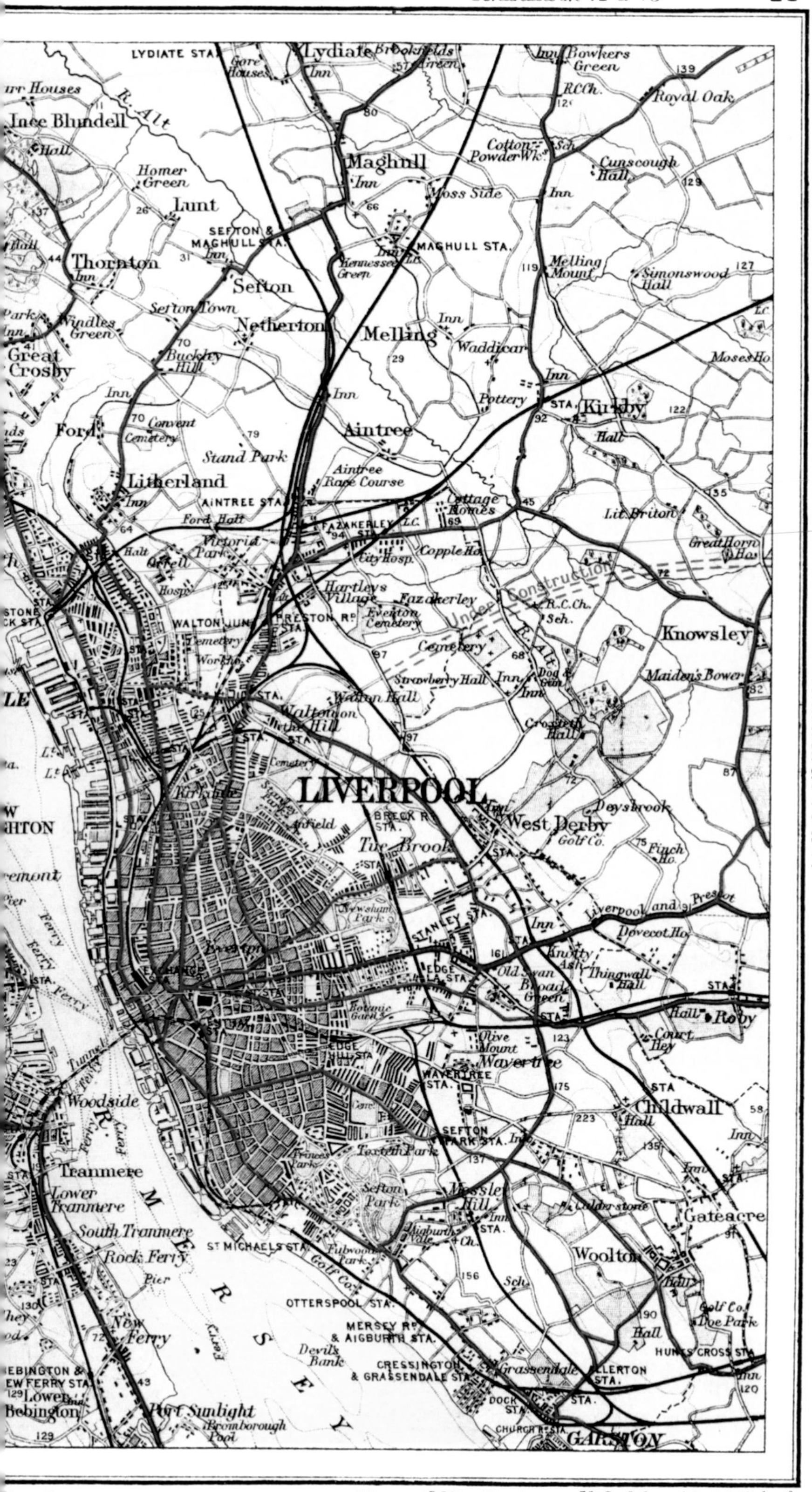

Lydiate Sta.
Lydiate
Bowkers Green
Royal Oak
R. Alt
Ince Blundell
Hall
Homer Green
Lunt
Maghull
Moss Side
Cunscough Hall
Cotton Powder Wks.
Sefton & Maghull Sta.
Maghull Sta.
Thornton
Sefton
Sefton Town
Netherton
Melling
Melling Mount
Simonswood Hall
Windles Green
Great Crosby
Buckley Hill
Waddicar
Pottery
Kirkby
Ford
Convent Cemetery
Stand Park
Aintree
Aintree Race Course
Litherland
Aintree Sta.
Cottage Homes
Lit. Briton
Ford Hall
Fazakerley Sta.
Victoria Park
Copple Ho.
City Hosp.
Great Horn Ho.
Hartleys Village
Fazakerley
Under Construction
Walton Jun.
Preston Rd.
Everton Cemetery
Cemetery
R.C.Ch.
Sch.
Knowsley
Strawberry Hall
Dog & Gun
Maiden's Bower
Walton on the Hill
Walton Hall
Croxteth Hall
LIVERPOOL
Kirkdale
Breck Rd. Sta.
West Derby
Deysbrook
Golf Co.
Anfield
Tue Brook
Finch Ho.
Stanley Sta.
Liverpool and Prescot
Dovecot Ho.
Knotty Ash
Thingwall Hall
Old Swan
Broad Green
Exchange
Edge Sta.
Roby
Botanic Gard.
Court Hey
Edge Hill Sta.
Olive Mount
Wavertree
Wavertree Sta.
Childwall
Woodside
Sefton Park Sta.
Tranmere
Lower Tranmere
Toxteth Park
Princes Park
Sefton Park
Mossley Hill
Gateacre
Calderstone
South Tranmere
Rock Ferry
St. Michaels Sta.
Fulwood Park
Golf Co.
Aigburth Vale
Woolton
Pier
Otterspool Sta.
Golf Co.
Doe Park
New Ferry
Mersey Rd. & Aigburth Sta.
Devil's Bank
Hunts Cross Sta.
Cressington & Grassendale Sta.
Grassendale
Allerton Sta.
Bebington & New Ferry Sta.
Lower Bebington
Port Sunlight
Bromborough Pool
Dock Sta.
Church Rd. Sta.
Garston
M E R S E Y


Main Roads ▬▬ Railways STA. L.C. (Level Crossing)

John Bartholomew & Son, Ltd. Edinburgh.

Continued on 46 & 47